Antony
12/1/87

If
I Live to Be
100 . . .
Congregate Housing
for Later Life

If
I Live to Be
100 . . .
Congregate Housing
for Later Life

Vivian F. Carlin, Ph.D.
Ruth Mansberg

Parker Publishing Company, Inc.
West Nyack, New York

© 1984, by

PARKER PUBLISHING COMPANY, INC.
West Nyack, N.Y.

Library of Congress Cataloging in Publication Data

Carlin, Vivian F.,
    If I live to be 100—congregate housing for later
life.

    Includes index.
    1. Old age homes—United States—Case studies.
2. Aged—United States—Social conditions—Case
studies. 3. Communal living—United States—Case
studies. I. Mansberg, Ruth,   . II. Title.
HV1465.C37 1983   362.6′1′0973   83-22153
ISBN 0-13-450387-2
ISBN 0-13-450379-1 {PBK}

Printed in the United States of America

Foreword

We are all aging—as individuals and as a society. Increased longevity has spurred the search for alternatives to the rocking chair in the old age home and has made decisions about how we will live, work, and play in old age critical to our health and well-being, and the welfare of our families and our nation.

One of the most complicated choices we have to make is where to live when we are old. Economic, social, and psychological factors all feature in our selection of the setting that we hope will offer the most opportunity for a healthy and satisfying life.

Dr. Carlin and Ms. Mansberg have written a very useful book that expands our knowledge about the choices available to us. They have selected one alternative, Lakeview—a residential community that embodies the best of small town community and urban vitality—and present their story about it in informative and interesting detail. They share their insights, derived from the experiences of real people in a real situation, and provide us with their analysis of the reasons why older persons thrive here. The authors have thoroughly researched the facts they present, and they have written a highly readable volume.

The Lakeview lifestyle will not be suitable for everyone, but the ideas presented by Dr. Carlin and Ms. Mansberg should prove most useful and stimulating for all persons planning for their later years. The book is nontechnical, but professionals would do well to include it on their bookshelves. It is a valuable resource.

As a social worker and a gerontologist, I recommend it highly.

Audrey Olsen Faulkner, Ph.D., ACSW
Director, Institute on Aging
Rutgers University

Introduction

A great deal of advice is being handed out today on how to exercise and eat for good health and long life. It is not our intention to add to that collective wisdom. Instead, we want to tell you about a congenial, invigorating, and very beneficial living environment for old people.

The lifestyle we describe here is not unique to this one place; it exists throughout the country. Whether it appeals to you or not, we hope it stimulates you to think about your own future. Because, sooner or later, if you live long enough, you too will grow old. In fact, chances are better than ever before in the history of humankind that you could live to be 100.

A few years ago that thought might have been depressing, but so many doors are now being pried open—by old people themselves and by people who study aging and the aged—that the landscape has brightened considerably. We are discovering that life can be sweet all the way through. It's not just what old people are saying but what they are doing: traveling, practicing the arts, learning crafts, caring for children, going to school, consulting, advising, teaching, enjoying sports, even running in marathons. The list is as extensive as that of the activities of young people, since the old are actually us—with extra years, or, as cartoonist George Booth has said, "All of us are children; only our bodies get older."

In her book, *The Measure of My Days,* Florida Scott-Maxwell said, "We who are old know that age is more than a disability. It is an intense and varied experience, almost beyond our capacity at times, but something to be carried high."[1] Unfortunately, all old people cannot carry their age so well or so high. With a little help, however, many can do very well indeed, avoiding the unhappiness of isolation or dependence and the high price—in economic and human terms—of institutionalization.

The pace of research in gerontology—the interdisciplinary field that deals with the elderly—has quickened in the last decade, along with increased awareness that our population is growing older, and social gerontologists trying to determine the types of living environment most beneficial to old people have come up with some useful findings. First among them is that age-segregated housing, despite the passionate antipathy toward it in some circles, facilitates the development of aging subcultures that insulate old people against feelings of isolation and loneliness and against society's negative attitudes toward the aged. The strength of an aging subculture is further enhanced if its members are fairly homogeneous with respect to sex, marital status, education, and social background. In addition, security and assistance with housekeeping and meals are important, especially for those who are older than 75, no matter how healthy.

The research upon which this book is based was designed to test these findings and possibly add some new ones. Originally conceived as a survey of several types of residential communities, it soon focused on just one—a middle-income congregate residence that seemed to epitomize a communal lifestyle for older Americans. Housed in a high-rise apartment building in a semi-urban town in the northeastern United States, almost 200 people, ranging in age from 66 to 95 (with a median age of 83), have created a cohesive and very active community. Each resident or couple has an apartment with a pullman kitchen and the usual safety and security features found in housing for the elderly. One floor of the building is used as an infirmary and long-term nursing care facility, and several of the lower floors are used for community space, including a dining room. All of the community areas and many of the apartments have a good view of the lake on whose eastern shore the building rises. Terrace gardens along the lakefront are cultivated and cared for by residents, an activity so popular that there is always a waiting list for garden plots. The lake is quite large, a locus for recreational activities in the area, and a source of continual pleasure to the residents. From it we have

derived the names we use for the town, Watertown, and the
residence, Lakeview House (neither of which is the actual
name).

The most striking aspects of Lakeview House are the
unexpectedly high level of activity and the independence of its
residents. And the activity is not confined to the building but
spills over into the town and beyond. A small administrative
staff and a minimum of rules and regulations encourage resident autonomy, so that the house is run to a large extent by a
residents' council and several dozen committees that, altogether, involve about 75 percent participation by the house
population. Emerging leaders serve as role models, in many
cases the older for the younger old. (Now that old age can be
seen as a 30-year stretch, such distinctions are necessary.)

It was the extraordinarily animated atmosphere that first
intrigued us. Each day, plans were made and followed: shopping, gardening, bridge, dates with friends and family, theater
and museum trips, paid or volunteer jobs, visits to patients in
the nursing unit, hours spent on duty at the front desk or in
the notions shop, preparations for a committee program or a
church bazaar. Physical ailments, of which Lakeview residents
had their share, were more often than not submerged in these
pursuits. Serious illness or loss called forth a network of
friendly concern and support. Yet, if one wanted to be alone,
strict respect for privacy was observed. Positive attitudes
toward aging were prevalent among Lakeview's people; they
accepted their own old age, usually with grace, often with
humor, thus avoiding the mental crippling of denial and despair.

How did this climate develop? What factors at this congregate residence were responsible for the flourishing sense of
community? Why, defying all actuarial predictions of a complete turnover of population in the first five years, were more
than half of the original residents still very much alive ten
years later?

To find out, one of the authors (Vivian Carlin) spent seven
weeks over a three-year period as a participant–observer at the
residence: talking, walking, eating, shopping, going to committee meetings and on trips with the residents. (Conse-

quently, Carlin is the "I" in these pages.) In this case, familiarity bred admiration, and the more we (both authors) learned about the people and the place, the more convinced we became that Lakeview's story could help a wide spectrum of the American public to confront old age—not with foreboding but with a genuine feeling of optimism.

In fact, research and work for this book dredged up many of the authors' own negative images of life in old age and transformed them. Above all, we came to realize the importance of planning for our later years.

By the year 2000, demographers estimate that one of every five persons in the United States will be over 65, and 44 percent of this population will be over 75 years of age. Though this future group is expected to be healthier and more vigorous than today's oldsters, delaying inevitable frailties does not eliminate them. To refuse to face future possibilities means that we leave the shaping of our lives to chance. And chance has been very unkind to many older people who end up trapped in deteriorating neighborhoods, rattling around in large gloomy houses they can no longer maintain, or drugged and imprisoned in nursing homes. Suffering from loss of friends, family, and a sense of belonging to society, these are the old people who sink into sloughs of illness, confusion, and despair.

Long the forgotten minority, the elderly are now becoming the subject of much societal soul-searching. A new militance by the gray set commands attention and action, rising community awareness results in some needed services and programs, and increased academic interest in geriatrics and gerontology promises to improve the environment and the choices available to us as we grow older. But basically each of us must choose and act while we still can—or someone else will make the choices for us.

The most remarkable thing about Lakeview's residents is that at a time of life when many stubbornly resist change they took charge of their own destinies and elected to join a community. Some were actually instrumental in drawing up the plans and working toward their fruition. Since congregate housing was a relatively new concept when they started, they were also pioneers.

Syndicated columnist Ellen Goodman has said: "Our whole society is aging, and few of us know what we want to be when we grow old. . . . There seem to be two dominating role models: those who behave as if 70 were really 55 extended a bit and those who have retired into emptiness. But we have too few people acting as contented guideposts, sending back positive messages of what is ahead. . . . We need to hear more about aging from those who have aged well. We need some people from the generation that taught us how to grow up to begin teaching us how to grow old."[2]

We believe we have found such teachers in the courageous and independent men and women living at Lakeview, and we invite you to come along with us to explore the community of elders they have created. We will also tell you about some of the other communal housing options available to older Americans and where to find out about them. Lastly, we list congregate housing facilities in the country and make some suggestions about what to look for if you choose this way of life for your later years.

Most of all, we hope this book will encourage you to think positively and plan for your old age. And we wish each of you at least 100 years of health and happiness.

Authors' note: Because of the keen sense of privacy of the residents of "Lakeview," all names have been changed, and the people portrayed are composites.

Vivian F. Carlin
Ruth Mansberg

Contents

Acknowledgment

Our gratitude goes to the "Lakeview" residents and management without whose help this book would not have been possible. The administrator and staff of the congregate residence were unusually helpful in allowing access to the site and in maintaining relationships with the residents. The resident leaders were particularly supportive during this study. The residents' giving of their time, allowing us to share in their private lives, and discussing openly their feelings about getting old, were invaluable. The way in which they faced the future was an inspiration.

V. F. C.
R. M.

1. A COMMUNITY OF ELDERS: The House and Its People

A home is not forever, but you can carry it with you to the happiest place you can find where you know you are welcome.

—*Kate Nolan, resident of Lakeview House*

Midway through the week of my first visit to Lakeview, my dinner companions turned the tables on me and began asking *me* questions. What did I think of the place? Was it what I had expected? Did I find the people strange, alien beings? The last question, asked with amusement, was answered in kind; I laughingly denied any such impression, while admitting that the people were not quite as I had expected.

It was the end of a bright midsummer day. Through the window wall of the dining room we could see the glowing orange disk of the descending sun and the pink haze it cast over the lake and the sails of boats returning to harbor. With me at the table were Frank Smithson, chairman of the Residents Council, who had made arrangements for me to sit with a different group of people at each evening meal for the week of my visit; his wife Doris; Agnes Drew, one of the newer and younger residents; and Kate Nolan, one of the earliest residents.

My first impression, I told them, was one of amazement at

1

the high level of activity in the house. Yes, I knew beforehand that close to 200 people lived there, and I knew the meaning of a congregate residence, but I also knew that most of the residents were in their seventies and eighties.

"And you expected a bunch of crotchety ancients supine before the flickering tube," Kate Nolan interposed. The others laughed.

"Don't feel too badly," Kate went on. "It's a common reaction. Most people on their first visit steel themselves for what they think of as an old folks' home. I was 69 when I signed up for an apartment here eight years ago. My family, my friends, even my doctor thought I was crazy. 'You don't need that yet,' they all said—as if I had consigned myself to Purgatory."

"And what's wrong with an old folks' home?" Doris Smithson asked. "When I was a little girl, I often visited my grandmother in a gentlewomen's home—that's what it was called then. I thought it was a lovely place. I made up my mind then—and can remember telling my mother—that I'd like to live in a place like that when I got old."

Frank Smithson gently chided his wife: "Obviously, my dear, you are unusual. Most people think of an old age home as an unhappy place, else why would Kate have run into the kind of reaction she did? I've heard the same from many others."

As a professional, working in my state's agency on aging and in the process of completing my doctoral studies in gerontology, I should have known better. But my subconscious fears were just as deep-seated as yours probably are. People like Doris Smithson, who have had loving relationships with aging relatives early in life and retain happy memories of them, are rare today. It would take several years of exposure to the kind of people I befriended at Lakeview before I could dredge up my own fears and come to terms with them. This book was born of that experience. It is meant for all who shudder at the thought of growing old and who equate all types of special housing for old people with nursing homes and similar institutions.

From the beginning, it was not only the amount of activity at Lakeview but its quality—the sense of purpose and good spirits of the residents—that impressed me, so much so that it was only after I had been there for several days that I became aware of how many people used canes. Whenever I spoke about the lively atmosphere and asked residents whether they thought it unusual, they invariably answered, "No, it's been this way ever since I've been here," or, "Well, we're a lively bunch," or something in that vein.

It was the newcomer among them, Agnes Drew, who understood what I meant. She said she had been struck by the same feeling on her first visit and that it had been a deciding factor in her choice of Lakeview. "Now that I've lived here for a few months, I think I've discovered the reason for that liveliness. It's because most people enjoy each day and plan and look forward to tomorrow." Recalling the years she had spent as companion to an older woman, she said, "The contrast between my old friend and the people here—though many are older in years—couldn't be greater. My friend lived only in the past, in her memories. Relinquishing the present made her helpless and dependent. It was terribly depressing after a while."

I believed then, and still do, that she had caught the essence of life at Lakeview—the strong momentum to go forward rather than look back. What engenders this momentum and keeps it going? Is there something special about the people? Or is it the place and the way it is run? These and a hundred other questions crowded my mind during the week of my first visit and drew me back for many more. But before I can tell you what I learned, a few definitions and facts are needed.

What is *congregate housing*? The term covers a variety of living arrangements but generally means a housing complex structured so that each individual has a self-contained living unit. It may be just a studio apartment, but it will have at least a kitchenette or plug-in kitchen unit and a bathroom, in addition to a living room–bedroom. The resident's own furnishings are used, with the possible exceptions of carpeting, drapes, and appliances. Services provided can range from one to three meals a day, housekeeping help, linen service, 24-hour security, and possibly a medical clinic, intermediate care, or nursing care facility, or a combination of any two or all three.

Gerontologists—members of the interdisciplinary field that deals with the study of aging—define congregate housing as a "residential environment which incorporates shelter and services needed by impaired, but not ill, elderly to maintain or return to a semi-independent lifestyle and to avoid premature institutionalization as they grow older." Congregate housing is a relatively new concept, combining aspects of independent living and a sheltered environment. It is also called "communal housing" and, in England, "sheltered housing." (I like to think of congregate as the opposite of isolate housing.)

Lakeview (a fictitious name for a real place) is a prime and fairly early example of a congregate residence. Located in a town I will call Watertown in the northeastern United States, it opened for occupancy at the end of 1968 with the first residents moving into apartments on the upper floors while the rest of the interior was being completed.

Sponsored by a national religious organization, Lakeview was originally conceived by a dedicated churchman, Miles Abbott, after he had visited a retirement home for the elderly in Denver in 1960. Abbott was so impressed with the type of living arrangement he saw there that when he returned to the East he asked the national church board to authorize a study of specially designed housing for older people. A committee was established the following year, and Abbott was appointed its chairman. After three years of investigating various housing alternatives, the committee decided on a residence with support services that would offer the most independent environment possible. It took another three years to explore various communities in the search for a suitable building site.

Early in 1966, a nonprofit housing corporation was formed, with Abbott serving as its chairman until 1969 and again from 1974 to 1976. He is still a member of the board, which consists of seven members and meets monthly. A mix of ministers, doctors, engineers, and businesspeople have been board members over the years. Abbott describes them as "devoted churchworkers, with above-average intelligence—successful people with a high level of sophistication and, above all, extremely dedicated."

Between 1968 and 1971, apartments were available upon application, but after that there was a waiting list that grew until, by 1976, the waiting period for apartments was five years.

Of the residents who moved into Lakeview House during the first two and a half years of rent-up period, more than half still lived there ten years later—in defiance of all the actuarial projections of a complete turnover of residents every five years. As one resident joked, "They treat us too well here—we don't die." Actually, it is the residents who set the tone and many of the rules. Management's role, as we shall see, is kept to a minimum.

As a group the residents are somewhat atypical of their generation and much more representative of the generation now advancing toward old age. With very few exceptions, they are at least second-generation Americans; they are also better educated, and more of them are single and working women than is true of their peer group. In the summer of 1976, when this study began, there were 163 female and 25 male residents at Lakeview. The overwhelming preponderance of women can be accounted for by several factors: first, there are three women to every two men aged 65 in the general population, and the disparity continues to grow with age; in addition, older men continue to live in family settings much longer than older women do and are less likely to live in special housing facilities.

The median age of residents at Lakeview was close to 83 years, the age range was 66 to 95 years, and the average age at date of application was 75. (These figures continued fairly steadily throughout the three years during which this study was done.) Forty percent (74 individuals) had never married, and an equal number were widowed or divorced; 40 residents (21 percent) were still married and living with their spouses, two couples having married at Lakeview.

Almost all residents were high school graduates, some had master's degrees, and a few had doctorates—a level of educational achievement unusual for people of their generation, especially for the women. The majority had worked all of their adult lives until retirement, including some of the women who were widowed while still quite young. A third of the residents followed professional careers as teachers, ministers, nurses, social workers, and librarians. The next larger segment (22 percent) were white-collar workers—secretaries and office workers—and an almost equal number (21 percent) had been housewives who never worked outside their homes except as volunteers. A small number were wealthy widows who had never held jobs and were accustomed to living in large homes attended by servants. Among the professionals were many former high school teachers, several college professors, and department heads at small schools and colleges; others had been magazine editors, administrators, missionaries, and staff members of service organizations like Red Cross, YMCA, and the United Fund. A number of residents worked at new jobs after retirement, a very few held part-time jobs at the time of this study, and many were active in churches or other community organizations. David Arnold (78), for example, tutored prisoners in a penitentiary. Several residents served as volunteer aides at the local hospital. Alida Barnes (76) was volunteer administrator for children's activities, which included playschool, nursery school, and Sunday school classes at a nearby church.

As for religion, the vast majority (90 percent) was Protestant, about 20 percent of them belonging to the same denomination as the nonprofit housing sponsor; five percent were Catholic; three individuals were Jewish; and the rest did not list any religious affiliation. There were no blacks, Hispanics, or Asians. It would be difficult to determine whether this was because none had applied or because such applicants had been discouraged, although the latter is less likely.

Generally, the people who live at Lakeview have similar backgrounds. They are well educated, mannerly, self-reliant, prizing privacy and independence, and with a tradition of service to others. A fairly homogeneous group, they feel comfortable together. And sociologists, for the most part, agree that such homogeneity is a necessary ingredient, or variable, for a sense of community in housing for the elderly.

One of our contentions is that the locale is another important variable, and—at least for the type of resident at Lakeview—Watertown is a nearly ideal location. A medium-sized semiurban community, it is located about an hour away from two large cities. Excellent public transportation via intercity buses and trains, in addition to a good local bus system and modestly priced taxi service, give welcome mobility to residents who no longer drive. From 40 to 50 residents who still use their cars pay a monthly rental for parking space in the underground garage or in the outdoor parking area which is less expensive. Drivers frequently take passengers or do errands for other residents. Opportunities for shopping and for cultural and civic activities in town are numerous. And city amenities, only a short ride away, make it possible for residents, most of whom moved to Lakeview from the surrounding area, to visit family and friends, to shop, and to attend theaters and concerts as they had before.

The building itself rises twelve stories high on the shore of the large and beautiful lake that makes this section of Watertown so picturesque. The lake can be seen from most of the indoor and outdoor community areas and from many of the apartments. Sailboats, power craft, and water skiers brighten the scene during clement weather. In winter, when the lake freezes over, skaters and iceboats with colorful balloon sails create pictures as pretty as any Currier and Ives print. The garden terrace at the rear of the building extends close to the lake shore, and its plantings—small trees, bushes, and a lush array of flowers—add to the charm of the scene. Though none of the residents had chosen to live there because of the view alone, it became an integral and cherished part of their lives.

The front of the building by contrast is on a busy town street alongside other apartment houses and facing a row of older one- and two-family houses across the road. A bank, the town library, and a small grocery store are only a block away, and a large shopping area with a variety of stores and services is about a quarter of a mile away, an easy walk. Watertown Hospital is a half-mile distant. From the street the building looks quite handsome, of good modern design and economy of line. A bright awning protects the front entrance, located close to the sidewalk with a circular drive enabling people to be picked up or dropped off at the entrance.

Immediately upon entering the building, you are in the lobby, which is cheerful, neat, and usually bustling with activity. A few comfortable chairs form a sitting area off to one side. Mailboxes and a reception desk face the sitting area, the desk being occupied throughout the day by a staff member or a resident volunteer. Just beyond the reception desk, separated only by a glass partition, are the staff offices. On a typical morning, even in the cold of winter, residents are seen entering and leaving the building on various errands, and those returning often carry parcels, books, and newspapers. A van may drive up to the entryway, followed by several cars. Entering passengers are usually animated, obviously looking forward to going somewhere.

Inside and through the lobby, a corridor running the length of the building is used as a community space; it contains a billiard table, shuffleboard, card tables, and informal sitting areas. A bulletin board and a small table holding copies of the day's newspapers are near the corridor entry, and just a few steps away is the administrator's office, its door usually standing open. Next to the office is a small notions and stationery store run by the residents; beyond are the maintenance supervisor's apartment and the library, a pleasant book-lined room. One wall of this large community area is window glass and faces the lake, so that the corridor seems to widen to include the outdoors. At the back end, a large enclosed lounge with bridge tables and comfortable chairs has three glass walls. (Bridge is a favorite pastime at Lakeview, and regular games are set up by numerous groups.) Adjoining the lounge is an upper terrace, with more tables and chairs, overlooking the gardens and the lake. On the level below, reached by the rear elevator, is the dining room, a simply furnished, L-shaped room, glass-enclosed on two sides for a fine view of the lake. Because the architect was able to take advantage of the sharp slope of the land, a second level below the dining room is still at ground level. The utility room, maintenance shop, housekeeper's office and supply room, residents' laundry room, arts and crafts room, and a large assembly room with two window walls looking out directly at the garden terrace and lake are located here.

What was done, one of the early residents told me, was to "take a mudhole and a lot of concrete and—voila!—a lovely terrace. Of course, the fact that it runs alongside the lake has a lot to do with it." Garden plots, sectioned off by concrete dividing strips, are cultivated and cared for by the residents with great devotion. On my first tour of the building, Reverend Craig Winiford, who was my guide, pointed with pride at the women working in the garden: "Mabel Lewis is 82 or 83, and Annie Harkin is even older, I think, but they're still puttering around out there." He told me, too, that he had worked a plot for six or seven years but had given it over to another eager gardener on the waiting list because of a problem with his back the year before. At the time, Reverend Winiford was 92.

As we strolled along the terrace, I realized it was large enough to make walking completely around it even once a good constitutional for residents who need protected areas in which to walk. Because it is relatively level, without curbs and traffic, it is easier and more secure than the town streets for people using canes or other aids. Outdoor chairs, benches, and a table and umbrella form convivial resting and conversation spots. It is a rare day when the terrace is not being used by at least a few strollers, and on a fine day many will be walking about or sitting and talking and, always, watching the gardeners at work and the activity on the lake.

Each resident or couple at Lakeview has his or her own apartment. There are 170 in all, ranging from small efficiencies and studio alcoves to one- and two-bedroom units, each a complete unit including a pullman kitchen with stove, sink, and small under-the-counter refrigerator. Front-facing apartments have a view of the town, while most others have at least a partial view of the lake; those facing the back and sides of the building, particularly on the upper floors, have the most spectacular views. Apartments on each floor are on a double-loaded, fairly long corridor, with an elevator at each end that necessitates a long walk for some people. The fact that the mailroom and lobby are at the front and the dining room, assembly hall, and terraces at the rear of the building also creates complications and causes some grumbling.

One complete floor, the second, houses the nursing care facility and infirmary. Registered nurses are on duty at all times, and a medical clinic is held twice a week. Some of the residents use the house doctor as their general practitioner; others go to Watertown or nearby towns for their medical care. Lakeview's nurses will give injections and perform other medical services prescribed by physicians for residents in their own apartments. There are no nursing aides on staff available to assist residents confined to bed in their own apartments, but management can usually help find such private assistance. A resident convalescing from serious illness or surgery may occupy a bed in the nursing unit if one is free. There is a time limit of 60 days, however; after that a committee reviews the case and decides whether the resident is to be given 30 days notice to vacate his or her apartment. The nursing unit looms large in the life at Lakeview; it is regarded with a mixture of gratitude for its presence and loathing at the thought of ending up there—an understandable ambivalence that will be explored in a later chapter.

Residents guard their privacy zealously. An unwritten rule requires that every visit be prearranged in person or by telephone. Except in an emergency, no resident will stop in at another's apartment without the prior approval of the occupant, though they may be the best of friends. More than in most apartment houses, however, apartments here are used for informal social gatherings—predinner cocktail parties, luncheons with a few friends or relatives, and bridge parties.

Except for draperies and carpetings, each apartment is furnished by its owner, some very lavishly and some quite simply. The first apartment I saw was Kate Nolan's. She invited me up to her sixth-floor "snuggery," as she called it, on the evening we had dinner together. "Well, this is home," she said cheerfully, flinging the door wide. "Forgive the mess. I'm not much of a housekeeper—never have been, which is one of my good reasons for living here." She added matter-of-factly that her weekly cleaning day was two days later, on Friday.

Mementoes of Kate's years abroad decorated her apartment, most noticeably some lovely scrolls, a few intricately carved ivory and jade figures, and small oriental rugs placed here and there on the carpeted floor of the main room and the sleeping alcove. Books and magazines were everywhere—in and on two waist-high bookcases along one wall, on and under the chairside table, coffee table, small dining table, and in the alcove's bedside table and headboard shelf—an eclectic collection judging by the titles, Agatha Christie paperbacks keeping company with Erik Erikson and *Psychology Today* with *Reader's Digest*. There was no television set in sight. When I asked her about it, Kate opened the closet door in the sleeping alcove and pulled it forth. "I only watch it when I'm stuck in bed for a while, or when I can't fall asleep at night. Otherwise, I prefer to read," she said.

As she showed me around, Kate joked about the small refrigerator under the kitchen counter: "This lowdown box is the bane of our lives here. You've got to get down on your belly to clean it—sheer torture for old bones. You're sure to hear a lot of complaints about it."

All of the apartments in Lakeview House have the same kitchen. And I did hear frequent complaints about the refrigerator. The saving factor for those people who find it extremely difficult or impossible to clean is that arrangements can be made with the housekeeping service to take care of it during the resident's weekly cleaning hour, which generally includes changing bed linens, vacuuming floors and upholstered furniture, and cleaning and mopping up in kitchens and bathrooms. Dusting is considered the individual tenant's responsibility. For other chores, like polishing furniture and cleaning closets, housekeepers may be hired for after-hours or weekends.

In addition to weekly housekeeping, the monthly fee includes one meal a day—dinner six evenings a week and at noon on Sunday—served in the communal dining room. Breakfast and lunch are also available for a small charge, which is added to the monthly bill. At most, a half-dozen residents breakfast in the dining room with any regularity. Lunchtime numbers are larger but vary with the weather and the day's activities; on a cold, snowy day as many as 60 residents may be found having lunch in the dining room. Any resident confined to his or her apartment because of illness or injury may have meals brought up for a small additional charge, but dining alone without cause is discouraged. "Even the most reclusive among us must dress and come down to the dining room for dinner," Frank Smithson told me. "It's not just for nutrition, though that's important, but for at least one hour of socializing."

Only one resident complained to me about this arrange-

ment, saying that she preferred to have her main meal in the
early afternoon and often went out for lunch with friends,
skipping the evening meal at Lakeview. Most residents, however, look forward to dinnertime, arriving at the dining room a
bit before five o'clock and, in a steady flow, between then and
six-thirty.

On my first visit the original dining times of five and six
o'clock, in two separate sittings, were still being observed.
Early diners tended to crowd the very small anteroom, expressing a great deal of annoyance at the indignity of it. Those who
chose the second sitting suffered the crowding augmented by
exiting early diners. Second-shift diners saw themselves as
being more lively—the cocktail partygoers and stay-up-
laters—and were slightly scornful of the others. Complaints
about the food were endemic then, too.

A change made in 1977, when a professional caterer took
charge, improved the quality of the food and the logistics in the
dining room. Seating was made continuous from five to six-
thirty, eliminating the predinner crush outside the dining
room. Meals are selected a week ahead from a menu distributed
to every resident, allowing choices of appetizers, entrees, and
desserts. These are recorded on slips that are laid out alpha-
betically on a table in the anteroom, to be picked up by residents entering the dining room and turned over to waitresses.
Local high school girls wait on tables at dinnertime and are
regarded with obvious fondness by many of the people they
serve. Though some acerbic comments about the food are still
heard now and then, critics are fewer and milder than before
the changeover.

Everyone dresses for dinner, not formally but in going-out
clothes: men in jackets and ties, women in dresses and suits. A
hostess is on hand to seat people, but prearrangements with
friends to share a table are common. In fact, dining appointment calendars can become quite complicated, with different
companions scheduled for each day a week or more in advance.

Residents' guests are welcome at meals and, unless the
party is larger than five, advance notice is not required.
Luncheon parties for as many as 50 people have been arranged.

On all of my visits to Lakeview, a total of seven weeklong

stays over a three-year period, I found the dinner hour the most convivial time of day. A serious illness or death in the house might lead to a subdued atmosphere. Otherwise, conversations were animated, dealing with the day's activities and future plans of individuals and of the community. News of family and friends, television programs, films, books, plays, and the like were all topics for lively discussion. Talk of politics, however, was rare; this was surprising, since most residents were faithful newspaper readers. When asked about this, several people explained that controversial issues are usually left for private discussion, though most people preferred to avoid arguments—public or private.

After dinner was always the best time to talk with individual residents, who invariably invited me to their apartments. Except on rare occasions, a holiday party or special program, evenings were free of planned events, and residents were agreeable, even eager, to have company. And so, my evenings at Lakeview were usually spent listening to life stories, learning why and how these people arrived at this place when they did, and how it affected them and they it. It was during such visits that I learned about the Smithsons, Kate Nolan, Agnes Drew, and a host of others.

Frank and Doris Smithson, who had moved to her family's house on the outskirts of Watertown after his retirement and lived there for seven years, came to Lakeview because the old house seemed too large, too difficult to maintain, and too lonely. "So many of our friends were connected with the school where Frank taught, and they scattered all over the country after retirement. And so many died, friends and family—until we felt quite alone," she explained.

Frank Smithson was 82 when I first met him. A vigorous, portly man of medium height, he spoke very slowly and precisely, measuring his words as though addressing a group of children. Long association with young adolescent boys had probably established this speech pattern, for Smithson had spent 43 years—his entire working life—at a boys' school, first as an English tutor, then as assistant headmaster, and then as headmaster. The school, situated in a rural area about an hour's drive from Watertown, has a good reputation in the region and still caters to the children of upper-middle-class families. Smithson and his wife return at least once a year for class reunions and also make the trip for special celebrations to which they are invariably invited.

Frank never knew his natural father, a British army officer who deserted and disappeared soon after his son was born. Frank was raised by his mother and grandmother in Sussex, not far from London. When he was nine, his mother married an American high school teacher from Cleveland who had been traveling in Britain on a year's sabbatical. Fifteen years older than his new wife, he proved to be a generous and loving husband and father. "I consider myself very lucky to have had him as a father. Though it was some time before I got used to my new American surroundings, he did everything possible to make the transition easier. It was a terrible blow when he died just before my college graduation."

Doris Jewett Smithson, four or five years younger than her husband, was a native of Watertown, the only child of a once prominent family in the town and the state. It was through her father, a member of the boys' school board of directors, that she first met Frank. Before that she had attended a women's college, attained a liberal arts degree, and then had traveled abroad for a year with her mother and a young woman cousin of about her age. Petite, fine-featured, and vivacious, she must have enjoyed the attention of many young men during that postgraduate tour of the world in the roaring twenties. "I always manage to have fun at everything I do. But that trip was so exciting, I'll never forget it," Doris told me, her words tumbling out quickly and her hands fluttering as she spoke. Her blue eyes sparkled in the fair-skinned face crazed with networks of fine wrinkles. "It was de rigueur then for children of the well-to-do to make the grand tour after finishing school. And it really is a splendid way to let off steam before settling down. It seems to be coming back into fashion, too, only nowadays the young people don't always wait to finish school, and they seem to prefer traveling vagabond style."

They made a balanced pair: the man sober and steady, the woman bright and mercurial. She confessed with mock shame that she had only taught school—first grade—for a few years before their marriage. After that her life consisted of keeping house and raising their child, a son who now lived in California. She also taught Sunday school and did volunteer work for their church and, Frank boasted, "had the most beautiful garden on the school grounds." Most of their summers while Frank worked had been spent abroad in the British Isles and Western Europe. After Frank's mandatory retirement at 65, they moved to the Jewett family house on the outskirts of Watertown, confining their travels to two trips a year to the West Coast for visits with their son, his wife, and their three grandchildren.

As members of the denomination sponsoring Lakeview House, the Smithsons renewed their contact with the local church and took a keen interest in the project. Each time they came to town to shop, they noted the progress of construction. After the building was completed, the church ran tours for members of the congregation, a few of whom soon signed up for apartments. But the Smithsons were reluctant to abandon the old Jewett home. They visited Lakeview frequently as guests of the residents from their church, having lunch there on shopping days in town and an occasional Sunday dinner, and they joined an afternoon bridge group.

"Before long, we were coming to Lakeview two or three times a week. Then, one cold, dreary winter day, as we watched our fourth soap opera of the afternoon while pretending to read, I went to the window to look at the lights in town just beginning to show in the dusk. We hadn't been able to drive to town for three days because of the weather, and we missed it. Doris came up beside me, and we stared out at the snowy landscape as we did so often in those days. Suddenly, we looked at each other and blurted out simultaneously, 'Let's get out of here and move to Lakeview!' " Frank's broad face broke into a grin as he said this, and he laughed heartily when his wife said, "Don't think that put a stop to soap opera for me. I still have my favorites and watch them every afternoon—when we're here. And if I miss an episode, there's always someone to fill me in, because so many people here watch them. But with all there is to do for the rest of the day, it doesn't seem quite as foolish as it used to."

If life experiences could be laid out on a scale, Katherine "Kate" Nolan would come from the opposite end relative to the

Smithsons. A social worker with a master's degree, her work had often required travel, and she had lived in several countries including Taiwan. She had never married.

When I first met Kate she was 77 years old. A big, raw-boned woman, she must have been statuesque when younger. Stooped posture, her head thrust a bit forward of her body, attested to many hours of sitting at a desk and "a touch of late-blooming arthritis," as she put it. Large, irregular features gave her face a craggy appearance, but the beautiful green eyes glowing through thick spectacle lenses and a brilliant smile saved it from ugliness. Of the gleaming teeth she later told me, "The top are borrowed, but most of the bottom ones are mine," explaining that she had suffered from amoebic dysentery while traveling around in China and that part of the toll had been the loss of many teeth.

"Actually, I never recovered my health after that tour of duty, which is one of the reasons I agreed to retire at 65. That's a decision I still regret," Kate confided softly.

A few years after retirement, she was hospitalized for a detached retina and had just recovered from that when she was struck by a heart attack. It was during this second recovery period that she decided to investigate retirement homes. "I had moved around a good deal during my lifetime, always telling myself that a home is not forever, but you can carry it with you to the happiest place you can find where you know you are welcome. But with limited income you tend to get stuck in a rut. I saw it happen to many of my friends, even though the neighborhood we lived in was going from worse to awful," Kate recollected. "But I really had to prime myself. Moving takes almost more energy than you can spare when you get older."

The children of an "anti-Presbyterian" and a "failed Catholic," as Kate characterized her parents, she and her two sisters grew up in Greenwich Village in New York City. Her father, who had studied for the priesthood and left the seminary just before ordination to marry her mother, was a professor of Greek and Latin at New York University. Her mother wrote poetry, painted street scenes, befriended other artists who filled their house from morning to night and sometimes longer, and marched in the ranks of the suffragette movement.

"My mother didn't bother with us children very much. She insisted on doing her own thing. When she had a few moments, she would shower us with affection, but she was always off like a butterfly to the next flower. My father adored her and tolerated all her excesses. 'She had a very circumscribed childhood,' he would say gently." After a brief, thoughtful pause, Kate continued, "I learned an enormous amount from my father. My mother? Well, perhaps I should credit her with teaching me that a woman can be free and independent. Certainly, she made life interesting for everyone around her."

At the time we talked, Kate's family consisted of nieces and nephews scattered around the world. One nephew visited her occasionally when a business trip brought him to a nearby city. A niece, who lived a half-hour drive away, telephoned her every week and stopped by at least once a month to lunch with Aunt Kate, sometimes bringing a daughter or daughter-in-law and a small child or two with her. Holidays were shared with this niece, or with a friend and her daughter who often took both women on a jaunt for the day.

Agnes Drew, who had been widowed young and had lived and worked in Chicago for most of her life, had come to Watertown to visit her brother and stayed because she was able to get a job as secretary to the director of the town's Chamber of Commerce. She was quiet and introspective; direct and witty when she spoke, which was rarely. Whenever we talked, it was about the place and the people, and her observations were always cogent. But I learned very little about her until much later. From her appearance, I thought at first that she might have been a fashion model, but a closer look revealed that she lacked the vanity and flair that seem to go with that calling. Smartly dressed, very trim, and looking at least ten years younger than her 71 years, she continued to work at the Chamber of Commerce while living at Lakeview.

After several conversations, I was able to piece together a somewhat sketchy history of her life. Her father had been a farmer in the Midwest, the third generation of his family to work the same land; he had been killed in France during the first world war when Agnes was 13, the oldest of five children. After her father's death, her mother had sold the farm and settled the family in Chicago. Three years later, Agnes left school for a job as a bank clerk to help support her brothers and sister. In the next ten years, taking business school courses at night, she rose from clerk to teller to the bank president's secretary. When she was 22, the son of one of the bank's clients, owner of a large grain company, became interested in her and, after a brief courtship, proposed marriage. But the opposition of his family forced the couple to live in the limbo of a long, unofficial engagement until they were grudgingly given parental consent to marry.

"I was a bride at 27—and a widow before my next birthday," Agnes said bitterly. "A few weeks after our honeymoon, we discovered that Lenny had cancer. He died in my arms four months later." She sighed and waved her hand as if to brush the memory away, saying, "But that was a long time ago."

Though she had some money from her husband's family, Agnes returned to her job at the bank after his death; she stayed there for 36 years. Following a complete reorganization at the bank, which came when she was near retirement age, she was forced out in favor of someone who was familiar with the computer systems that had been installed. Unable to find another job, she agreed to serve as companion to an old friend of her mother. After the woman's death, Agnes Drew gave up her Chicago apartment and traveled, visiting each of her three brothers and a large family of nieces and nephews and their offspring. "I was a virtual stranger to them. And I'm not a good traveler—too set in my ways. But I'd had my fill of Chicago, and it was a way of getting around the country and deciding where I wanted to settle," she explained.

While staying at her youngest brother's home in a small town near Watertown, she met one of his friends at a dinner party. When the man complained to her about the difficulty of finding decent staff for the Chamber of Commerce office he directed, she offered her own services. "The salary is laughable, but since I'm not dependent upon it, that's okay. The important thing is that I'm in harness again, the work is fairly interesting, and the conditions are pleasant. It's good."

Finding an apartment was difficult, because rentals are scarce in the area. Agnes settled for a third-floor walkup flat in one of the older sections of Watertown from which she could walk to work, but she had scarcely moved in before the place was robbed. Before the year was out her apartment was burglarized three times. A mugging in the downstairs hallway was the final insult. Knocked down, her handbag snatched, she landed in the hospital with a broken shoulder and a couple of cracked ribs. "Lying in that hospital bed gave me plenty of time to think. And the more I thought, the more it seemed that Lakeview might be the best answer. I knew a good deal about it from the literature in the Chamber office and had even led several tours through the building. Why it never occurred to me before, I don't know. Possibly because none of us likes to think that we're getting old," she admitted a little sheepishly. "Well, I told myself that's stupid and had someone from the office bring me an application. I filled it out before I left the hospital."

During the four years she had to wait for her one-bedroom apartment, Agnes rented a small house near her brother's, bought a car, and took to driving to work. "I've kept the car," she told me. "It's my escape valve when I feel I need one—though I rarely do anymore."

I said that she seemed to be a loner, and because of that her choice of Lakeview surprised me a bit. "Well, there are two good reasons for my choice," Agnes answered. "First is safety; I feel secure when I walk through the doors of this building. Second is the assurance that I won't put anyone in my family through the ordeal of nursing me through a long and chronic illness. I've paid my own way, and if I have to end up in the nursing unit here, so be it. It's as pleasant as such places can be, and I'd be surrounded by friends."

She paused briefly and continued quietly, as though answering an unspoken question: "Yes, I have made a few friends here—more than ever before in my life. That's because the community is set up so that we all respect one another's rights, especially the right to privacy. Yet we're never really left to feel alone. It was one of the best decisions I ever made—coming to live at Lakeview."

2. LINGERING IMAGES:
Why Change Is Important

*Happy is the man who finds wisdom. . . . It is more
precious than rubies; and no treasure can compare
with it. Long life is in its right hand; in its left hand
riches and honor.*

—*Proverbs 3:13–16*

After only a short time at Lakeview, it struck me that life there
was a potent antidote to many of society's myths about old age.
Contrary to the standard image of the old as sickly, senile, and
helpless, the people in this congregate residence were remarkably active, capable, and independent. They were living proof
that old age is not some sort of unavoidable disease but a stage
of life that can be very rewarding despite the diminution of
some of our youthful powers.

And some experts have been trying to tell us this. Listen to
Dr. Robert Butler, former director of the National Institute on
Aging: "Recently we have been able to prove that one's learning ability, memory, and mind deteriorate to only a minute
degree as one gets older. Only five percent of people over 65
have any noticeable impairment."[1]

Yet the old images linger, even among the majority of
senior citizens. A recent Louis Harris survey revealed that
people over 65, when asked to characterize their contem-

poraries as a group, harbored the same miserable stereotypes as those under 65—not surprising when you consider that those over the line cling to the same ideas they held before they reached it. The vast majority of oldsters polled by Harris also said they believed themselves to be exceptions, since they felt quite vigorous, in fair to good health, mentally alert, and with the added benefit of many years of experience that had endowed them with more patience, understanding, and capability in solving problems. (It appears that it is always "they" who are old, while "we" stay young.)

Why this aversion to the old? Aside from our reluctance to face the ends of our own lives, there must be an historical basis. Is it because the old are considered weak and useless? That may have been so at the dawn of civilization when weak members of nomadic groups might have been left behind to die, a custom practiced until the recent past by some primitive tribes with meager resources. Or did it start in ancient Greece where the worship of ideal beauty centered on youth? The Greeks believed that as youthful beauty, vigor, and strength began to fade, life became increasingly dreary and unrewarding. In their view, long life was a curse rather than a benediction. Among the Hellenic philosophers, Plato was virtually alone in objecting to his contemporaries' obsession with the physical. He introduced the idea of aging as a natural process and, invoking the value of the spirit, expressed the belief that experience and knowledge could compensate for the loss of strength and beauty.

The people of the Old Testament took this a step further: for them the spirit was to be elevated over the flesh. Beauty is vain, they said, and only wisdom and reverence for the Lord are praiseworthy. "Happy is the man who finds wisdom. . . . It is more precious than rubies; and no treasure can compare with it. Long life is in its right hand; in its left hand riches and honor" (Proverbs 3:13–16). Long life and honor were the rewards for fidelity to God and obedience to his laws. Thus, the Hebrew patriarchs, great in their wisdom and fealty to their deity, lived to extreme old age. According to Scriptures, Abraham died at 175 "in a good old age, an old man full of years," "the days of Isaac were a hundred and fourscore years," and those of his son Jacob, 147 (Genesis 25:7, 35:28, 47:28). The Bible is full of references to good men who lived long and died old after a full life. And Isaiah, in his prophecies of a golden age for the righteous, promised, "There shall be no more thence an infant of days, nor an old man that hath not filled his days: for the child shall die a hundred years old . . ." (Isaiah 65:20).

The decline and death of the physical being are accepted as inevitable in the natural order of life; only the pursuit of wisdom and spiritual growth depend upon human will. "In the morning they are like grass which . . . flourisheth and groweth up; in the evening it is cut down and withereth. . . . The days of our years are threescore and ten; and if by reason of strength they be fourscore, yet is their pride, labor, and sorrow; for it is soon cut off, and we fly away. . . . So teach us to number our days, that we may apply our hearts unto wisdom" (Psalm 90:5–12).

Throughout, Judeo-Christian teachings enjoin us to revere and honor our elders. At the same time, the Greco-Roman influence—the idolatry of physical beauty—remained and often, as in modern times, gained ascendancy. In past centuries the two views could coexist with relative ease, because so few people lived to old age. Furthermore, the old were keepers of the wealth—the coffers, the estates, the farms, flocks, ships—thus commanding respectful treatment from the young and especially their heirs. Secular literature, however, continued to record aging's grim infirmities, senescence, and other signs of decay; perhaps the best known example is the passage in Shakespeare's *As You Like It* that depicts the seven ages of man, ending with "second childishness and mere oblivion, sans teeth, sans eyes, sans taste, sans everything." Old age, then as now, was regarded with a mixture of respect, fear, despair, and loathing.

During the industrial revolution, with the advent of more democratic societies in western nations, the old were forced to relinquish some of their power. Youth took the reins, and the old were shunted aside and expected to die off quietly while the young and vigorous fought the wars and got on with the job of building nations—and all but the sturdiest of the old obliged. With modern advances in the biological sciences and medical arts, more of us are living into old age. But living how? And for what? "Empty-handed old people without any role in the life of the next generation," Margaret Mead has said of the new legions of older Americans.

Does old age have to be a time of emptiness and isolation? The answer, of course, depends to some extent on each of us—on how we have lived, what we have learned, whom we have loved, and the host of physical and emotional factors that go into the making of a mature individual. Equally important are the cultural values and public attitudes that set the stage for us throughout our lives.

How we see ourselves is generally a reflection of the way society sees us. In youth and middle age, we can easily define ourselves in terms of our careers, our friends, and our roles as parents and homemakers. In later years we lose this kind of identity and, unless we can substitute new roles, we tend to look backward and live in the past as so many old people do. With the growing population of the elderly, that is those over the age of 65, who now constitute more than 11 percent of the U.S. population, the demand for changes in societal attitudes and actions has quickened, and this has become manifest in the burgeoning studies of gerontology and geriatrics.

In 1970, only about 400 schools in this country offered at least one course in gerontology; ten years later, more than 1,300 schools offered such courses, and it has been predicted that every college and university in the country will have a program in gerontology by the year 2000. There are now gerontology centers and institutes in more than a dozen colleges and universities, large and small, across the country, as well as a national institute and agencies on aging in most states. Conferences and symposia on aging, once rare, are now organized on regional, national, and international levels and held with increasing frequency. Early in 1982, the first department of geriatrics to be established at an American medical school was announced by Mount Sinai Medical Center in New York City. Although many of the nation's 126 medical schools had centers or institutes for the study of health care problems of the elderly, this was the first time that geriatrics was given equal status with other medical fields by integrating it into the curriculum as a required course for all students.

Study and research and the exchange of information are bringing new hope for an improved quality of life in old age. Better understanding of preventive health measures and of psychological needs should lead to a more healthy and vigorous elderly population. Even the cultural stigma attached to growing old in our society is being attacked through education and the media, and a new message is being conveyed: We are all headed this way, and we will all be as different from each other then as we are now. In fact, the destruction of stereotypes and the recognition of human diversity, no matter what our ages, may be the most significant finding of the flourishing new science of the old.

Future generations may well consider long life one of the greatest achievements of the twentieth century. A child born in the United States in 1900 could expect to live 47 years. Today the average lifespan is 74 years, an increase resulting from improved sanitation, nutrition, and immunization which reduce the risk of dying in infancy and childhood. In 1980 there were more than 32,000 centenarians, as compared to the 1970 count of about 7,300.

And the old today are not what they once were. For increasing numbers of people the extension of life accompanied by relatively good health has come to mean a gift of years to be used in new ways—to start new careers, to learn new skills, to begin new adventures. If the present trend toward a general aging of the population continues, coming generations of healthier, more vigorous, and better educated older Americans should be needed and welcomed into the work force and the voluntary sector for most of their lives. Even today, a few lucky souls pick up speed as they approach retirement age and, freed of family cares, launch themselves on successful business or artistic ventures or second careers.

Expectations of longer life may also be responsible, at least in part, for the startling changes in the way we all live now—the longer period of adolescence, greater flexibility in career and marital choices, shifting family relationships.

Knowing that we have more time to switch tracks and change direction has made us a little bolder in experimenting with different lifestyles. "Years ago, only the young, during the interval before they got into the responsibilities of adulthood, were able to live experimentally. Now you're seeing a new group of older people, who no longer live for duty and responsibility. These people are able to grow even more in their later years than they did in their youth," says Dr. James E. Birren, director of the Ethel Andrus Gerontology Center at the University of Southern California.[2]

For all of the exciting prospects implicit in longer life for greater numbers of us, there are at least as many problems to plague and bedevil us—individually and as a society. How can we increase job opportunities for older workers without alienating the younger ones? Can we manage an income support system sufficient to maintain decent levels of dignity and comfort? What about the cost, quality, and availability of medical care? Can we afford community-based programs and services for the elderly who wish to remain in their own homes? What provisions will be made for special housing for frail old people who can no longer manage on their own? Will we accept new living arrangements in old age?

All of these questions are being addressed today with varying degrees of success. But one of the most persistent and recalcitrant problems—the shortage of decent, affordable housing in this country (and not just for the elderly)—has grown worse over the past decade. Cities—once good places for old people to live because of public transportation, neighborhood cohesion, and the proximity of health, social, and cultural facilities—are now degenerating at a frightening pace. Instead of the convenience and comfort found in former days, older residents are being victimized by crime and hurt by the general neglect of urban services. Other old people live in lonely isolation in suburban or rural houses, often too large and difficult to maintain, uncertain about where to go and fearful of change, especially of institutionalization.

In general, a safe and comfortable place to live becomes more important to all of us as we grow older. Throughout our lives, where we live determines to a great extent how we live, but this is especially true when we have lost some of the vigor, resilience, and mobility of youth. During the years when school, jobs, recreation, and other activities of busy adult life keep us on the move, home may be only the place where we sleep—and it may change as frequently as we change jobs or, in recent years, lifestyles.

For most older people, the circle of life shrinks as mobility diminishes, more time is spent at home, and the place itself becomes very important. Increasing difficulties encountered even when coping with ordinary needs—shopping, cooking, banking, housecleaning and repairs, medical and dental care—are compounded when home locales are changed. A new supermarket, bank, or physician's office can present an overwhelming set of obstacles to a person who has reached a stage of life where he or she is barely managing by rote.

The psychic investment in home seems to increase with age, too; it becomes the sanctuary for memories of family life, loves won and lost, career and scholastic achievements, triumphs and tragedies. For many, leaving home means losing precious mementoes. Ghosts of the past become surrogates and consolers for the love and attention missing in the present.

The current generation of the aged lived through two world wars, the Great Depression, and an explosion of population and technological innovation unprecedented in the history of humanity. Many in this generation were immigrants and have been worn down physically by lifetimes of hard work; they are ill-equipped culturally and educationally to cope with the swarm of new mechanical and electronic marvels. (When my mother was a small girl, there were still horsedrawn trolleys on the streets of New York City, radio and telephone were in their infancy, and television was the stuff of science fiction.) These are the people—the poor and moderate-income old—who have been left behind in deteriorating city and older suburban neighborhoods, who barricade themselves behind triple-locked doors, and struggle to preserve a last vestige of the lives they built so laboriously through the long, hard years.

Recognition of this strong attachment to home and the traumatic effect of moving on elderly individuals has resulted in increased home and community services: outreach programs, senior centers, lunch programs including meals-on-wheels for the homebound, friendly visitors, homemakers, and visiting nurse services. In age-dense neighborhoods, where the population warrants such programs and funds are made available for them, even the frail elderly are able to remain in their own homes, sometimes until the end of their lives. Support services of this kind and the relatively new medical and social day care centers for the elderly also benefit the semidependent aged who live with younger family members, while relieving some of the pressure on the caretaker family. The social, psychological, and economic value of these community programs is undisputed; their cost, in monetary terms, is generally lower than the cost of maintaining patients in institutions.

One of the many studies corroborating the need for support services was a survey of 182 senior housing authority managers, who were asked to estimate the number of their tenants in need of such services. On the basis of her sample, Dr. Wilma Donahue, director of the International Center for Social Gerontology, who conducted the survey, concluded that more than 3 million old people nationwide could use an assisted living arrangement. "If the services are not provided," Dr. Donahue warned, "the entire 3 million may be forced to resort to nursing homes, 80 percent of them unnecessarily."[3]

Actually, only a small percentage of the elderly population is in nursing homes at any one time. Of the 26.8 million people over the age of 65 in the United States in 1982, about 1.3 million (5 percent) were in institutions, including nursing homes. Just how many were there because they had nowhere else to go has been variously estimated at one-third to as much as two-thirds of the institutional population.

Most old people lived in family settings (16.1 million) and about a third lived alone or with nonrelatives (7.6 million). A large majority of the last group—6 million—were women. With advancing age, the proportion of the elderly living in family settings decreases while the proportion in institutions rises.

It is sometimes difficult to extract the human story from statistics, but in the case of the elderly in this country the numbers are very revealing; they tell us that more women than men survive into old age—146 to 100 at age 65—and the disparity continues to grow with age, that more than three-quarters of the men (75.5 percent) are married—almost half of them to women under 65—whereas only a little over a third (38 percent) of the much larger number of women are married, most to men older than themselves. Of the approximately 16 million women in the 65-and-over age group, 52 percent are widowed and 9 percent single or divorced, which adds up to more than 9 million. Since only a small number are in institutions, where do these 9 million women alone live? And what about the 2.5 million men alone? How do they manage?

Some of them do very well indeed, especially those under 75. Like their married contemporaries, they have a variety of lifestyles. More than two-thirds live in the nation's metropolitan areas, the rest in rural areas. Those who are completely independent have homes of their own—apartments, condominiums, mobile homes, homes in retirement communities and senior housing complexes. Those who are semidependent may live in congregate residences, group homes, and living quarters shared with relatives or friends. More dependent older adults may find themselves living in relatives' homes, sheltered boarding homes, and foster homes, and there are intermediate care facilities—convalescent and skilled nursing homes—for the partially or temporarily disabled. Anyone who lives to a great age may go the full gamut from completely independent living to long-term nursing care. The trick is to find the best mode of living before a crisis arises that catapults you prematurely into the least desirable surroundings.

Social service workers who search out the distressed elderly tell heartrending stories of apartments or houses filled with debris, infested with vermin, with heat and other utilities shut off because bills are lost and forgotten amid the clutter. Although many are poor—one out of four over 65 and half of those over 75 live at or near the poverty level—the awful conditions in which some isolated old people live are not restricted to the poor.

Dr. Andrew Farber, a psychiatrist and member of a state-sponsored crisis team in one of New York's wealthiest counties, reports, "I go in and the houses are like weird museums. There are plants with dust you could stick your fingernails into, stacks of newspapers, and charred pots and pans. That's one of the key signs; that's when I know they need help. If they put food on the stove and forget it, it means the possibility of fire."[4]

Some of the elderly found by the crisis team, often alerted by shopkeepers or neighbors, had outlived their doctors and were no longer under any medical supervision at all. Some continued to take medicines prescribed for them years before, though the drugs were often useless and sometimes harmful because of physiological changes. Many suffered nutritional disorders because they snacked instead of bothering to prepare meals.

Kate Nolan, whose application to Lakeview House had been met by family and friends with disapproval, described the plight of one of her old neighbors in the city. "Sarah was a sturdy woman in her mid-seventies, quite healthy. Oh, a touch of arthritis that made walking a bit difficult and the kind of bronchial condition that many people who live in big cities seem to get when they get older. Her husband died about twenty years before I knew her, so she'd been living alone in her apartment for a long time—and she seemed to like it."

"She was something of a loner," Kate continued, "refusing to join any senior groups in the neighborhood, but she played bridge with a few of the neighbors two evenings a week. On nice days, she'd go off and spend time browsing in department stores. But her greatest pride was her apartment; it was crammed full of bric-a-brac and furniture, and she kept everything spotless. She also liked to cook and bake. So she kept pretty busy. During the winter months, she rarely went out. She'd call and have her groceries delivered.

"Oh, another thing," Kate recalled. "She refused to use a cane. That would have helped with her arthritic legs, but she said it made you look old—and she was quite vain and stubborn about that. Well, in early December of my second winter here at Lakeview, she fell on the icy pavement on her way to catch a bus to her doctor's office. That was the beginning of the end," Kate said, shaking her head sadly.

While Sarah was hospitalized with a hip fracture, her apartment was vandalized—silver stolen, china smashed, stuffed furniture and mattresses slashed. Although her son, who had come in from the Midwest several times, tried to repair some of the damage and restore order, the shock of the changes she found when she returned to the apartment, added to the state of helplessness caused by the injury, threw Sarah into a profound depression.

"The last time I saw her," Kate said, "on one of my periodic visits to friends in the old apartment house, she was pitifully apathetic. A homemaker came in for several hours a day, but both she and the apartment seemed slightly unkempt. It was sad. Soon afterward, I was told, her son took her out to Chicago and placed her in a nursing home near there, close to his home. I wrote once, but a letter came back from the management saying that she had died."

We agreed that the same series of incidents could have thrown a younger person, too. Of course, the prognosis for recovery would have been much better. But Kate refused to accept bad luck as the cause of Sarah's troubles. "If she had gone into a place like Lakeview a few years before, I'm quite certain she'd never have had the accident. I think she'd have adjusted to using a cane—so many of us do. As for the destruction of her precious things, it was inevitable with the rise of crime in the city. It had to happen sooner or later. Of course, she'd have had to give some of them up before coming here, but whatever she kept would be perfectly safe. And I think she'd have enjoyed life here and could easily have lived another ten years."

All of us have heard stories, from friends, relatives, and the news media, of old people in distress. Some of us have personal experience with aging relatives, grown dependent upon us because of accident, illness, or deteriorating health, who have slipped from proud independence to varying stages of dependence. If it is a gradual decline, we can help the old person plan an alternative living arrangement. But it may take all of our powers of persuasion.

It was the Smithsons who persuaded Tom McAdams to come to Lakeview. "It wasn't easy to get him to submit the application, and he almost went out like a used lightbulb during the three years he had to wait to get an apartment," Doris Smithson remembered.

When I met Tom at Lakeview, he was a spry man of 82. He had been one of Frank Smithson's colleagues at the boys' school, where they both taught for many years. His wife had died six years before, and after her death he had insisted on staying on in their home. One son and his family, living about 90 miles from the McAdams house, looked in on him once a month or so and helped with repairs and the heavier chores. "That first spring after his wife died, Tom planted his vegetable garden as usual," Smithson told me. "But at harvest time, he left the stuff rotting on the plants—never picked a thing. It was weird. And that was the first indication his family had that something was wrong."

The following spring, there was no garden at the McAdams house, and the old man developed reclusive habits, scarcely responding to his children and grandchildren when they telephoned or visited. During the winter, the younger McAdams got a call from a neighbor who was worried because the house had been dark for several days and no one answered when she knocked. At the house, he found his father huddled in bed under a pile of quilts. The house was a shambles—clothing piled everywhere, dirty dishes filling the sink and lining the counters, open food cans and boxes scattered about. The electricity had been shut off because, as he later discovered, the bills had been ignored for months. Ignoring his father's weak protests, the son bundled him into the car, locked the house, and took the old man home with him.

"But living at his son's home didn't seem to help at all, except that he was fed and clothed," Frank continued. "Tom remained despondent. He rarely spoke to anyone, never went out, just sat in front of the TV set staring at the screen or dozing. He nearly drove them all crazy."

The Smithsons recalled that they had moved to Lakeview a few months before Mrs. McAdams's death. "We went to the funeral and visited him several times after that, and we knew he was suffering. He'd always been an outgoing, rather jolly type, but he'd become glum and untalkative. We thought he'd come out of it after a while, but when he seemed to get worse we began urging him to visit us here, to look the place over and think about moving in. That was the only time I saw him show any life. He'd get angry, say that he wasn't planning to move anywhere, that this had been his home for 32 years and the only way he'd leave would be to be carried out," Doris said.

The younger McAdams and his wife brought Tom to Lakeview to see the Smithsons. After several visits and much coaxing, he reluctantly agreed to apply for residence. "It's a lucky thing we didn't lose him during that long wait," Frank added. "But you can see how well he's doing now, and it didn't take too long for him to perk up once he was here." Indeed Tom McAdams appeared very alert and cheerful when I met him.

Sarah and Tom are only two of the many old people who make the precipitous drop from complete independence to inertia and despair. The circumstances that cause them to give up on life can be external—illness, accident, injury, shock caused by violence or the death of someone close—or it can be a state of mind induced and nourished by isolation, loneliness, and fear. With assistance, concern, and love, this surrender of self can sometimes be reversed, as it was with Tom.

It is said that depression is the major disease of old age in this country. One commentator on the subject asks, "How much of senile behavior—loss of memory, loss of orientation, confusion . . .—is the result of the aging process itself, and how much the result of the situation into which we thrust the elderly? How much is caused by physiological changes in the brain and body, and how much by social influences?"[5] Except for the cumulative damage to the brain caused by successive small strokes or the effects of Alzheimer's disease, most of the symptoms lumped together as senility are actually symptoms of physical or mental disorders that can be treated and often corrected. Some of the causes of senile behavior are as simple as improper diet or the side effects of medication.

Given their vulnerability to symptomatic senility, why do so many old people insist on living alone? There is, as we said, the strong attachment to home and the concomitant fear of change. Another reason is pride in independence, the feeling that "I've managed alone all these years, and I can still do it." Related to this is the unwillingness to be a burden to anyone, the fear of becoming an annoyance, being treated impersonally, and losing identity. Other reasons might be an exaggerated need for privacy, an inability to get along well with other people, a refusal to accept one's own aging, and any number of others depending upon individual personality. But overlying all of these reasons and intricately woven into them is the common prejudice against shared or communal living arrangements with peers, summed up in the pejorative use of the term "old age home." Any one or a combination of these reasons can prevent an otherwise sensible person from admitting the need for a change and exploring the available options before a problem has reached crisis proportions, leaving the individual no choice.

It is true that a few people do manage to reach very old age living in seeming independence. We say "seeming" because most of them invariably depend upon a network of support— from families, friends, social agencies, churches, or hired help. Longevity seems to favor those individuals with intense interest—in business, art, or organizational activities. Pablo Picasso, Louise Nevelson, Artur Rubinstein, and Georgia O'Keefe are some of the famous octo- and nonagenarians who come readily to mind, all of them with the strong backup force of an entourage of younger apprentices and assistants.

Most people, by the time they reach the age of 75, do need some help. Even with the best community resources available, they must still spend a good deal of time by themselves when they live alone. As mobility and self-reliance diminish, demands on family and friends increase. Those lucky enough to have understanding and concerned people close by, who can and will commit themselves to steady assistance, may be able to hold on to their old way of life. Others will be moved into younger relatives' homes, usually the homes of children who are themselves approaching their sixties and looking forward to some years of freedom to travel and enjoy life without the responsibilities of child-rearing and jobs. There undoubtedly are successful arrangements of this kind, built upon foundations of good, loving relationships. More often, the situation is stressful for the aged parent and the adult child. So widespread have the problems endemic to this living arrangement become that a whole new vocabulary has been invented to describe it: pressure-cooker environment, sandwich generation (for the aging children of aged parents), women in the middle (for the daughters and daughters-in-law on whom most of the responsibility falls).

The National Institute of Health, in a workshop report on older women, points out that nearly two-thirds of women over age 65 are widows, that half of the women living alone have incomes of $3,000 a year or less, and that those in their seventies had the lowest fertility rate of any generation of women in the United States (since their child-bearing years coincided with the depression years of the thirties and World War II). Therefore, the report concludes, "these older women can expect to live the last years of their lives without a husband, on limited income, and with few if any children to provide financial, emotional, or social support."[6]

That's a rather grim picture of old age! And it forces us to realize how many do not have families to rely on. No matter how emotionally painful reliance on relatives can become, at the very least they are the ones who can be counted on in emergencies. For the true loner, without family or devoted friends, a crisis often signals a swift descent. Any incapacitation, unless it is very short-lived and can be handled by a social agency—if there is one in the community and if the stricken person or an acquaintance knows enough to contact the agency for help—can land the elderly individual in a nursing home, the most dreaded of all possibilities. And every person alone knows this; it's a chance they take.

Yet every day valiant battles are fought by aging people who cling to their old homes, fearing change, while all about them change wreaks havoc with the quality of their lives. The very force they seek to deny by staying invades their turf, destroying familiar landmarks and comforts. First, loss of job and career status devours their self-esteem, death continuously robs them of friends and family, and crime-infested streets daily threaten their very existence. Increasing isolation and fear often bring confusion, despair, and ill health. Yet they resist change, preferring to suffer the ills they know to the loss of independence, dignity, and control over their lives envisioned in some dreaded institution.

This terrible fear of institutions rooted in the consciousness of old people comes from several sources. Early memories may have set the pattern. An excerpt from an 1890s essay, "Life in New York Tenement-Houses as Seen by a City Missionary," is illuminating: "There are many poor, upright, God-fearing old people who struggle against fearful odds to keep body and soul together, and yet they drift daily toward the almshouse on Blackwell's Island, the last and most dreaded halting-place on the way to Potter's Field. I have nothing to say against the administration of the almshouse or the treatment of its inmates, but I do not wonder that old men and women who have led a good moral life would rather die than be stranded on the island and take up their abode among the broken wrecks of humanity which fill that institution."[7] Morality may not have played as large a role in the fortune of the "inmates" of almshouses as the minister–author believed, but the judgment of their ultimate abode is certainly hellish.

Old impressions of workhouses and poorhouses—from experience or hearsay—are reinforced by visits to hospital wards and media coverage of nursing home and boarding home abuses, building a lifetime distrust for all institutions and motivating the struggle to hang on to one's cherished freedom. Though admirable, this struggle can also be self-defeating. For an extreme case, but one that without doubt is illustrative of similar scenes taking place in any modern city as you read this, we go back again to the last decade of the nineteenth century, this time "Among the Poor of Chicago."

"The poorest and most wretched household we found that day was that of an old soldier, a gray-haired man of education and (at some time) of intelligence, once a lieutenant in a volunteer regiment. He was wounded at the battle of Fair Oaks. There he lies, grimy and vermin-infested, in a filthy bed, with a young grandchild beside him in like condition, and a drunken virago of a woman, ramping and scolding in the two rooms which constitute the family abode. She is quite the most repulsive being yet met with. A little inquiry develops the fact that this man was in the Soldiers' Home in Milwaukee (and could return there to remain, if he wished), well fed, clothed, and cared for, and that he left there because: 'You see you can't stand it to be kept down all the time and moved back and forth, and here and there, whether you like it or not.' And he moved his black paws back and forth, and here and there, on the dingy bedclothes, to indicate how the Home deprived him of his freedom—his 'liberty' to pass his time in the living death which his present condition seems to the onlooker."[8]

Freedom is a mockery if it means squalid surroundings, constant fear of assault, and long hours of imprisonment and loneliness when daylight hours grow short, as it does for so many of our old, rich and poor. It can also mean being trapped in a self-perpetuating cycle of malnutrition, depression, and ill health. To generations of old people, however, the words "old age home" have conjured up a vision more fearful than any suffering they have endured living with relatives or on their own.

And it is not just the old. Too many of us, of all ages, try to erase all thoughts of old age. Paradoxically, this tendency seems to get stronger as we grow older. Not only do we dread thinking about our own aging, but we desperately side-step any reminders—including old people. Add to this fear the prejudice against any type of planned housing for the elderly, and we have built a barrier against planning for our own futures, distorted ideas that prevent us from making wise choices, and we tend to stick with what we have and hope for the best.

No one knows exactly how many old people are unhappy in their homes but afraid to move. As we pointed out before, a helping community and family can go a long way toward providing contentment and eliminating the need for change. But some older adults have sought change. And over the past 30 years we have seen a variety of living arrangements created by and for them. Today about 10 percent of the elderly population lives in communities built for older Americans. Adult/ retirement communities, residences, and housing complexes, for those who can afford them, are risen and rising from sea to shining sea, the growing population of the elderly having made them profitable. Congregate housing, shared housing, and group living offer more sheltered and usually less expensive alternatives; they are sometimes the next step after leisure activity types of retirement communities. In fact, the possibility of the need for a second move is an important consideration in late-life planning. (Other considerations and more details about housing are discussed in chapter 8.)

As always in our society, there are many choices for the well-heeled and a shortage for the poor, which accounts for the large numbers of old people living in squalor or wandering the streets of our cities as "bag people."

Astute and courageous people, young and old, have pioneered and are continuing to work and plan for decent living environments for old people at all income levels. Most of us will have to become informed and involved, and we will if we can conquer our fears and prejudices. The possibility of living to be 100 should be cause for jubilation, not lament. But how can we rejoice in years marred by fear and isolation? With very few exceptions, the people at Lakeview House chose to live there because they looked into the future and saw their need for a haven, a safe and congenial home. In many cases they came because of the enthusiastic testimony of friends.

Kate Nolan, for example, owed her introduction to Lakeview to Betty Reardon. She and Betty had been college friends. "After graduation we kept in touch, but just barely, with once-a-year Christmas messages and meetings every couple of years, either at class reunions or for lunch on the rare occasions when I was in New York," Kate explained. "Then, during the year or so that I worked in the city before going off on the China assignment, we saw each other quite frequently. After that we corresponded faithfully and, when I returned, I settled in New York, and we saw quite a lot of each other until Betty moved out here."

Eventually, Kate followed her friend's lead and applied for an apartment. It was barely within her means, she said, whereas most other housing alternatives were not. "What kept me from doing it straight off was my preference for big-city living—New York or Boston, say—for the cultural advantages. As it turns out, being here hasn't deprived me of much at all. Betty and I and a few other women still travel into the city once in a while. Not as frequently as we did in our first years here, but there are concerts, theaters, and museums closer to home, and we enjoy those, too."

Pointing out the window at the lights shimmering on the lake and glittering from the houses and the highway beyond them on the far shore, she said, "That view and the feeling of safety and being surrounded by good friends are more than I dared hope for."

Once, on a later visit when our acquaintance had deepened, I asked Kate why she had never married. "Maybe because I was bigger, smarter, and harder-working than most of the men I knew," she joked, her wit intact despite failing health and, worse for a book-lover, failing vision.

When we discussed family, Kate grew philosophical: "It's amazing how panicky you get as you grow old—with or without family. If you have children, or younger brothers or sisters, you're scared every time you feel a twinge that you're going to become dependent on them. And if there is no one close to look after you, you're scared silly because there is no one. And that's what makes places like Lakeview so important; no one wants to burden relatives or friends, no matter how much they love you." I was to hear echoes of this theme over and over again.

She advised me to talk to Betty Reardon about this. "Both of Betty's daughters were eager to have her come live with them. They're busy gals, with jobs and community work, and they insisted that it would be a boon to have her at home looking after things. And Betty would be a definite asset—she's so bright and energetic. The girls got into quite a heat over who would win her and then, typically for Betty's girls, agreed to share her—half and half." Kate laughed and said again, "Ask Betty why she preferred living at Lakeview."

Betty Reardon was a forerunner of today's woman, balancing a career as a retailing executive at a New York department store with homemaking for her husband and daughters. "Actually, I wanted to be an economist," she told me, "but it was a difficult field for a woman to break into in those days. As it turned out, I loved my job and was very good at it. Best of all, my husband was cooperative, the apartment was easy to manage, and the girls were very good, God bless them." Her face shone as she spoke.

A plump, animated woman in her late seventies, her eyes still bright blue, Betty had pretty features and deep smile wrinkles at the outer corners of her eyes and mouth. She was widowed in her early sixties and retired from her job a few years later, picking up the slack by increasing her activities in the church. She was appointed to its first housing advisory committee and later became the only woman member of the housing corporation's board. "It was all very exciting— investigating the different kinds of homes and communities," she recalled. "There weren't as many choices then as there are now—and some were terrible and others quite pleasant. But there was no question about it; after all the reviews and reports, we decided on a congregate residence—though it was a very new idea. The decision was unanimous. Later, we had to work out the financing, and that wasn't easy. But the really hard part was finding the site. And I think we did quite well, don't you?" she concluded happily.

It was apparent that Betty Reardon had invested personal as well as altruistic concern in her work with the original committee and housing corporation, developing as deep a love for the place as she would have for a house she had built with her own hands. And she actually said as much, describing the cabin in the Adirondack Mountains that she and her husband had built when their daughters were young teens. "That's the only place I've loved more than Lakeview. That little cabin meant more to me than any of the apartments we ever lived in. After John had his stroke," she went on pensively, "when the doctor finally said he could be moved, I took him up there to stay. It was early June. At the end of the month, our girls and sons-in-law and all the grandkids came up for a week. On the day before they were to leave, John fell asleep sitting in his chair in the late afternoon sun with all of the young people shouting and running about playing games. He never awoke." After a moment she added, "It was a beautiful way to go. Our Maker must have loved him."

About Lakeview she explained, "I think I knew from the very beginning that I would come here to live. I've never liked living alone and, though my daughters are dear and wonderful, I've always believed that, as adults, we should live separate lives."

"Why?" I asked. "Kate says they were eager to have you and that you all get along so well."

"That's because we do live apart," Betty answered, laughing. "Oh, I'm sure it would have worked out fine," she hastened to say. "After all, we do love each other and are polite and civilized. But our interests and energy levels are different, and I think we'd soon clash—politely, of course. And they'd feel constrained, having to invite me with them wherever they went or curtailing some of their activities in deference to me. I sense it after a while, even on just a short visit. And I definitely don't want that—to put a crimp in their lives. Or, for that matter, in mine."

I admired her for her independence and self-assurance. Late-onset diabetes had robbed her of "one of the great pleasures in life—rich desserts. You'd think I'd lose weight, wouldn't you? No such luck!" That self-mockery was the closest thing to self-pity I ever heard from her, nor did she ever exhibit what Coleridge called "that sign of old age, extolling the past at the expense of the present." It seemed to me that Betty Reardon, one of the founders, planners, and original residents of Lakeview House, embodied all that was best about it—the spirit of independence, the optimism, and the strong sense of community.

3. AT THE CONTROLS:
Resident Activities

The council's main purpose is to serve as a self-governing organization so that residents can decide on the kinds of activities they want to be involved in and the rules they want to live with.

—Rev. Craig Winiford,
Lakeview resident and first
chairman of the Residents
Council

The downstairs assembly room was full by seven-thirty in the evening when Frank Smithson, chairman of the Residents Council, called the meeting to order. He welcomed his audience and said, "I'm glad to see so many glowing faces—with scarcely a new freckle or wrinkle among them. I hope you've all had a fine summer and stored up lots of energy, so that you're eager to begin our fall activities." Chuckles and murmurs of assent were heard—and the business of the meeting began.

As the minutes of the last meeting, in May, were read by the council's secretary, I looked around the room. It had a seating capacity of 200, and every seat seemed to be filled. Since only two staff members—Lakeview's administrator and the activities director—were regularly invited to attend the monthly council meetings, most of the residents must have been there. They all listened attentively as the treasurer's report and various committee reports were presented.

First to speak was Ruth Dobbins for the Hospitality Committee. She introduced two residents who had moved into the house during the summer. They were greeted with polite applause. Then, the editor of the monthly newsletter, explaining that she would be undergoing cataract surgery the following week, asked for a volunteer to assist the new editor, who had been serving as her assistant. Next, the Garden Club representative reported that annuals were being potted and brought indoors to decorate the lobby, lounges, dining room, and nursing floor, which, she added proudly, the club had supplied with fresh flower arrangements all summer.

Other reports, announcements, and calls for volunteers came from the notions shop, the program committee, the music and arts committee, and the housekeeping watch committee. Now and then a question was asked or someone offered to fill a vacancy. But the only piece of business that aroused any show of feeling was the report by the nursing unit volunteers, ten women who regularly spent time with patients.

Under the leadership of Karen Burgher, the NUVs, as they called themselves, had persuaded the administrator to allow the most fit residents of the nursing floor to have lunch in the main dining room instead of their day room on weekdays. The plan had been instituted during the summer, and I had noticed about a dozen people, most of them in wheelchairs, sitting at tables near the entrance to the dining room during lunch hour. From comments by other residents, I understood that a few were so upset and angry over this development that they had gone to Ben Gordon, the administrator, to protest. Ms. Burgher spoke of this and asked Gordon to take the floor.

"From my own observations and reports by staff and volunteers," Gordon began, "this arrangement has been very beneficial for the nursing unit people. I don't see that any objections can be taken too seriously in view of the good results," he added firmly.

"Why don't we take a vote on whether it should be continued?" a woman in the audience proposed.

"Go ahead, if you like. But no matter how the vote turns out I want you to know that we plan to continue for as long as it's good for the patients and does no harm to anyone else," Gordon warned.

Several voices called out, "Hear! Hear!" including Rev. Craig Winiford who sat beside me. And when Smithson asked whether there was a motion on the floor for discussion, only nays were heard. Whereupon he shrugged and went on, "Since you have the floor, Ben, why don't you fill us in on the safety committee's plan for fire drill training."

The brief flare-up over nursing patients in the dining room was one of the few times in Lakeview's history when administration overruled residents, Rev. Winiford told me afterward. As it turned out, Gordon reached a compromise some months later with the minority opposed to this ruling: The patients were served lunch in the dining room every weekday except Friday—the day most favored, in addition to weekends, for inviting guests and having group luncheons.

I had dined with the reverend and his wife Lydia and accompanied them to the meeting at his invitation, which, he assured me, had been approved by the council's executive board. With the true courtliness born of early instruction and nine decades of practice, Craig Winiford was very solicitous of my welfare throughout the evening. In the dining room, he had urged me to take the chair with the best view of the outdoors and had insisted on ordering another dessert for me when I exclaimed over how good it was. During dinner and as we made our way to the assembly room, he had carefully explained the structure and functions of the Residents Council, its executive board, and some of the committees, of which there were at least two dozen, he said.

Lydia Winiford would interject a gentle reminder now and then and laugh at her husband's occasional witticisms. She was small and very lean; he was tall and lean. A bit quicker than he, she was in her late eighties and he in his early nineties; both used canes but were quite active. They had just returned from three months spent at their summer cottage in Maine. "We're there mid-June to mid-September, but we always make certain to return in time for the council meeting in the fall," Lydia said.

Winiford had been presiding minister of the largest church of his denomination for 45 years, a position from which he retired when he reached age 75. Soon after I met him, he commented that he was "living proof of the marvels of modern medical technology, complete with pacemaker, hearing aids, sturdy spectacles, and a back brace." Even with his specs, his vision was very poor, but he managed well with his wife's help and an indomitable spirit that enabled him to compensate.

Rev. Winiford had seen Lakeview through from initial concept, as a member of the original search committee, to residence in the house when it opened. He continued as an active member of the sponsor's board for several years after he became a resident and was also the first chairman of the Residents Council. He explained that the council was initiated by the first administrator and held its organizational meeting in January 1969, four months after Lakeview was occupied by the first contingent of 32 tenants. Every Lakeview resident automatically became a member of the council, which met once a month except during June, July, and August. There were no dues, but over the years fund-raising activities had evolved to pay for some of the improvements at Lakeview that the sponsoring corporation could not afford. A canopy over the front walk outside the building was one such amenity; others were holiday and party decorations and refreshments, program and music equipment, and so on.

"The council's main purpose, of course, is to serve as a self-governing organization so that residents can decide on the kinds of activities they want to be involved in and the rules they want to live with," said Winiford.

There are a few basic rules and regulations established by the administration and accepted by each person who comes to live at Lakeview. (We will discuss these later.) But the Winifords could remember only one other instance when the administration set policy without the full agreement of the residents. "It was during the first year the house was open. I was chairman of the council then, and there was a big to-do about whether and where smoking would be permitted," Rev. Winiford recalled. "A few people insisted that it be permitted in the common rooms, especially in the dining room. Others were equally vociferous against. Our administrator at the time, Rev. Cotwold, stepped in and ruled against. And the rule has remained. Smoking can only be done in private apartments. And we settled for the same rule on drinking—alcoholic beverages, that is."

"Later on, we bent that rule a bit so we could have wine punch at our Christmas parties," Lydia commented wryly.

The Winifords, who preferred early dinner, rarely went to the cocktail parties held in various apartments in the house by some late diners, but they assured me that very little alcohol was consumed during these predinner socials. As an occasional guest, I was able to confirm this. Snacks, fruit juice, ginger ale, and wine were always served, and the hostess (it was seldom a host, though it might be a couple) invariably knew which of her five to ten guests drank hard liquor. I attended several cocktail hours at which no one drank anything stronger than wine. No matter, the conversation and camaraderie were just as potent, and everyone moved on to the dining room with raised spirits.

The knowledge that they were in control and the nature of the residents, most of whom had spent their lives in service careers, combined to spur them on to work and plan for the community. More than half of them were either council officers, directors, or active members of committees. Not only were there more than 100 active residents but at least 60 percent served on two or more committees or posts and about a dozen were involved in as many as five or six. Among those not actively involved, almost half had once been but were not able to continue because of illness or advanced old age, a small number were new residents who had not yet ventured into an activity, and the remainder were either too old and frail when they moved in or were uninterested in community activities. The uninterested ones comprised a very small group, some of whom satisfied their social needs with bridge games, shopping, travel, and family visits; a few others spent their time in solitary pursuits.

Virtually every aspect of life at Lakeview was affected by resident input. Aside from maintenance, meals, and housekeeping, most services were originated, administered, and often funded by residents: programs, hospitality, library, gardens, substitute staffing, safety, and communications via newsletter and bulletin board. Whenever the need arose, a committee was formed or an existing committee picked up the reins.

The program of fire drills was a good example. Although the building had the fire prevention and safety equipment then required by law, there had never been any practice drills. Nor had there been a fire—until early one spring morning when a smoker dozing in her bed in a sixth-floor apartment woke to find her mattress smouldering.

Marie Panauer, the smoker, described the ensuing confusion. "Luckily, I smelled the smoke and jumped out of bed. But I was stunned. Finally, I got my wits together and ran out into the corridor yelling 'Fire! Fire!' and banging on doors. Soon people came out and began running about in their robes and pajamas, tripping over each other. But no one seemed to know what to do. A few people ran to the emergency exits and began rushing down the stairs. Meanwhile, in my apartment, what had started as a smouldering mattress became a blazing bed."

A few cool heads had prevailed, however, and by the time the Watertown Fire Department arrived on the scene, fire extinguishers had been used to squelch the flames, and the firemen had only to stamp out the dying embers.

"It could have been disastrous, though," Ben Gordon told me. "A few people at the other end of the corridor slept through the whole incident, and some of those who walked down the stairs became ill. One man had a heart attack. Thank God it was mild and he recovered.

"As for me, I felt very remiss for not having set up regular drills, some sort of training," the administrator confessed. "I knew I would have to do something about it—and soon. As usual, the residents were way ahead of me. The safety committee called an emergency meeting that very day, right after breakfast, and came to me in the afternoon with a tentative plan."

The plan called for two fire captains on each floor to be responsible for rousing every tenant. Each fire captain was to appoint a messenger, one to alert the fire captains on the floor above and one on the floor below. Two other appointees were to be in charge of fire extinguishers. Several scheduled drills were held during the next two weeks, followed by a surprise drill at eleven-thirty one night.

When Ben Gordon was asked to speak at the September council meeting, he reported that he had contacted the town fire department as requested by the safety committee, and arranged a date for a review of the drill procedure. It was to take place later that month when most of the residents who traveled or lived elsewhere during the summer would have returned.

Perhaps the most pleasant and certainly the most profitable venture run by the residents was the notions shop. It was the brainchild of Betty Reardon and Dorothy Grainger, born during Lakeview's second winter, which was a particularly cold one. Several people had fallen on the front walk in January; one had suffered a serious hip injury and another a broken ankle. A Residents Council proposal to install a canopy over the front walk had been turned down by the administration as too expensive. And growing reluctance to leave the building was having a depressing effect on everyone. Dorothy Grainger came in on a discussion of this at lunch one stormy, bitterly cold day, bringing a package with her.

"The cards just arrived in the mail," she announced cheerfully to the four women seated at a table glumly watching the walls of swirling snow outside. She opened the parcel, took out a few packets, and handed them around.

"They are lovely. Your niece does beautiful work," Betty Reardon exclaimed as she looked through the sheaf of hand-drawn and painted note cards.

As the women ate lunch and chatted, Betty suddenly said, "I just had a great idea. We asked Dorothy to get these cards for us and we're paying for them. If you charged us a little more than your niece asked for, Dorothy, you'd be making a profit. Right?"

Dorothy began to protest. But Betty cut her off impatiently, eager to get her thoughts spoken. "Why couldn't we have a little shop—with cards like these, other stationery, small gift items, and trinkets—maybe some toiletries as well? We could sell them at a small profit and use the money to buy things for the house."

"Like a canopy," Dorothy chimed in. "What a wonderful idea!"

"Sure is," Kate Nolan agreed. "It's also a lot of hard work."

"When were we ever afraid of a little hard work?" Betty said, her thoughts racing ahead to sources of merchandise for the shop. "We could sell crocheted and knitted items made by our own people—Addie's mittens and socks, Julia's scarves and hats, Denny's paintings, Corinne's mugs and pots. The town senior club and the churchwomen might be able to supply us with a few things. And later on we can buy from commercial suppliers—greeting cards, stationery, whatnot. . . ."

"Let's call it that," Dorothy burst in. "The Whatnot Shop!"

Kate smiled indulgently at their enthusiasm. The other two women, Margo and Paula Tourain, sisters in their seventies who were involved in many of the musical activities at Lakeview, expressed some doubt about the practicality of the enterprise—questions about who would do the buying, selling, stocking, and recordkeeping. Betty and Dorothy, undaunted, came up with all the answers. Right then and there, the five women formed the nucleus of the Whatnot Shop committee, stopping in at Ben Gordon's office to talk it over with him and to find out what space could be allotted for the little store.

"I was flabbergasted," Gordon recalled. "Oh, I warned them that it would be a tremendous job, and I pleaded lack of space. They said, 'Not to worry,' they would get the manpower and find the space. In the end, there was no way I could deter those determined ladies."

A small supply room between Gordon's office and the library was emptied and used for the shop. It opened six weeks later carrying in-house crafted items and any others, like Dorothy's niece's note cards, that could be obtained on consignment. With the profits, a catalog and commercial supplies were ordered. Betty and Dorothy managed the store, and it was staffed by resident volunteers.

Two years after its opening, the library-side wall was moved for an expansion that doubled the space, and a year or so after that a window bay extension out into the corridor was added. The expansions were paid for with shop funds—but only after the canopy over the front walk had been put up.

When I first entered the Whatnot Shop, it was five years old and thriving. Betty Reardon, at 79, was still chief manager, assisted by Jane Drummond, a younger woman of 71, a retired accountant who handled all the bookkeeping. Dorothy Grainger, who had had a double mastectomy a few years before and was very frail, still kept her hand in as a regular sales volunteer twice a month. When the volunteer list grew long enough so that their services were no longer needed, Kate Nolan and the Tourain sisters, whose interests lay elsewhere, dropped out. Shop hours, originally ten-thirty to twelve-thirty on weekdays, had expanded to include an hour on Tuesday and Thursday evenings.

"It's been successful beyond my wildest dreams," Betty told me proudly. "Besides that famous canopy, the Whatnot has paid for carpeting all of the corridors, for a movie projector, slide projectors, a lectern. Best of all, so many of our people have become involved—creating things to sell and working in the shop."

She picked up a framed sheet of parchment with the Lord's Prayer lettered in exquisite calligraphy and decorated with scroll and leaf designs colored in delicate pastels. "You'd never guess who did this—Deirdre Danivan. And she's working on another for us."

Betty was right. I never would have guessed. Deirdre Danivan was one of the three residents who always seemed confused and forgetful. Because she regularly took breakfast in the dining room and there were rarely more than three or four others, I sat with her several times; it was not a very pleasant experience. She repeated phrases over and over again and was constantly searching in her pockets or purse—for a key, a handkerchief, a letter, or photo. She showed me the photo of her dead husband at least a half-dozen times one morning. Her nervousness and confusion were very trying, and most of the residents ignored her. A few—Kate, Betty, and Lydia Winiford among them—made an effort to be kind, stopping to chat with her for a few minutes, helping her rediscover the way to the elevator or mailboxes.

"How does she manage in her own apartment?" I wondered.

"Her stove is disconnected, for one thing. That's why she has all her meals in the dining room," Betty said. "Otherwise she spends a good deal of time up there, watching television and puttering around. I guess she feels safer in familiar surroundings. One of her neighbors often shops for her and knocks on her door to remind her that it's time to go down for lunch or dinner."

Deirdre Danivan was one of the few residents at Lakeview who had not come to live there of their own volition. When her confused mental state became apparent, one of her sons applied for the apartment on his wife's mother's recommendation. This woman, Nelly Blackmore, was one of Lakeview's "socialites," as I came to call them. Nelly assiduously avoided Deirdre, except when her daughter and son-in-law came to visit two or three times a year.

Deirdre had never worked outside her home, devoting herself exclusively to family matters. She was the youngest child and the only girl in a family of six, and she had lost three of her brothers in the same year that her husband died, the year she turned 70. Frail, delicate, and birdlike, she wandered about the corridors of Lakeview like a lost soul.

How had Betty discovered her talent? She had invited Deirdre to lunch in her apartment one day with two of her more tolerant friends. Deirdre had penned a thank-you note and slipped it under Betty's door the following morning. "I was amazed," Betty said, "and immediately got after her to do some calligraphy for the shop. I bought the parchment paper and suggested the Lord's Prayer. Now people are ordering favorite psalms and poems. And it's had a calming influence on Deirdre. She's still confused and absentminded, but I think she looks a little brighter—not quite as lost and lonely, if you know what I mean."

It was difficult for me to judge, since I had not met Mrs. Danivan before. But her lack of focus made her an oddity in this house full of alert and purposeful people.

On a typical morning, residents occupied themselves with personal chores and volunteer activities. The laundry room was busiest then. In the crafts room adjacent to it, activities director Lynne Battelle offered instruction and assistance in ceramics, weaving, sketching, and painting. The few regulars who used the large sunny room as a studio rarely consulted Lynne, but there were always others in various stages of learning who came in for a half-hour or an hour to work on a project. Residents waiting for their laundry often stopped in to watch or to chat with Lynne and with friends. During the weeks preceding a holiday, Lynne organized morning workshops to craft simple gifts like Easter baskets, stuffed bunnies, and decorated eggs for children of family and friends and for patients in the pediatric wards of Watertown Hospital. Pre-Christmas workshops were especially popular, producing toys, ornaments, and miniature nativity scenes.

Banks, shops, and the town library—conveniently close for most of the residents—might be visited mornings or afternoons, depending upon the other activities scheduled for the day. One morning a week, a bus was available to transport people to a large shopping mall; it was usually quite full. Residents with cars often invited friends in the house along on shopping and sightseeing trips, as did outside friends and family members.

Lunch out was a treat frequently indulged in by those who were most mobile and could afford it. Carrie Sutter, an 83-year-old woman with severe arthritis, once asked me to join her for her weekly lunch out. Using two canes, she laboriously made her way to a diner two blocks away at least once a week in good weather, with or without a companion.

"Of course I prefer company," she said. "But if my friends are busy, I go by myself. I do so enjoy having lunch out."

It took 20 minutes to complete the short walk. But it was worth it; not so much for the lunch, which was simple fare, but for the conversation, which was fascinating.

"I've always been very independent," Carrie began when I asked her to tell me about herself. "I was an only child, the apple of my parents' eyes. They were middle-aged when I was born and really regarded me as a miracle.

"We lived in a small town. My father was the only attorney there. I wasn't allowed to go to school until I was 12. My mother gave me lessons that my father helped her prepare. By the time I got to high school, a private school for girls close enough to home so that I could spend weekends there, I could read Latin and Greek, knew algebra and geometry and a good deal of law. Of course, I was backward socially. But adolescents were much more restricted then than they are now, and it didn't seem to make much difference to me."

After two years at school, the young Carrie took her qualifying exams for college entrance. Though she passed with high grades, none of the colleges would accept a 14-year-old female.

"So I stayed home and studied on my own. I was fascinated by the ancient world and all fired up about the new archeological discoveries. My parents were very generous, and I was able to send for all the journals and books I needed to keep up," Carried continued. "When I turned 17, I applied to several East Coast universities involved in digs in Greece, Asia Minor, and Egypt for a staff position. None would have me. They advised me to complete my education, 'but not here, as we do not accept female students.'

"Well, to make a long story short, I finally entered Barnard College in New York as a classics major, was graduated after three years, and became a teacher of ancient history at a public high school in the city." She laughed. "I wish I could say it was a truly rewarding experience, but history—and particularly ancient history—was of little interest to my pupils. They all seemed to be concentrating on becoming bank presidents or army generals."

World War I started soon after Carrie began her first year of teaching. She had been traveling in Europe with her parents—a graduation present—at the time of the assassination in Serbia that sparked the war. Except for the death of a distant cousin and the increasing restlessness of her students, Carrie confessed that the war scarcely made a dent in her life. "My greatest concern was over the possible destruction of treasures of antiquity. It took me a long time to grow up emotionally. By the next great war, I no longer worried about the destruction of temples and statues," she said.

Her life fell into a pattern—teaching, haunting libraries and museums, quiet summers with her parents—until her marriage at age 32 to a man 25 years older, an archeologist. Her father had died the year before, and she had returned to the small New England town of her birth the following summer with the intention of staying on with her mother.

"Robert and I had met just before Papa died, and we corresponded while I was at home. When Mama insisted that I go back to my work, I returned to the city and my teaching job.

We were married on Christmas Day, 1925. I think I loved his profession more than I ever loved him. But Robert was just as prejudiced as the others against women in the field. What I had envisioned as a partnership soon turned sour."

During the second summer of their marriage, Carrie, in her fourth month of pregnancy, disobeyed her husband's injunction against joining him at a dig in Egypt. She followed him there, making the long, arduous journey by herself. Conditions were primitive, and when she miscarried and nearly lost her own life as well, his recriminations and her guilt loomed between them.

"After the divorce," she went on quietly, "I understood clearly that I could not pursue my goals through another person. I demanded and finally gained entry to postgraduate school. For the rest of my life, except for the lean years of the Depression when funds dried up and during the war years of the early forties, I worked at various sites in Greece, first as a poorly paid sorter, gradually working my way up to assistant to the chief archeologist."

After her retirement at age 72, Carrie continued to lecture and write papers for archeology journals; she still submitted an occasional paper from her roost at Lakeview during the three years I knew her.

When had she come to live at Lakeview? And why?

She had moved into her one-bedroom apartment in 1973, having applied at the urging of Margo and Paula Tourain. They had all taught at the same school and were old friends. "They fed me and dragged me along to concerts during some of the most difficult times of my life. And there I was, almost 80, still full of energy but with legs that were getting more and more balky about taking me where I wanted to go. Margo and Paula had visited an aunt here. They were smitten by the place and very persuasive. They insisted that I apply when they did, warning me that I wouldn't be accepted if I got to the point where I needed a wheelchair. They were right, of course; I'm much better off here than alone in a city apartment.

"You know," she added pensively, "my mother lived to be 94. She stayed alone in the old house all that time, except for a nurse–companion toward the end. But I told myself if I'm going to live for 10 or 15 more years, I don't want to spend them in virtual solitary confinement. That, more than anything else, made me decide to come here."

Carrie Sutter was Lakeview's volunteer historian. When I met her she had almost completed a small volume. She also wrote amusing and informative sketches about her life as an archeologist for the monthly newsletter and continued to submit book reviews and articles to professional journals. Despite her "balky legs," she often went along on house excursions to theaters, concerts, and museums.

Group trips were most appreciated by residents with limited mobility, like Carrie Sutter, but they attracted many others as well. On days when trips were scheduled, a noticeable holiday air prevailed at Lakeview House.

One summer day I boarded a chartered bus headed for a restaurant lunch and summer stock matinee with 40 residents and Lynne Battelle. In her role as activities director, Lynne took charge of trip planning. "Most ideas come from the residents themselves," she told me as we settled into our seats. "They keep up with the culture scene through their newspaper and magazine reading and will drop into the crafts room or leave a note in my mailbox with suggestions. They're a very lively bunch, always alert to what's going on."

Lynne would do some preliminary investigation of the ideas submitted to her, prepare a list of possibilities, and post it on the bulletin board along with a meeting date for discussion of the list. Although she called the group the excursion committee, she described it as unstructured, without officers or regular meeting dates. A core of three or four residents always showed up when a meeting was held every couple of months, Lynne said, and as many as 15 more might join them in the crafts room to go over the tentative list. Only after these interested residents had approved the trips and suggested a schedule did Lynne proceed to make the arrangements—hiring buses, reserving tickets, and calling museums to schedule group tours. Overnight trips of two to four days duration were planned three or four times a year.

Excursion announcements, dates, and prices were printed in the monthly newsletter and notices posted on the bulletin board with signup sheets. Plays and concerts and museum, mansion, and garden tours were usually fully subscribed for a busload of 40. Occasionally a trip elicited enough interest that an extra van or two had to be hired. "Once we needed two buses. It was for a play starring Douglas Fairbanks Jr.," Lynne recalled. "Whenever an old-time performer is featured, we have a good turnout. But well-known young performers are very popular, too."

Lynne was also responsible for arranging transportation to several church and hospital events that had become Lakeview traditions. In mid-December, for example, residents who had knitted mittens, mufflers, socks, and hats took them to a large Watertown church where they helped trim the "Warm and Woolly Tree," as it had come to be called. On another day before Christmas, residents brought the toys and ornaments they had crafted and packed in bright holiday wrappings to the hospital and gave them out to patients. A pre-Easter trip had been added more recently for residents who found the Christmas season visits so gratifying.

"It's a sight to see, the way the kids' wan little faces light up when they get the gifts—and a hug and a kiss besides. Of course, it's sad to see them ill. But we always come away glowing a little," Lynne said.

The hospital and church gifts projects had been initiated years before by residents who served as volunteers at the hospital and with church and community poverty programs. During the three years I visited Lakeview, at least ten women were volunteer aides at the hospital and a dozen or so worked with various church and social agencies. (More details on outside volunteer activities are given in chapter 4.)

Ella Compton, a former nurse and hospital administrator, became a volunteer soon after moving to Lakeview in 1973. "By that time I had also had experience as a patient," she told me, "having been laid up for several months with hepatitis and pneumonia. Because I have no family to speak of, I accepted a friend's offer to stay at her house until I recuperated fully. It was during that time that I saw Lakeview for the first time, when we came to visit her friend, Addie Padgett. Have you met her?"

I had, I answered, and found her most agreeable—a bright, sunny person, well-loved by all who knew her.

Adelaide Padgett's happiness and appreciation for her new home at Lakeview, and the physical surroundings and atmosphere had so impressed Ella that she decided to apply for an apartment. "I was 67 then, unhappily retired, without family ties and, though recovering from my illness, uneasy about my health and about what the future might hold."

Earlier in her life, Ella had lived in an apartment, but she had moved to a small house in her late forties, enjoying the quiet and privacy for twenty years. "I hated the thought of leaving my little home. At the same time, I found myself dreading the loneliness when I had to go back there after my stay at Ilana's."

Two years on the waiting list gave Ella time to do battle with her fears. Whenever she felt depressed and lonely, she would jump into her car and head for Lakeview to visit Addie Padgett, often with their friend, Ilana Gross. (Ilana, a former nurse and hospital colleague of Ella's, had persuaded her husband to apply for residence at Lakeview. And the Grosses, too, were on the waiting list.)

"Addie is a wonder. She's ten years older than I am—going on 82, I think—yet she's still doing volunteer work at the hospital three afternoons a week. And she only cut down from five a year or so ago. She's also on some house committees, program and hospitality and maybe one or two more.

"I can't tell you how much she raised my spirits whenever I came to see her. I'd really slipped into a low frame of mind, a feeling that life was over, that there was nothing left to do but wait for death."

Ella laughed at her old self. "Since I've lived here I haven't had much time to be gloomy. Addie recruited me for hospital work at once. I also play bridge two evenings a week and garden mornings. Ilana and I share a garden plot."

"Were the Grosses enjoying life at Lakeview, too?" I asked.

Ella told me that Ilana had been widowed before a two-bedroom apartment became available. In fact, the two women had talked to management about sharing the large apartment. They were told that only married couples and blood relatives,

like the Tourain sisters, were permitted to share apartments.
(On the other hand, I later learned, a married couple was not
required to have one apartment. One couple, the Gilberts, were
allowed to take two separate apartments, a small studio which
Dr. Gilbert used as a study and a one-bedroom unit.)

"In my opinion, it's a silly rule," Ella declared. "If Ilana
and I had been allowed to share her apartment, there'd be an
extra one-bedroom place, and they are scarce. I think the wait
now is five years! And what would Ilana have done if she
couldn't afford the cost of the large apartment?"

According to Ella, the death of Teddy Gross had "thrown
Ilana for a loop." Because they had not seemed a close couple—
living in the same house but leading quite independent lives—
the depth of Ilana's grief had surprised her friends. One daughter, a troubled and troublesome child who had run away at 17
and never returned, could not be located in time for the funeral.
When the news of her father's death caught up with her, she
sent her mother a brief note saying she was sorry to hear the
news but felt that her parents were strangers.

"No sympathy from that quarter," Ella said. "I guess Ilana
felt completely alone for the first time in her life. I spent as
much time with her as I could before I moved in here. Luckily,
her apartment came through a few months later. She moved in
and took to Lakeview like a duck to water. But Addie and I
have never been able to get her interested in the hospital or
committee work. She keeps busy with social things—bridge,
cocktail hours, luncheons, trips. And she enjoys the gardening."

Ilana was one of the few residents who restricted their
activities almost exclusively to social life at Lakeview—the
group I think of as "socialites," most of whom were affluent
widows accustomed to spending their time in this way.

This is not to say that residents who worked with house
committees and as outside volunteers did not participate in
social activities; most of them did. I would venture to say that
at least 75 percent of the residents played bridge. Numerous
games were held in the afternoons and evenings, in the terrace
lounge and in apartments. Some bridge groups met regularly
every day, others one or more days a week. The Smithsons

belonged to a group that played two afternoons a week (as they had done even before they moved into the house, you may remember) and split up for an evening once a week when Frank joined a men-only game.

Kate Nolan, who called herself the "world's worst player," nevertheless joined a friendly game twice a week. Even when her sight was failing, the other players rigged up a "helping hand" system so that she could stay in the game; they recruited an extra player to arrange Kate's cards and cue her on the plays, and to fill in when Kate grew impatient and tired.

When one member of a foursome was confined to her apartment after an injury or noncontagious illness, the game was held there until she recovered. Several women told me how grateful they were for the diversion during such times.

Formal programs, ranging from simple slide shows of residents' travels to concerts by professional musicians, were frequently scheduled in the afternoons, less frequently in the evenings when some residents preferred playing bridge or retiring to their apartments to relax, read, write letters, sew, and watch television.

The program committee, working with the music and arts committee, was on constant alert for talent and opportunity. Residents who traveled knew they would be asked to describe the sights they had seen; accordingly, most of them returned from their journeys with slides and notes, prepared to share their experiences with the others. Age alone did not seem to be an impediment to travel. People who were healthy enough and wealthy enough went off on trips to countries and continents all over the globe. Two women in their late seventies took a three-month tour around the world. Their talk and slide program was given in three parts on separate afternoons.

Musicians among the residents prepared programs in keeping with various holidays and accompanied or introduced other programs and lectures with musical interludes. The Sunday program, often a lecture by a visiting minister, was preceded by hymns or other compositions played on the organ or piano by a resident. The house choir sang carols at Christmastime and gave a few concerts during the year; some of its members also sang for the nursing unit patients at weekly singalongs. Dramatic readings, poetry readings, and art lectures illustrated by slides were other resident offerings. To fill in when live performers were not available, programs of recorded music or short films and travelogues would be shown by members of the program committee who were in charge of the projection and sound equipment.

Professional and amateur artists were also invited to perform: town and school choirs, chamber music groups, drama groups, authors, museum curators. Relatives and friends with special talent or knowledge were often prevailed upon to present programs. All arrangements were made by the committees involved and costs paid by the Residents Council from a fund maintained for this purpose. Management was seldom involved, but staff members had a standing invitation to attend and sometimes did.

Residents also took complete responsibility for holiday parties, shopping for and preparing refreshments and decorations. Only when furniture had to be moved—chairs for the Christmas party held in the corridor area or setting up the tree—was the maintenance staff called upon.

Dinner, of course, was the universal social occasion in the house. Most of the residents dressed for dinner, albeit informally. Depending upon the inclination of the individual, dinner dates might be made a week or two in advance, or on the same day, or seating might be left to the dining room hostess. The buzz of conversation filled the room each evening, and many of the diners exchanged pleasantries with the young waitresses as well.

The hospitality committee wisely arranged a schedule for each newcomer so that he or she sat with a different group of residents each evening for the first two weeks. Newcomers might protest that they already had friends at Lakeview and wished to dine with them, but they generally agreed afterward that meeting some of the others had been interesting and enjoyable and, in many cases, had resulted in new friendships.

I did observe certain patterns in the dining room. Couples usually sat with other couples. "The wives are afraid we single women will steal their men," Agnes Drew remarked wryly when I commented on this.

It was true that some of the wives maintained a proprietary watch over their husbands. At the same time, some couples seemed to have close friends among the single women, and I pointed this out to Agnes. "Those are special couples, like the Winifords and the Smithsons, and you'll notice that the women they befriend are always the least threatening types." She mentioned no names, but I knew whom she meant; Kate Nolan, Addie Padgett, and Carrie Sutter were examples of the independent, nonflirtatious women who could be accepted by wives without fear. "I guess we never outgrow our petty jealousies," I said. Agnes and I both laughed.

For the few single men, socializing was awkward. Tom McAdams told me that he felt like "the prize rooster in the barnyard" when he first arrived. But he soon got used to it and began to enjoy all the attention. "So what did I do?" he asked ruefully. "I went and got caught by this chicken," and he squeezed his new wife's arm. McAdams and Harriet Pembroke, a 67-year-old widow, had married at Lakeview the previous May. He was a resident for three years and she had been there a year when the wedding took place in the garden terrace and lounge, one of two memorable wedding celebrations during my visiting years.

The strain of being a single man surrounded by an overwhelming number of women is not unique to Lakeview, however, and most of the men I spoke with reported that they had had similar experiences elsewhere in groups of their contemporaries. "If anything, most of the women here are more reserved and more careful to observe the old-fashioned proprieties. And it's rare for anyone, male or female, to trespass on your privacy," David Arnold observed. "Still, there's always that undercurrent when I'm the only man at a table or in a group."

David, who was 78 when I met him, had been a history professor at a large eastern university, a widower for 20 years, and a Lakeview resident for five. He managed to cope, he said, by keeping to himself much of the time; he tutored prisoners at a penitentiary, drove about exploring the countryside, and wrote historical monographs for academic journals.

"I'm not around for lunch, and I don't play bridge or attend cocktail parties, though I'm frequently asked. About the only house socials I go to are the monthly men's lunches and some of the holiday parties. I do attend many of the evening and Sunday programs, which are usually quite interesting. And I feel obliged to be at Residents Council meetings, though I've never really contributed anything.

"I know I'm labeled 'aloof,' but I'm grateful for the freedom to be that way and still have my creature comforts taken care of," he added.

David Arnold seemed content with his life as he had made it. The odd note was his attendance at the men's lunch. I asked him why he went. "Loyalty to the others," he answered softly. It was a small thing but a token nevertheless of the feeling of community that could be aroused even in a confirmed loner.

The men's lunch was Frank Smithson's idea. He realized the constraints on single men in most social situations and thought it might give them a chance to loosen up and converse more easily. After polling the dozen or so single men and the 16 married men and getting a good response, the men's lunch was launched. Two years later it was still attended by virtually every male resident. Frank avowed that he learned more about the Lakeview men at the monthly midday meals than he ever could before. The others were equally appreciative.

One man, Vincent Cantin, was especially pleased. "It's the only time I feel a little like I belong here," he said. Vince had run a home construction company in Watertown. It was taken over by two of his sons after a fall from a ladder in his seventy-first year left him lame. "They kicked me out," he said with mixed anger and pride. His wife had died three or four years before. Vince couldn't remember exactly when, sadly claiming that the accident had injured his head as well as his back and leg. One of his three daughters lived close enough to visit him fairly often and to take him home with her for holidays; he spent weekends at the home of his married son, the other son having been divorced. It was a large family with many grandchildren and great-grandchildren.

Vince frequently grumbled about living with "all these old people" and looked forward to "getting out" on weekends. He took little interest in any of the house activities and spent most of his time in his studio apartment, watching television and whittling wood. The figures he carved were very nice. Betty Reardon tried to get him to make some for the Whatnot Shop, but Vince refused; he wanted them for his family.

After about a year, Vince left Lakeview to live in his son's home. In a Christmas note to Frank Smithson, he wrote that he was much happier there. He wasn't at all sure his son and daughter liked having him live with them, he said, "But after all, our kids do owe us something in our old age!" Lunch and cards with cronies at a church senior center helped him pass the time. Although he lived on the outskirts of Watertown, he never once returned to Lakeview for a visit.

Cantin's was a rare case in Lakeview's history. He was one of three residents who left voluntarily. Another male resident had moved to a retirement community in Arizona, and a woman had left to share a home with her daughter who was widowed. If there were others who wished to leave, they did not speak of it. The majority of residents seemed to have adapted successfully, contributing to and enjoying the congeniality of the community according to individual inclination and capabilities while retaining the measure of privacy desired.

Everyone was encouraged to participate in shaping life in the house; no one was compelled to do it. The socialites—Ilana Gross, Nellie Blackmore, and others—preferred to live as if it were an apartment hotel. The workers and contributors regarded it as a cooperative community that flourished under their care and guidance. But everyone agreed on one thing: it was home.

4. GOOD NEIGHBORS:
House and Town

In a sense we're all ambassadors from the house to the town. And everything we do helps us earn the right to be called citizens of the town, instead of being thought of as outsiders who happen to occupy a building here.

—Abel Johnson, Lakeview resident and Watertown social services agency volunteer

One of the criticisms of age-segregated housing is that it leads to a closed society. That may be true when a large number of old people are concentrated in a retirement community in an isolated area. But in an urban setting it need not be.

Most residents of Lakeview House would laugh if you told them they lived in a segregated or closed society. For one thing, they would point out, their ages spanned some 30 years. More important, they would tell you, they regarded themselves as apartment dwellers who, as long as they were physically able, were free to come and go as they pleased. Even when their mobility diminished they could claim the pleasure derived from the constant flow of visitors to the house. In many ways, they would say they had more freedom than their counterparts living alone—freedom from the fear of criminal attack, from sudden illness with no one near to help, from lack of companionship, and from the energy drain of heavy housework and meal preparation.

"It's a shame," one woman commented, "that there's so much bias against group living for old people. We've all encountered it, even from people who should know better, like our doctors. You know . . . the pitying and pained expression, 'Oh, poor dear, she's gone into an old age home.' "

When I discussed this with administrator Ben Gordon, he said, "There's nothing wrong with age-specific housing per se. The difficulties arise when the surrounding community rejects a place and its people. Or when residents are overprotected and restricted. That's when you get an ingrown or closed society.

"You have to consider the attitudes of the residents, too," Gordon continued. "Remember that all of our residents chose this place with a fairly clear idea of what they wanted. First, of course, they wanted an environment that was fairly safe and secure. But they certainly didn't come here to live in seclusion and to block out the rest of the world. On the contrary, like most people everywhere, they wanted to continue interacting with the rest of society. And they have plenty of opportunity to do that—here in the house and in the town."

Lakeview's location was certainly a major factor in affording opportunities for interaction with society, and the residents who made best use of those opportunities served as role models for the others. Because of its urban setting Lakeview also provided for a continuity of living patterns that was comforting and comfortable.

A substantial number of the residents belonged to one or another of the local churches, the major denominations being well represented in Watertown. Those who were sufficiently mobile attended church regularly; the others were able to hear visiting clergymen at the Sunday afternoon programs in the assembly room.

Many residents maintained memberships in local and county historical societies and museum, library, and art support groups, as well as in area chapters of national organizations like the American Association of University Women, the League of Women Voters, and the Lions Club. They attended meetings whenever possible, and a few were officers or directors.

Concert-going, museum visits, and theater attendance in

the Watertown area and nearby cities, aside from Lakeview's group trips, engaged those people who were fond of such activities. And convenient transportation—by bus, taxi, and railroad—facilitated excursions to local and city events and visits to friends and relatives. The town supplied local bus transportation at reduced rates, and the private taxi services offered discounts as well.

"If we lived off in the woods somewhere, it would certainly be more difficult—maybe impossible—to get to concerts like these," Margo Tourain once told me after describing a concert she and her sister had gone to the afternoon before. I had seen them leave the building, dressed warmly against the blustery January winds, setting out on the half-mile walk to the county art center, home of a music series to which they subscribed. They could have taken a taxi, as they did on stormy days, she explained, but they opted for the exercise and fresh air that afternoon. Margo boasted that they had missed only two concerts over a span of three years, both times because of illness.

The proximity of religious, cultural, and community organizations, important as these were to many of the residents, was overshadowed by the convenience of more basic services, such as shopping, banking, and health facilities. Being able to take care of these needs was of prime importance, enhancing feelings of self-reliance and independence. One new resident recalled how timid and fearful she had become when faced with banking and shopping chores in her former community in a nearby city. "The first week I was here, a couple of the women insisted that I join them so they could show me around. And you know the old adage, 'There's strength in numbers.'. . . Well, it sure worked for me," she said with obvious pleasure in her new-found, or re-found, confidence.

It's difficult to measure the economic value of the residents' trade to the town. The nearest stores and the bank acknowledged steady trade from the house. The bank, estimating deposits by residents at over a half-million dollars, made an extra effort to serve them by sending a teller to Lakeview once a week to assist those people who were unable to get to the bank.

Lakeview's value as an employer should not be forgotten

either. There were approximately 50 full- and part-time jobs—
in the office, housekeeping, maintenance, kitchen, and dining
room; and the house had earned an excellent reputation as a
place to work. Most residents and employees developed a reciprocal regard for each other. Indeed, some of the staff became so
fond of certain residents that an illness or death affected them
as deeply as if the favorite person were a family member.

Perhaps the greatest returns to the town from Lakeview
came in the form of the volunteer services of its residents.
Churches, the hospital, and the local office of the county social
services agency were the major beneficiaries. It was, of course,
a reciprocal exchange from which the volunteers gained a
deeper sense of belonging to the larger community and a
chance to defeat those feelings of redundancy that so often
afflict idle old people.

Besides the holiday gift-making and giving at churches
and hospitals described in the last chapter, regular volunteers
joined with other church groups to help raise funds for community projects, sewed clothing, repaired items, and assisted
church missions in other ways. Paula Tourain played the organ
at Sunday services, and her sister Margo assisted the choir
leader. Two Lakeview women were assistants to the secretaries of their respective churches, another wrote articles for a
church magazine and prepared and delivered talks for church
groups, and still another wrote a weekly column on church
activities for a local newspaper.

At her church, Alida Barnes was considered "a precious
jewel," to quote the minister. As coordinator of all child and
youth programs—preschool, afterschool, and Sunday school—
she spent at least four hours Monday through Friday and two
hours on Sunday mornings in her church office.

Alida was 76 years old when I met her and had been doing
the job for six years, without pay. "I wouldn't dream of asking
for money," she declared. "The church can't afford it, and I don't
need it. I get a good pension and Social Security. Besides, I often
feel that it's I who should pay for all the joy it brings me."

A tall, imposing woman and straight as a ramrod, Alida
was known as "Big Teacher" by the young people under her
supervision. She had taught in a public elementary school for

30 years in the same city in which she was born and grew up, and she had been assistant principal and then principal of that school. Her contract mandated her retirement at 65.

"For almost 45 years that school was home and family to me. My parents died young, and my only brother lived in Michigan; his family still lives there, though I rarely see any of them. I can't tell you the sinking feeling that struck me when I walked out the door of that building on my last day."

A summer of travel helped to buffer the blow. "But when fall came, I had to fight an irresistible urge to set off for school every morning after I woke. That winter I had a bout with pneumonia—me, who'd never been sick a day in my life. Then I fell and broke my hip. It was the most awful time of my life. Like being in a black hole."

Friends saw Alida through this dark period, but it was a church acquaintance, Betty Reardon, who first told her about Lakeview. The congregate residence was in its planning stages then, and Alida was very resistant to the idea of leaving the city, so she paid little heed to Betty's talk. Betty, who was on the board and deeply involved in the project, was constantly bubbling over with enthusiasm.

"I was almost rude to her," Alida recalled. "But she was very kind. She sensed my despair and went to the pastor to recommend me for the job of director of an afterschool study center the church was starting that fall. The salary was minuscule, a token really. But I jumped at the chance."

During the long hours spent organizing and running the study center ("I never worked so hard in my life!") Alida and Betty became good friends, and she listened to Betty's progress reports on Lakeview with a more open mind. "Gradually, it dawned on me that this kind of housing might be a good way for old people to live. But I still refused to accept the fact that I myself might be getting old. It was only when Betty told me she was moving to Lakeview that the reality hit me. Here was Betty, energetic and vibrant and just as attached to city living as I was, going to live in an old age home! And miles away, in another world, it seemed to me."

The building was in the last stages of construction when Alida saw it for the first time. The model apartments were on an upper floor, the tenth. It was a Sunday at the end of summer, a lovely golden day, and the lake was alive with fluttering sails and darting boats of all kinds. "A stunning view," Alida remembered.

"I left Betty with the group of people she and the pastor had been showing around. Incidentally, I couldn't help noticing that some of them were younger than I was. And I walked outside and through the neighboring streets." There she saw the stores, bank, library, and diner nearby and the shops and office buildings a bit farther away. Not many people were about, but she realized it was Sunday and most of the shops were closed. Buses went by now and then, and she checked off the bus stops on the walk back, noting the one at the corner of the building site. Just before reentering Lakeview House, Alida stood in the doorway looking at the row houses across the street. "They reminded me of the rundown brownstones on my street in the city, though these were wood and asphalt shingle. I remember thinking that anyone who lived in an apartment here wouldn't have to worry about being with old people all the time. As soon as you stepped out of the building, you'd be in a real town with people of all ages."

With the day's observations simmering in her mind, Alida became sharply aware of the dilapidation and filth in her own home neighborhood. Hurrying through the ominous streets and back in the apartment she had occupied for more than 30 years, with the door double-locked and chained, the contrast was shattering.

"For days after that I argued and raged against the part of me that clung to the old familiar places, no matter how miserable they had become. I reminded myself over and over again of the many times I had promised myself to find a new apartment in a better neighborhood. Finally, after about a week, I asked Betty for an application."

Before filing the application, however, Alida consulted the church pastor. The study center was running smoothly, he assured her, and the young man who was her assistant could take over. Not entirely pleased with her dispensability, she asked him to find out whether a place might be available for her at the Watertown church. After inquiries he informed her that the congregation had been contemplating expansion of its children's programs and was eager to discuss it with her. In fact, the Watertown minister had offered to set a date for a meeting at the city church, since he had long planned a visit to see the study center in operation.

And so, Alida Barnes at the age of 70 transferred her career allegiance from the city of her birth and what she had thought would be her lifelong home to another, smaller city which she endowed with the same devotion for nine more years. Stricken by a massive stroke in her office at the Watertown church in the fall of 1978, she died a week later at the hospital only a few blocks away.

At the memorial service, the church building, though fairly large, was too small to hold all of the mourners. Old students came from the city with children and grandchildren who had been students at the school and study center. Colleagues and friends from the city and from Watertown were there, too. At the end of the eulogy the minister said, "Alida Barnes lived and died doing what she liked best—overseeing our education. We were all part of her family. And we mourn her passing as we would that of a beloved sister and mother who was also a great teacher."

Hospital volunteers from Lakeview were almost as numerous as church workers and equally dedicated. They helped at the reception desk and in the record rooms, gift shop, and library; they sorted and distributed mail. They read to patients and wrote letters or made phone calls for them. Ruth Dobbins was assistant to the director of volunteer service at Watertown Hospital, a job she took over from another resident, Arlene Clark, who became too ill to continue and then entered the nursing unit at Lakeview where she was one of the favorite patients. (Ruth Dobbins, you may remember, was also in charge of hospitality at Lakeview during much of the time I spent there.)

Ella Compton, whom you met in the last chapter, was recruited as a nurse's aide because of her training and experience, and she was paid a small sum for her four hours three afternoons a week. "I'd do it for nothing, if need be. But it's nice to have some pin money," she confided.

The most outstanding hospital volunteer was Adelaide Padgett. Watertown Hospital gave a dinner to honor her for six years of faithful volunteer service; by then she had broken the record for continuous hours served by any volunteer in the hospital's history.

To my surprise, I learned that Addie had never done any community work before coming to live at Lakeview. "I was always too busy being a wife and mother and then a grandma, and enjoying it too much, to work outside. I loved cooking and baking, partying and entertaining. Except for church and PTA, and being a den mother and Girl Scout leader, I really didn't do much outside of home."

From her descriptions of life at the Padgetts, her five children—three daughters and two sons—must have had a happy time of it. Parties, camping trips, and family gatherings with numerous aunts, uncles, and cousins brightened their growing years. Indeed, when I met her sons and daughters, their undisguised fondness for one another and for their mother corroborated the picture she painted of a close and loving family.

When she was widowed at 75, Addie's bright outlook was temporarily dimmed by grief. Members of her family stayed with her at the old family home in relays or took her home with them for long periods, never allowing her to be alone. Buoyed up by her children and their children, she soon regained her sunny disposition. "They were all so dear and kind," she said. "I'm afraid I really shocked and upset them when I decided to move to Lakeview."

How had it happened?

Arlene Clark was a good friend and neighbor in the small suburban town not far from Watertown where both families had lived for many years. Arlene, then a widow for several years, had sold her house and moved to Lakeview shortly before Addie's husband died. Months later, after a visit with her, Addie announced to her family that she had applied for an apartment at the residence. "Oh, how they fretted!" She laughed at the memory. "They couldn't comprehend that I was lonely, that I needed the company of people my own age. Finally, they all gathered together and descended on the place, the whole Padgett clan, including some of the grandchildren—a grand delegation, you might say. After seeing Lakeview and learning more about it, most of them gave their approval. And I moved in in the summer of '71, never regretting it for a moment, then or since."

We were talking in the living room of Addie's two-bedroom apartment on the seventh floor. She had seated me in her favorite cushioned rocker so I could enjoy the sight of the lake shimmering below in the last light of day. Framed photographs were everywhere, showing bright faces ranging from those of infants to adults in their sixties and seventies. The room was cosy and clean but cluttered with an eclectic collection of odds and ends, many of them handmade—some crude and others finely wrought—which were obviously gifts from children. Now and then, when she referred to someone in her conversation, she would rise from the armchair opposite me, pick up one of these treasures, and say, "Johnny made this for me," or, "Mary gave this to me last Mother's Day." Not all were gifts from children in her own family; some had come from patients at the hospital.

It was Arlene Clark, then assistant to the director of volunteers, who had involved Addie in work at the hospital. "I requested work in the children's wards, and that's where I spend most of my time now. We read, or draw pictures, sew, do puzzles. I help feed the little ones and help the older ones with their school lessons. Sometimes I wangle small favors from the nurses or get the kitchen to prepare a favorite food. I do whatever I can to make the strangeness a little less frightening and the place more homey. And God bless them, I love them all, every one of them."

Here, I thought, was a woman who never tired of mothering. Echoing my thoughts, Addie said, "Don't you think I'm lucky to do what I love best, caring for children, even in my old age?"

Actually, her generosity of spirit was not confined to children. Addie Padgett was considerate of all in the Lakeview community and was one of the most admired and loved of its members. Many of the hospital volunteers and a number of the people who worked for the local blood bank and the social services agency credited her with inspiring them to take up their volunteer jobs.

The social services agency was another recipient of much volunteer time given by Lakeview people. Of the 20 or so involved in any one year, a significant number spent at least one day a week doing clerical work at the office. Children waiting for free inoculations were often comforted by Lakeview volunteers and rewarded with finger or hand puppets or other small toys made by residents. Adults filling out forms were also given aid and comfort by the volunteers.

During the week before Christmas, cookies and toys made at Lakeview were distributed to children at the agency office by Abel Johnson, a yearlong volunteer, dressed for the occasion in a Santa Claus suit. It was Abel who coordinated the gift-making activities with Lynne Batelle. "I'm not much good at making things myself, but I dearly love giving them away," said Abel, a stout, jovial widower who had been national director of a charitable organization for most of his life.

Said Lynne, "Mr. Johnson is such a funny man. He places orders. He'll come to me and say, 'We're going to need six dozen puppets, fifty pairs of mittens, and as many cookies as your ladies can bake.' Or he'll ask for ten dozen yarn dolls. Or five dozen of whatever pops into his head that week. I always answer by saying, 'We'll see what we can do.' And he always comes back with, 'Oh, you're such a smart young lady, I know you can do it.' He's a puzzle," she concluded, laughing good-naturedly.

Abel Johnson was one of Lakeview's hardest-working volunteers. He often spent up to six hours a day, five days a week, at the social services office sorting mail, dispensing information, checking applications, filing, lifting boxes "too heavy for the girls to handle," even using his car to drive to the county's central office on urgent errands. At 73, he was healthy, strong, and brimming with energy. A good family man, or so it seemed, since his son and daughter were frequent visitors at Lakeview. He had lost his wife about ten years before and had been a Lakeview resident for four years. He married Minerva Tredsill, a fellow volunteer at the agency, about the same age as he, who had moved into Lakeview a couple of years before.

Minerva seemed as languid as Abel was energetic, but in her own slow way she accomplished a good deal of work, or so I was told by the social services agency director. They made a delightful couple.

So appreciative was the social services staff of the work of Lakeview volunteers that they sponsored a special annual luncheon for them. Also invited were several residents who assisted teachers at the county's day-care center, which was run by the agency.

Among other volunteer jobs done by residents was tutoring of students with learning disabilities at the local elementary and high schools. And several Lakeview people with interesting backgrounds were signed up as speakers for school enrichment programs. Kate Nolan, for example, was called on at least two or three times every year to give a talk on her experiences in China; and Carrie Sutter periodically lectured on anthropology and the ancient world. All school volunteers and interested retired teachers and educators from Lakeview and the town attended Elders Day at the regional high school, sitting in on classes and joining the students for lunch and afternoon rap sessions. These intergenerational exchanges, always stimulating and challenging, were reported to me by residents as high points of each year.

A professional librarian helped out a few days a week at the local library, and several people assisted the county arts center with programs and subscriptions. Lydia Winiford, working in her apartment with materials sent by the Library of Congress, transcribed books into Braille. David Arnold tutored prisoners at the state penitentiary. And Dr. Mayhew Gilbert used his doctorate in psychology and his experience as a minister to counsel prisoners and probationers.

Altogether, Lakeview people racked up an excellent record of service that was widely acknowledged in the town. Some of the more visible volunteers acquired nicknames over the years. Abel Johnson was called "Mr. Jolly" by staff and clients at the agency. A little girl at the hospital, unable to get answers to her questions from the nurses, said, "I'll go ask Grandma Dear," pointing to Addie Padgett, and the title stuck. Counting the cookie-bakers and the toymakers along with Mr. Jolly and

Grandma Dear and all of the other active volunteers, virtually every resident gave some time and effort to the Watertown community. Even some of the socialites contributed knitted items.

Of the very few who were paid for their work, in addition to Ella Compton at the hospital, there were Agnes Drew in her job as secretary to the president of the local Chamber of Commerce, a former dentist who did consultations at the hospital's dental clinic, and a tax expert who taught adult education courses on financial management.

Whether paid or unpaid, Lakeview people working in the outside community took their jobs very seriously and were regarded by their "employers" as hard-working, conscientious, and dedicated. In a serious moment, Abel Johnson once summed up their status this way: "In a sense, we're all ambassadors from the house to the town. And everything we do helps us earn the right to be called citizens of the town, instead of being thought of as outsiders who happen to occupy a building here." It occurred to me that, in a larger sense, they were all ambassadors from the territory of old age as well, representing the continued usefulness of an often stigmatized and scorned segment of the population. The rewards for each person in renewed self-pride and the pleasures of accomplishment, seldom consciously sought, were ample repayment for their efforts.

Many communities fear and reject proposals for housing for the elderly. A variety of reasons is usually given: the project will create too much traffic, lower real estate values, bring in people of different socioeconomic classes. In cases where government subsidies are promised, communities fear the eventual loss of local control. Since Lakeview's sponsor had decided against applying for government funding, it did not have this strike against it. Nevertheless, before the Watertown site was purchased, the search committee encountered opposition in several other towns. A combination of luck and diplomacy was instrumental in effectuating the purchase of the site and obtaining town approval for the building. First, an institutional building already occupied the land, so a zoning change was not needed. Then, Lakeview's sponsor agreed not to seek tax-exempt status. Through negotiation, however, agreement was reached on a maximum tax limit of no more than 15 percent of gross rental income and the building was given a limited-use classification which made possible a 25 percent reduction in its assessed valuation. Even with these provisions, the completed facility paid a healthy tax of more than $100,000 per year. Town officials also demanded and got a prohibition against any commercial development on Lakeview's grounds which might compete with local merchants; therefore, plans for a beauty and barber shop and small grocery store in the building had to be dropped. In addition, the Watertown zoning board required what the sponsor considered an overabundance of parking space. The sponsor's estimate proved to be true, and some years later Lakeview's board was able to convince the town board that the extra space was not needed for parking and received permission to use it to expand the building's recreation area.

This kind of negotiation to obtain building approval is to be expected and, unless widespread opposition by townspeople arises, it is manageable. The location of the Lakeview site, in a mixed area of apartment, commercial, and recreational uses, blunted townwide opposition. But several of the earliest residents remembered encountering hostility, silent and spoken, from people in the immediate neighborhood. Eventually that antagonism evaporated, probably because of the work of Abel Johnson's "ambassadors," as well as the upkeep in the building's appearance and the cheer and friendliness of the residents.

Once I asked the mailman—a friendly, middle-aged man who always stopped in the lobby to chat with residents and knew many by name—how people on his route felt about Lakeview now that it had been open for eight years. His answer was, "They don't think of the people here as strangers anymore. They're just neighbors, like everyone else, and good neighbors at that."

Part of the successful integration of Lakeview into the community may have been the result of early community relations efforts and to the continuing cordial "open-door" policy (modified only by security requirements). For example, hundreds of guests were invited and came to a spring housewarming party in the first year the building was occupied. Tea, coffee, punch, sandwiches, and cookies were served by residents with the help of women from some of the town churches and dining room staff. This developed into an annual affair, the June Garden Party, attended by residents, their friends and relatives, and town and church friends.

Art exhibits and garden tours also kept the doors open to familiarize townspeople with the building and its occupants. The gardens actually became quite famous in the surrounding area and were visited by schoolchildren, garden clubs, and horticultural groups, winning some awards and feature articles in a magazine and newspapers. An outdoor art exhibit each spring, displaying works by residents and other town artists, offered the best of both nature's and people's creations, and an indoor exhibit in mid-November also open to guest artists, brought many viewers and buyers. All exhibitions were mounted by Lakeview's Art Committee, which also prepared show catalogs and designed and sent out announcements. Committee members were responsible, too, for maintaining the regular art displays in the common rooms and for changing them monthly.

Two wedding parties, and 80th and 90th birthday celebrations given by the families of several residents over the years, also brought guests from near and far.

Even on days when there were no special events scheduled, friends and relatives were always in evidence—being greeted in the lobby, at meals in the dining room, and strolling on the terrace and through the corridors. Guests were especially noticeable on weekends, when many children and young people were about. A few visitors were seen regularly at dinner on Sunday or at lunch and dinner on a particular day of the week or month. Occasionally a visitor would stay in a resident's apartment overnight to look after someone who was ill or because the visitor was far from home.

With all the traffic into and out of the building, there was never a sense of isolation or confinement. Even those who seldom left the building and had few visitors could enjoy the sights and sounds of the outside world brought in by the guests of other residents and by guest artists and ministers.

Cooperation between the town library and the house library had evolved over the years to the point where the former regularly loaned the house 30 books for six weeks at a time. Before that, Lakeview's library had consisted of books donated by residents and an initial stock of paperbacks purchased with a grant from the Residents Council. The public library's revolving collection was welcomed and eagerly read, especially by the shut-ins. A library committee, headed by Rita Dorrancy, working with several other former librarians kept order in the pleasant little room opening on the ground-floor corridor.

Two later innovations, both forms of exercise—one mental and the other physical—started several years ago. The first, a Great Decisions Discussion Series, used material prepared by the foreign policy association at eight weekly sessions to stimulate thought about national and international issues. Discussion leaders invited in from the town included the mayor, a newspaper editor, social worker, high school principal, bank president, and real estate broker. (I was told by Kate Nolan that several of these leaders, who had not previously been acquainted with Lakeview people, had registered surprise at their knowledgeability and the intensity and quality of the discussion.) A dozen people attended the first series in the spring, which was so well spoken of that 14 more signed up for the fall series and a second group was formed. The Great Decisions program served as an outlet for residents with strong political interests and convictions, since controversial discussion seemed to be assiduously avoided during ordinary social contact among residents.

The physical exercise arrived in the form of a weekly class by an instructor from the Watertown YMCA. It was suggested to Lynne Battelle by a new resident who was attending classes at the Y, and together they had persuaded the program director there to schedule a class at Lakeview on an experimental basis. Attendance was so good that classes were soon changed to twice weekly. Some of the exercises were quite vigorous, but everyone seemed to enjoy doing them.

The Y also served as an outside resource for several Lakeview residents who regularly used the gyms and pool there. One woman, so badly crippled by arthritis that she had to use a walker, was a daily swimmer. Her daughter, a town resident, drove her to the Y where they both swam each morning. In many ways this pair exemplified the repaired relationships between family members that could result when an aging relative moved to a good congregate residence.

Valerie Platt and her daughter had lived together in a house in Watertown for most of their lives. Widowed at 25, Val was left with her three-year-old daughter Trisha and a little money from her husband's insurance. A clerical job in the office of a small manufacturing plant on the outskirts of town enabled her to keep up payments on the little cottage near the lake that the couple had moved into the year before Mr. Platt's death. As Trisha grew, so did the town and the company for which Val worked. By the time she was 40, Val had advanced to the position of office manager, a job she kept until her retirement in 1960.

Had she ever thought of marrying again? I asked this woman, now in her eighty-first year, bent and wrinkled, but with still discernibly pretty features.

"I was tempted to once or twice, but I hated the idea of giving up my independence," she answered. "At the beginning, after George's death, I was devastated. But things changed when I realized how well I could manage on my own. And Trisha was always such a good child, helpful and obedient. She still is." (It was odd to hear the gray-haired, 59-year-old Trisha, a stout and sturdy person, referred to as a child.)

"When she got a bit older, into her teens, she was good company, too," Val continued. "And we did so many things together—swimming, skiing, boating, skating, traveling. . . . Now, with this terrible arthritis, there's only the swimming and a movie or play once in a while. It's really the main reason I moved here—I got to be a terrible burden on Trisha. I miss our little house, but I do get to spend holidays there, and at least I know she's looking after it."

Trisha's version of her mother's move to Lakeview revealed a more complex pattern. She told me that until her retirement Val had led a generally happy, busy, well-rounded life. She had her own friends and Trisha had hers with a few overlaps. And though they shared the same living quarters each went her separate way, Val to her job at the company office and Trisha to her teaching job at a small college where, by the time I met her, she was a full professor of sociology. Some but not all of their summer vacations were spent together on travel tours. Because they were the only remaining members of her mother's family and had lost touch with her father's family, they always spent winter holidays together, either at home or, in later years, at hotels in warmer climes.

"Mom was always fun to be with. Even after she turned 65 and had to retire, she seemed to enjoy puttering around the house and spending more time with her friends. Her arthritis kept getting worse, but at first she tried very hard to keep active. After a few years, though, a definite change came over her."

The more incapacitated Val became, the more cranky and unpleasant she became, according to Trisha. "She'd always been very independent and hated to ask anyone to do anything for her—except me, of course. And I'd grown so used to doing for her, I really didn't mind. In fact, the few times I've tried living away from home, I've missed it. So it wasn't the help she needed that created problems for me; it was her increasing resentment and anger and the way she piled it all on me. She'd be talking to a friend at home or over the phone and be like her old self, interested and cheerful. But after the friend left, she'd turn on me—grim, bitter and complaining, an entirely different person. It got so we could scarcely speak to each other without shouting."

From our conversations, I gathered that Trisha herself was having problems at about the same time—the start of menopause and an accompanying mental state which she labeled "my identity crisis." Despite her background and education she could not suppress the irrational feeling that her mother's personality change had triggered her own decline. In any case, counseling by a colleague convinced her that she could not regain her own equilibrium while under continual personal attack by her mother.

"We were both off-key, but there were too many years and too many emotional ties for us to be able to help each other, and the situation steadily became more unbearable. At the same time, I knew I couldn't just leave her to live by herself. Finally, I told Mom I was going to move out, closer to school, and that I'd hire a housekeeper–companion to come and live with her. Can you imagine my surprise when she said no, that she'd been thinking about it, too, and that she wanted to move to Lakeview?"

Val had seen Lakeview with a group of church women and knew several who had applied for residency. It was 1969, the first year the house was open, and apartments were immediately available. Trisha made her first visit with her mother to choose the one-bedroom apartment Val subsequently moved into. Describing her feelings that day, Trisha said, "I arrived feeling terribly guilty, as if I were doing something awful to my mother. After seeing the place and talking to some of the people, I felt as if a tremendous load had been lifted from my shoulders."

Almost as soon as the decision to separate was made, relations between mother and daughter improved and, for all the seven years Val had lived at Lakeview, they continued to be good. Besides the time spent together each day on the trip for their morning swim and to the theater now and then, Trisha appeared faithfully for Wednesday night dinner every week and often joined her mother for Sunday dinner and the afternoon program. She no longer took summer vacations with her mother, but they were together for the Christmas to New Year week at the little house on the shore of the lake across from Lakeview. "Sometimes, toward the end of that week, we slip back into those rotten old roles as antagonists," Trisha told me. "It's interesting, though, how Mom reacts. She'll suddenly stop grumbling when I lose my temper with her, and she'll go and sit by the living room window and gaze across the lake at this building. It's as if she's homesick!"

Another resident's grandson, a sophomore at the college where Trisha Platt taught and a frequent visitor at Lakeview, spoke to me about similar changes in his family's life and his grandmother's since she had come there to live. "Granny's much happier since she came here, and nicer, more like she was when Gramps was alive. I'm glad, because when she lived at our house everyone was very nervous."

I asked him what he meant, and he explained, "Well, my

mother was always on edge. She and Granny didn't argue much, but I could tell because she'd yell at us, my kid sister and me, a lot more than she ever did before. And she fought with my Dad a lot, too."

What about Granny? "Oh, she seemed to be sad all the time, and she got sick a lot. I suppose that made Mom nervous, looking after her and all." He thought for a moment, then added, "It's funny, because we always saw a lot of them, my grandparents, I mean. They only lived a few miles away. I used to ride over on my bike all the time, especially when Mom started to work all day."

When I complimented the grandmother, Matilda Fenninger, on her grandson's loyalty as demonstrated by his frequent visits, she laughed and said, "Greg is a sweet boy. We've always been very close, 'secret conspirators' his mother always calls us. She thinks I spoil him rotten. But I just can't deny the charming rascal anything, and he doesn't ask for much." She later confessed that she often gave him money, "because he always seems to run short." Although it troubled her a little, it also gave her great pleasure.

The doting grandmother—a fresh-complexioned, white-haired, diminutive woman—gave the impression of having more power and energy than her small frame could contain. Born at the turn of the century, married at 18 and a mother at 19, Matilda felt she still had her whole life ahead of her when her only child, Greg's father, went off to college. "That's when I decided it was time for me to go to college, too," she related. "It wasn't as easy then as it is now for middle-aged women to enroll, but I was stubborn and pushed my way in. Five years later, at age 42, I was the oldest and probably proudest graduate in my class." Her major in English literature and minor studies in education qualified her to teach, but an opening for a librarian in her home town seemed more attractive. She got the post and kept it for 24 years—"very good years," she claimed.

After her retirement, Matilda and her husband, who had retired the year before, sold their house (in a town adjacent to Watertown), bought a motor home, and traveled. "We had one good year before Karl became ill and we had to return here to the East. During his illness and after he was gone, I stayed at my son's home. I was weary and drained, unable to make any

decisions about what to do next, not really wanting to do anything. A bad time for me and the children!"

The family minister suggested Lakeview to her son and a
Sunday afternoon visit had pleased them all. "To tell the
truth," Matilda admitted, "I wasn't very enthusiastic about it.
Oh, the place seemed fine and the people nice, but I was so
lethargic and depressed I didn't care about anything. All the
same, I knew I was miserable and that I was making the rest of
the family miserable, so I went along. How fortunate I am that
they persisted! Otherwise, I'd still be without a home of my
own."

Matilda arrived at Lakeview in 1973. It wasn't long before
she caught the spirit of the place. During the following three
years and the three years that I knew her she worked as a
volunteer in the Watertown Library and on the Lakeview
Library Committee and was responsible for initiating and
monitoring the revolving collection; she was also instrumental
in bringing the Great Decisions discussions to the house. An
active member of the local League of Women Voters, she had
also chaired Lakeview's Sunday Program Committee and was
a key member, and she was a nursing unit volunteer as well.
Because of her work at the library and her presence at League
meetings and at her church, Matilda had many friends in the
town in addition to the ones she had made in the house.

Lakeview residents like Matilda, Alida Barnes, Addie
Padgett, Abel Johnson, and the others helped create the links
connecting the house to the town. They helped establish the
apartment complex as more than a conglomeration of strangers imposed upon a community, and they earned it and themselves the reputation of good neighbors. While doing so, they
enriched their own lives, adopting new roles to replace former
career and homemaking roles, and inspired many of their contemporaries to do the same. For most of them involvement in
the community meant more than just keeping busy; it fulfilled
the basic human need for affection and respect that stays with
us all of our lives. For the community, they were living
lessons—proof that talent, experience, and dedication do not
vanish in old age.

5. CARETAKERS:
Administration and Staff

*Rules and regulations were deliberately kept loose so
that residents could have a hand in setting up the kind
of structure they'd be most comfortable with and flexible enough so that it could be changed with changes
in the population. In other words, the founders wanted
to provide only basic services, thereby challenging the
people to contribute others according to their needs
and wishes.*

—Ben Gordon,
Lakeview administrator

Where were you during the blizzard of '78? I remember because
I happened to be on one of my weeklong visits to Lakeview
House. The snow began falling gently at midnight and picked
up in intensity through the night along with the howling
winds. That January morning we awoke to a white world with
sky, air, and earth full of snow.

Tim Kellman, the maintenance supervisor who lived in an
apartment on the first floor, got the first of many telephone
calls from Ben Gordon early that morning. Gordon could not
get his car out of his garage, which was blocked by a huge
snowdrift. He asked Tim to get on the intercom and announce
that it was unlikely any of the staff would make it in because of
the storm and to advise the residents to stay in the building. I
asked Tim why he thought the advice was necessary. "Ben said
some of the old troupers—those were his words—might take it
into their heads to go trudging out into the snow to get to their
volunteer work. And I wouldn't put it past some of them
either," Tim answered, chuckling.

Gordon then called Margaret Parsons, the head nurse who was on night duty in the nursing unit. She said she had no intention of leaving. "Even if I dared venture out in this weather, I'd never leave my post until my replacement arrived. I never do," Mrs. Parsons told me. As a result, she stayed through until the following morning, sleeping for a few hours in the afternoon and early the following morning, while nursing unit volunteers took over her watch.

Except for Tim and Nurse Parsons, the only other employees who came in that day were three high school students who lived close enough to walk. When they appeared in their arctic apparel in the early afternoon, these three—two waitresses and a kitchen assistant—were greeted with as much acclaim and applause as if they had climbed Mount Everest. New snow was no longer falling by then, but the wind was whipping the fallen snow about into shifting drifts. At about the same time, the electric power failed and the building went onto its emergency generators.

Most of the residents had breakfast in their apartments, as they ordinarily did. The few with disconnected stoves, like Deirdre Danivan, were invited in by neighbors, some of whom also brought trays to the apartments of those who were ill. Liz Roland, who headed the residents' staff substitute committee, stationed herself at the reception desk to take incoming calls. Before long she was joined by Rita Dorrancy, then president of the Residents Council, who announced an emergency meeting over the communications system.

By ten o'clock, everyone who was not bedridden was in the assembly room. Rita outlined the most urgent needs: care for the nursing unit patients and meals for everyone. Offers to assist the nursing unit volunteers came from many, and a kitchen corps was formed to check out supplies and come up with suggestions. Most people said they had enough food on hand to manage their own meals for the day. Afterwards, friends and neighbors talked about pooling their resources and cooking and dining in one person's apartment, and small parties were organized throughout the building. The kitchen corps set to work, cooking up a big kettle of soup and making sandwiches for the nursing floor people and for residents who wanted to eat in the dining room, knowing that they would have to serve themselves. There was a bit of complaining here and there, most of it mild and from chronic complainers, and a few disagreements about how things should be done. But generally, good humor and even a sense of adventure prevailed.

In the dining room, people sat around listening to some of the old-timers reminisce about early days in the building and the hardships caused by ill-fitting windows, crumbling ceilings, leaky pipes, and balky elevators.

The next morning, Ben Gordon got in early. After he had looked around and found everything in good order, he said, "At times like this I get the feeling that we're superfluous and that the residents could run the building very well by themselves."

Caroline Fitzby, the pretty young receptionist at the front desk, overheard him and countered, "The office staff maybe, but not Tim and his men, or housekeeping, or the kitchen crew. They'd surely be missed."

"And you, sweet Caroline, would be missed most of all," Ben assured her. And I knew this to be true from the residents' oft-expressed fondness for her. It was to Caroline that everyone turned for help with minor problems—calling for a taxi, delivering a message, contacting a relative, changing an appointment—and she always performed these tasks agreeably and well.

Caroline, a Watertown native, had come to the job directly from high school and had been there from the beginning. Her duties were to screen all visitors, to receive packages and mail, to sort and dispatch mail, and to answer questions and provide information. Her desk in the lobby was the radial center for all incoming and outgoing activity. Everyone stopped to chat with her, and some confided in her. She was often the first to hear about a quarrel, complaint, family problem, or some other difficult situation. If it threatened to become serious, she would alert the administrator.

Ben Gordon was Lakeview's third administrator and had held that position for five years by the time I completed my study. The two previous administrators had each stayed for about three years until recruited by the national church-sponsor for executive posts at new congregate residences in other parts of the country. All three had divinity degrees and had served as ministers, though Gordon's earlier background included Army service and business experience. He was rarely referred to as Reverend, seeming to prefer the use of his first name by staff and residents alike. I sometimes heard Tim Kellman call him "Chief."

The nonprofit housing corporation's seven-member board of directors appointed the administrator; he hired all other employees. Within the framework established by the directors, the administrator was charged with overall management of the residence. His office staff consisted of a secretary–office manager, bookkeeper, receptionist, and two part-time office assistants.

A supervisor, deputy, and two assistants made up the maintenance department staff. In addition to their routine custodial chores, these four men did building, plumbing, electrical, and boiler repairs; they also helped residents with heavy jobs like moving furniture. Newcomers were especially appreciative of their assistance in moving in and getting settled in their apartments. The maintenance supervisor was the only employee required to live on the premises. On his days off his deputy or one of the assistants took charge, so that at least one qualified person was always on call in case of emergency.

A head housekeeper supervised five full-time houseworkers who cleaned each apartment once a week, vacuuming, scrubbing bathrooms, and changing bed linens. Residents did their own dusting, furniture polishing, and closet and appliance cleaning, though extra help after hours and on weekends could be obtained through Anna Noble, the head housekeeper, for an additional fee. Common rooms—lounges, dining rooms, halls, lobby—and offices were the housekeeping department's responsibility as well; for this, several part-time workers were hired to supplement the regular housekeeping staff.

All departments appeared to function smoothly and efficiently. Employees seemed to like their jobs and got along well with residents and each other; there was very little staff turnover. Tim Kellman and two of his assistants had been at Lakeview for almost six years, and Mrs. Noble, Caroline Fitzby, and

Eleanor Green, the office manager, had been there since the opening of the house.

Changes made under each administration, frequently at the suggestion of the residents or the council, had helped clear up some early problems. Laundry, for example, used to be done by housekeeping and residents in the same machines, causing backups and inconvenience for all. The first try at a solution was to send linens to an outside laundry. Later, a small storage area next to the arts and crafts studio was fitted with laundry machines for the residents' use, and this proved most satisfactory.

Problems with kitchen and dining room management were the most persistent. For a long time the staff of mostly young people was not adequately supervised, and meals and service tended to be "slapdash," as some residents characterized it. They attributed this to the fact that Lakeview's administrators were ministers with no managerial experience in this kind of operation. "A hotel manager would be more suitable for the job," they said. Some extended their criticism even further, to the total management of the residence. Improvements were made under all three administrators, and dining room service changed for the better, but the food was still deemed mediocre by residents and visitors alike, including me.

When I returned a couple of years later, however, extensive changes had been made. A professional food service organization had been put in charge. The new director reorganized the kitchen; with the help of two dozen workers, including the student waitresses, menus had been transformed and the service, always pleasant, had become as efficient as that in any good restaurant. To the general relief of the diners, the two sittings at dinner, so long and widely criticized, had been abandoned. Instead there was continuous seating, by choice or prearrangement, with the assistance of two part-time hostesses. The house dietitian was consulted, as always, in planning meals for both the main dining room and the nursing unit.

One surprising observation on the dietary habits of the residents: Except for the small number on medically prescribed special diets, residents ate whatever they liked. Anxieties over fat, salt, and sugar consumption never seemed to trouble the majority of them. When I mentioned that I found this most unusual in today's diet-conscious society, the amused response invariably went something like this: "If I've lasted this long, it hardly makes sense to start worrying now."

A description of the staff would not be complete without mentioning the activities director. Lynne Battelle was second to hold that job, her predecessor having left after four years because of her husband's job transfer. I was told that both were very well liked, "mostly because they were never officious or condescending and took direction from the residents themselves," according to Caroline Fitzby.

The nursing unit had a complete staff of its own, headed by a registered nurse and consisting of six registered nurses, six practical nurses (four of them part-time), two housekeepers, an activities director, and a part-time secretary. Dr. Charles Bonner, on duty three mornings a week, was also on call at his Watertown office at other times. Residents could use Dr. Bonner as their personal physician, and those who did could see him during his infirmary hours if they wished.

Although the nursing facility was fully staffed and patients received total care, their lives were considerably brightened by the added attention contributed by resident volunteers. Elsewhere in the house, residents' contributions were of a more substantive nature. A large group of volunteers serving as office and reception desk substitutes during lunch hours, weekends, and staff absences eliminated the need for extra office personnel. Gardeners took over an area of exterior maintenance that would have had to be paid for otherwise. Hospitality people supplemented the work of the activities director and dining room hostesses. Funds for building improvements and equipment were raised by the Whatnot Shop and its large contingent of resident shopkeepers. In addition to affecting economies (much to be desired in those days of swiftly rising costs), all these efforts gave residents broader control over their surroundings and a great deal of personal satisfaction.

Liz Roland, head of the staff substitute volunteers,

summed it up for me: "We do everything here but hire and fire employees. The beauty part is that it creates such wonderful esprit de corps among all of us, residents and staff alike."

So many of the pleasant extras at Lakeview were introduced and maintained by its residents: bird feeders and bird houses in the garden and on the terrace were handmade and the feeders kept filled winter and summer; several tropical fish tanks in the main corridor, installed by a biologist resident, became the beloved project of another when the initiator died; a former high school shop teacher and a small group of amateur carpenters built shelves for the library and display cases for the Whatnot Shop, using power tools in Tim Kellman's workshop with his blessing. The art committee's work in beautifying community areas has already been described, as has the contribution of flower arrangements and plants by the Garden Club.

Undoubtedly, cases of friction between staff members and residents occurred just as they did between residents, but they were remarkably few. One could hear complaints about a sloppy houseworker, or a slovenly waitress, or an inept repair job. But cooperation, even affection, seemed to be the rule. Friendly exchanges about family and health were constants, except among the most reserved people. When a resident celebrated a happy event—a birthday or the arrival of a new grandchild (more likely a great-grandchild)—many employees joined in the congratulations. Sad news always elicited deep sympathies. And employees were accorded the same interest and concern by residents.

Caroline Fitzby's engagement in the fall brought general jubilation to the house. Before the wedding date the following June, the residents held a prenuptial party for the couple and showered them with gifts. "I couldn't have been happier if she were my own granddaughter," Doris Smithson said, expressing the sentiments of all.

Gifts to other employees on other occasions were made by personal choice. But each year at Christmastime a community gift was given. The Residents Council divided a sum of money set aside for this purpose among all staff members.

Caroline maintained that Lakeview's residents were "the

kindest, most considerate people" she had ever known. "I feel
as though I have a big family of aunts and uncles here." About
her job she said, "Sometimes a friend will ask me whether I
mind being with old people all day long. It's a question that
always surprises me, because I forget how old they are while
I'm here. They're fine and good and mostly fun to be with."

The office manager, Eleanor Green, a childless divorcee in
her mid-fifties, was not quite as laudatory. "People here are
intelligent and polite but a little too sociable, always coming by
to chat and interrupting those of us who are trying to get our
work done. I find that hard to put up with. I sometimes think it
would help if we had a house psychologist for them to talk to.
Then there's all the illness, the complicated arrangements to
be made, the deaths. It can be very depressing.

"Still," she added, "this is the best kind of place for old
people. They have a lot of freedom, and they stay very lively.
Listen, in ten years or so I'll probably be applying for an
apartment myself, so I shouldn't complain."

Eleanor's behavior often belied her criticism. She herself
was quite garrulous and seemed to enjoy long conversations
with some of the residents, especially the socialites, and she
told me she stayed two evenings a week to play bridge with
Nellie Blackmore, Ilana Gross, and Harriet Dexter. Furthermore, though she was not as cheerful and accommodating as
Caroline, I never found her unkind or uncooperative nor did I
hear any of the residents say she was.

Checking with Ben Gordon on Eleanor's hint about the
need for a psychologist, I received a not unexpected explanation. "For the most part these people are very self-contained
and private. You could call them reserved. For many in their
generation the idea of resorting to psychological counseling
would be an admission of something shameful. It's a cultural
characteristic. But they do seem to have found useful outlets
for their energies through most of their lives, nonetheless."

Did he encourage them to come to him with their problems? "Yes, and some do, because they regard me as their
minister and are much more likely to discuss personal things
with a minister than with a professional therapist or
counselor—not realizing, I suppose, that many modern minis-

ters are trained in psychology." Actually, he added, he knew of a few residents who had consulted private psychotherapists on the advice of their personal physicians. He gave as example Dorothy Grainger, after her serious surgery and treatment for breast cancer.

When I asked residents whom they consulted about difficult problems, I found that most preferred trying to solve them on their own; others had particular friends or relatives in whom they could confide; quite a few brushed the question aside, saying that they had long passed the age of mental agonizing and that all of their current problems required medical attention of the physical kind.

Given this attitude, which also included opposition to social workers and government assistance as encroachments on privacy and self-dependence, the absence of these services was understandable. Gordon also pointed out that the trustees, who had considered retaining a counselor, were aware of the antagonism, but conceptual and economic factors had also influenced their decision not to do so.

"The broad philosophy on which Lakeview was established was that it would not cover all of the needs of the residents. The thinking was that if everything needed were done for them, it would tend to create dependency and a psychologically unhealthy environment. Where would the incentive be for the residents to continue to be actively involved? Also, it would have made the entry fees and rents prohibitively expensive for most of our people.

"Rules and regulations were deliberately kept loose, too, so that residents could have a hand in setting up the kind of structure they'd be most comfortable with and flexible enough so that it could be changed with changes in the population. In other words, the founders wanted to provide only basic services, thereby challenging the people to contribute others according to their needs and wishes."

Entrance requirements were simple. An applicant had to be 62 years of age or older, in a good state of health and mobile (without the use of a wheelchair), and with sufficient financial assets to pay the costs. A $500 deposit was required with the preliminary application, which, when accepted, put the appliant's name on the waiting list. (Ten years after Lakeview opened that could mean a six- to seven-year wait for an apartment.) All but $50 of the initial deposit would be refunded if the application were withdrawn before a contract was signed. Before a person could become a resident, a complete financial statement, a medical report by a physician, and three personal references were required.

When an apartment became available and a contract was signed, an entrance fee and a month's rent had to be paid. At the time of this study, the entrance fee ranged from $13,000 to $40,000, and the monthly rent, which included the cost of congregate services (housekeeping, one meal a day, infirmary, nursing unit entry, and so on), ranged from $500 to $900, depending upon the size of the apartment.

In the ten years since Lakeview had opened, the entrance fee had tripled and the rental fee increased by about 250 percent. The contract for residents who moved in during the first five years had also been more liberal, stipulating that rents could be raised only a maximum of 5 percent each year for four years, after which it remained fixed, and monthly fees for the nursing unit were to be the same as for apartments. Contracts for the next five years allowed rent increases for a period of ten years. Several years later, all resident contracts were made open-ended, with no cap on rent increases, and apartment rates applied only to the first six months in the nursing unit, after which a patient had to pay an additional monthly charge.

The large increases in fees and the changes to a less favorable contract over ten years were the result not only of rapidly escalating costs caused by inflation but of the unexpected longevity of the early residents. Lakeview's board of directors had been advised by actuaries to expect a complete turnover of residents every five years. Ten years later, more than half of the original residents were still living there.

One result of the higher rates was that newer residents had to be wealthier. Another was the establishment of an endowment fund to help financially distressed residents and to improve and maintain building, equipment, and services without raising fees still further. The fund was administered by a committee of seven—three trustees chosen from the housing corporation's board, three residents chosen by the Residents Council for two-year terms, and Lakeview's administrative director, who was to be a permanent member. The endowment fund committee was responsible to the board of directors and required to make periodic reports to the residents. A memorial fund sustained by gifts from families and friends of deceased residents helped pay for some capital improvements.

Each resident at Lakeview was entitled to life occupancy and the use of all congregate services and facilities, including the nursing unit if that became necessary. Except for carpeting, draperies, and appliances, residents furnished their own apartments. If a resident died or decided to leave within the first three years of occupancy, a portion of the entrance fee was refunded. (After three years, the full fee became the property of the corporation.)

No restriction was placed on the choice of apartment; a single person could choose a two-bedroom apartment, while a couple might move into an alcove efficiency. Apartment sharing, however, was restricted to married couples and blood relatives. Anyone waiting to exchange one apartment for another had to pay the going rate at the time of the change, not the rate paid for the first apartment. Since this involved greater expense, even the couples who married at Lakeview—the McAdamses and the Johnsons—kept their original individual apartments instead of making the move to larger ones. Early residents widowed in the house invariably stayed in their first apartments, too, though smaller ones might have been more suitable.

As in any other apartment house, residents were free to do whatever they wished in their apartments as long as they did not unduly disturb or endanger their neighbors. Guests could be invited at any time and stay overnight. Card games, parties, luncheons, and all kinds of social gatherings were individual prerogatives, as were smoking and drinking which were not permitted elsewhere in the building. A strict rule by agreement between residents and administration, instituted after the fire described earlier, was that anyone who caused a fire in an apartment by smoking would be forced to leave the residence. The rule regarding pets prohibited four-legged animals of any kind. The only pets I ever saw in the building were caged birds, canaries and parakeets.

The most rigid rule was an unwritten one originated by the residents themselves; it concerned the right to privacy. Every visit by one resident to another, even by a close neighbor, had to be arranged in advance, in person, by phone, or by a note slipped under the door. A new resident, finding this strange at first, confessed, "Looking at all those closed doors, I sometimes feel I'd like to run up and down the corridor knocking at every one of them." It was an act that would have taken more courage than she had, she said. But the image of surprise and indignation it would have caused made us both laugh.

The preservation of privacy was one of the salient reasons given by residents for choosing Lakeview rather than some other type of communal living. As Ella Compton put it, "We each have our own complete little home—our apartment—so we can enjoy both the socializing and have our own life, too." And contrasting her life at Lakeview with her life at her son's home, Matilda Fenninger said, "I prefer this because I can have more time by myself, if and when I want to."

"My apartment is my refuge when I want to escape from the rest of the world for a while," Kate Nolan once told me. "At the same time I know that when I'm ill or need help, there's always someone I can call on to lend a helping hand."

Respect for privacy is a form of consideration for others, and kindness and consideration were highly valued. Despite their strict adherence to the rule against spontaneous visits, residents did manage to look after one another. When one fell ill, or failed to keep an appointment, or was missing from an accustomed place or activity, at least one neighbor or friend could be counted on to investigate and alert management if necessary. Good friends exchanged keys, shopped and prepared breakfast and tea trays for each other, ran errands, shared newspapers and magazines, and offered comfort in times of stress and sorrow.

In general, they were tolerant of individual foibles. The woman who had a habit of taking the remaining rolls from baskets on the dinner tables was alluded to as "one of our house eccentrics." Disoriented people were ignored or pitied but never ridiculed. Agnes Drew, with her usual perspicacity, expressed it this way: "You learn to keep your sense of humor in order to live with the eccentricities of other people, realizing, too, that you've got some of your own."

This highly developed sense of consideration might have been responsible for the avoidance of controversial discussions; few seemed willing to risk argument and the possibility of wounding the sensibilities of others. Religion and politics were seldom discussed in a general group but were confined to conversations with close friends. In all the time I spent at Lakeview, I never heard one resident trading insults with another; it just was not done. Resentment was invariably veiled in polite language. I knew, for example, that some residents regarded me with suspicion; they felt I was an intruder in their midst. Yet only one person expressed this openly, saying, "I do feel that you are invading our privacy by coming here and asking questions, no matter how worthwhile your reasons. After all, this is our home." Another type of reaction came from the woman who, upon catching sight of me on a return visit, quipped, "Watch out, friends, our anthropologist is back again to study us old folks." Others who felt the same way were evasive or made some excuse for not being able to talk with me.

Fortunately, these negative attitudes were limited to a few people, and the considerate nature of both residents and staff prevailed so that I usually felt welcome and could count on the cooperation and friendliness of many.

Personal reserve with strangers is one thing; fear of strangers is quite another. And there was little of the latter at Lakeview. Security was good, though not excessive. The front door was unlocked at eight-thirty in the morning (nine-thirty on weekends) and stayed that way until five in the evening. During that time the person at the reception desk could easily see everyone entering or leaving the building, and there was always someone at the desk while the door was unlocked. Visitors had to sign in and be announced. At all other times the front door was locked and could only be opened by a key, which all residents had. Visitors arriving before or after hours could only get into the building if met at the door by the person expecting them.

Security in each apartment depended on keeping the door locked. Also, an emergency cord in the bathroom could be used to set off a signal at the receptionist's desk and at the nurse's station in the infirmary, ensuring swift response no matter what the time of day or night.

Residents were requested to sign out at the front desk whenever they expected to be away overnight or longer. No other formal checking system was used. As noted before, however, residents checked on one another. If anyone was missing during the dinner hour who was not known to be away on a trip, the overnight book would be checked and, unless the person had signed out, the nurse on duty would be notified and the apartment visited. Routine daily checks of apartments whose owners were away was the responsibility of the maintenance staff.

Residents could be away for any length of time. A few of them spent two or three months away at summer homes, visiting family, or traveling. As long as the monthly rent was paid, the apartment belonged to its owner. Any resident in the nursing unit for a 60-day continuous stay, however, might have to relinquish his or her apartment.

All residents who were at home and well were expected to appear for dinner. Trays could be ordered at extra charge, but the practice was discouraged by management except in cases of proven need, like illness or convalescence. Since dinner was the one meal included in the rental and since most residents looked forward to it as the communal social time of the day, this rule had general approval. Residents could sit wherever they chose, guests were welcome, and no reservations were needed except for groups of more than five. After the changeover, when the two separate seatings were dropped, they could come to dinner any time between five and six-thirty. All told, dinner was enjoyed in a distinctly noninstitutional atmosphere.

Conversations were animated. The quiet people were usually the ones with hearing problems. Waitresses greeted diners and exchanged news and comments with those who encouraged their talk. Now and then a friendship between a resident and a waitress grew from such dining room dialogue. The student workers, most of them juniors and seniors in high school and preoccupied with plans for the future, sometimes consulted residents who had worked in fields the young people intended to enter.

Carrie Sutter corresponded with several former waitresses who were studying anthropology. One young woman, in preparation for her doctorate in archeology, was working at an excavation site in Jerusalem when Carrie and I spoke about this. "She was one of the first Lakeview alumnae to ask for my advice. Her interest had apparently been sparked by a lecture I gave at the high school, and she approached me after dinner one evening. It was the start of a lovely friendship."

Modestly downplaying her part in this student's progress, Carrie mentioned a few of the ways she had helped—suggesting colleges, reviewing application essays, writing letters of recommendation. "She's a brilliant, hard-working person. All I did was to give her a bit of guidance. I assure you, I've been more than repaid by her letters and by her visits when she comes home to Watertown, not to mention the vicarious pleasure I get from her descriptions of university life and work in the field."

One evening I saw Carrie hand a waitress a typewritten page. "Peggy is reading in anthropology and asked me to recommend some books," she said by way of explanation. "Actually, her interests seem to be veering toward social anthropology. She could use the help of someone like Margaret Mead instead of an old digger like me." But Peggy seemed unaware of her advisor's failings and gravely thanked "Dr. Sutter." (All employees addressed residents by their last names and courtesy titles.) Later, as the girl cleared the table, I noticed them with their heads together, deep in earnest conversation.

Talking to waitresses from time to time gave me some idea of the informal network that existed between residents and students. Men and women who had taught at colleges and universities were asked about the merits of particular departments at their former schools. If a long time had elapsed since the former academician's retirement and he or she felt unqualified to give advice, inquiries were made through friends and relatives. For almost every student worker interested in a particular field of study, there seemed to be at least one resident with some experience in that field who was willing, even eager, to help the young person. The help might range from as little as advice on choosing a school to as much as tutoring and contacting a former colleague with a request for assistance. When approached by a student, a resident who was unable to help often referred the student to another resident who could.

Kate Nolan had advised youths interested in social work and Chinese studies; one of her protégés had, in fact, become a Chinese language specialist in the State Department. Students interested in nursing would often consult with Addie Padgett and Ella Compton. Matilda Fenninger advised others who were considering studies in literature or library science.

A few of the graduates kept in touch with their mentors through letters or even return visits. (Kate Nolan was invited to the wedding of the young woman who became the China specialist.) Others were never heard from again. The continuing friendships were very gratifying, of course, but those who disappeared were never referred to as ungrateful, at least not in my presence. The attitude seemed to be, "It's their business to go ahead with their lives. If that means there isn't enough time for old friends and acquaintances, so be it," as Addie Padgett said one day when asked, "Whatever happened to young Mary Turner?"

For these people the process itself was important. It strengthened their engagement with life, their involvement in the future. To turn inward and dream only of the past would have meant succumbing to the one sign of old age most of them refused to accept. And they were encouraged to reject dependence and passivity by the unstructured nature of the small community. By keeping services basic and eliminating all but the most essential regulations, the founders of Lakeview House made certain that its residents' resources would be called on to fill the gaps. Consequently, the form the community eventually took was, to a great extent, the form its residents wished it to have—a direct result of their own ideas put into action.

6. A LOOK AT THE NURSING UNIT:
Residents' Attitudes

I was 85 when I moved in with the first batch of residents. I certainly wouldn't recommend that most people wait until they're that old! It was sheer luck that I was still healthy enough to get in and enjoy the wonderful community life for a few years.

All in all, I consider that God has been very good to me. I've had a fine family life. I've done interesting work. And I've had good health and been able to hear and see quite well for more years than most people get. And I found a pleasant haven in my old age.

—Arlene Clark,
Lakeview nursing unit
patient

In his scrappy book attacking agism, *It Takes a Long Time to Become Young,* Garson Kanin tells the story of a friend who is still active as a psychiatrist, professor, writer, lecturer, and research consultant in his 88th year. On being asked his views on death, this man said, "Oh, I don't mind the idea at all. I'm quite resigned to death, but—but just *not today!*"[1]

The same attitude prevailed among the residents of Lakeview. Rev. Winiford expressed it this way: "Most of us are too busy living to worry about dying." He acknowledged, however, that in a community of old people, where the illnesses and frailties of advancing age were ever-present reminders, it was not easy to escape from the realization of one's mortality. "But each of us, through a long lifetime, has developed his or her own ways of dealing with these thoughts."

How individuals come to terms with death is revealed in many ways—sometimes by direct reaction, more often obliquely by reactions to disease and physical losses and by the degree of acceptance of new ideas and relationships. A few Lakeview residents, for example, said they avoided making close friends in the house because they could not bear the pain of losing them.

A more typical reaction was Betty Reardon's on the day Dorothy Grainger died. "People die here all the time. We expect it. We know it's bound to happen. But when it comes to a dear friend, the sense of sorrow and loss is still terrible," Betty said, weeping. Dorothy and Betty had been partners in setting up the Whatnot Shop, and Betty had been a faithful visitor and comforter throughout Dorothy's long illness. It was not a lengthy friendship; the two women had known each other for only the four years that Dorothy lived in the house.

That some residents were capable of facing death squarely was proved to me by the 93-year-old woman who said, "I'm so glad I'm at Lakeview because there'll be less fuss when I go. I didn't want my children to worry about 'What shall we do with Mother?' while I'm alive. And after I'm gone, I don't want them to have to dismantle a large house and get rid of all the things I accumulated. I took care of that before I came here." And Dorothy Grainger, seriously ill with cancer, had given all of her prize possessions to friends and family during her last year. Other residents gauged their longevity by that of their parents. One might say, "My mother lived to be 90, so I suppose I'm destined to get at least that far."

Even a humorous approach to the subject surfaced occasionally. At dinner one evening, Ruth Dobbins remarked that she had been at Lakeview six years and hoped the next six would be as pleasant. Whereupon Kate Nolan said ruefully, "I don't think I'll be here in six years." Ruth then asked, "Why? Where are you going?" At that, everyone at the table, including Kate, chuckled. (Sadly, it turned out to be an accurate prediction. Kate Nolan died a little over a year later. We all mourned the passing of this woman of rare wit and generosity.)

Death and mourning were commonplace, an accepted part of life for most members of this community. Much more fearful than dying was the thought of becoming completely incapacitated and helpless, the fear of becoming a patient in the nursing unit. And yet, the presence of the nursing unit was one of the major reasons given for choosing Lakeview.

At the time the residence was built, in the late 1960s, the inclusion of a skilled care facility was an innovation. Fully staffed, it was licensed by the state and eventually approved for Medicare and Medicaid. The nursing unit, which occupied one floor of the building, also served residents as an infirmary, medical clinic, and convalescent center when beds were available. It was clean, neat, and well run, and a registered nurse was on duty and on call 24 hours a day, every day, for emergencies anywhere in the building. Nurses also helped residents in their apartments with eye drops, dressing changes, and needed injections. In at least one case, a nurse assisted a disoriented resident, who was forgetful about bathing, with weekly baths, shampoos, and changes of clothing.

Many residents spent time convalescing on the nursing floor. In later years, when all 30 beds were occupied, they might have to stay in the hospital. Others preferred living in their apartments while they recuperated after an illness or injury, with the temporary assistance of friends, relatives, or hired aides. A few of the wealthier residents, incapable of managing apartment living on their own, had aides come in to care for them on a permanent basis in order to avoid becoming nursing patients. This arrangement could involve a complicated schedule of home health care aides, many of whom could not be counted on to stay for long. Help from Lakeview's management, which was not set up to hire extra aides, was limited to recommending outside agencies. A resident living this way, therefore, might have to rely on some devoted relative.

One such person, Gertrude Loman, was totally dependent on the three or four aides who spent each day with her. She had been an assistant manager of a large city bank, at a time when it was rare for women to hold such executive positions, and had enjoyed the luxury and diversity of big-city living throughout her middle years. After retirement at 65, Gertrude continued the same way of life, adding extended travel. In her midseventies she began suffering from frequent bouts of pneu-

monia and other respiratory ailments that developed into em-
physema. Never married, childless, and with a circle of friends
decimated by moves to retirement places and by death, she
reluctantly came to live with her sister in Watertown. At the
urging of her sister's daughter, they both applied for an apartment at Lakeview. It was this niece and her husband who
briefly described Gertrude's background and who took care of
her affairs, including the employment of aides.

"Aunt Trudy was quite a livewire in her day," the niece
said. "But she's gone downhill fast, especially since my mother
died three years ago, about a year after they moved in here."
She sighed. "Well, she'll be 90 in a few months. I guess we can't
expect too much. Although I think some of the people here are
almost as old, and they manage beautifully. They really are
extraordinary, you know!"

The niece and her husband, in their early sixties, had
brought Gertrude down to the dining room to have dinner with
them, as they did at least twice a month. On other days dinner
trays were delivered to her room, except for the occasional
times when she felt well enough and had a cooperative aide
who was willing to accompany her to the dining room. Her
slow, shuffling gait and labored breathing made it a tremendous effort. Once seated, however, she seemed to enjoy her
dinner and the companionship, though she could hear very
little of the conversation; even with a hearing aid, she was
quite deaf.

On the evening we talked, the niece tried to comfort her
aunt, speaking directly into the ear with the hearing device
and repeating several times, "You'll be fine on the nursing
floor. It's only for two weeks, until we get back from vacation
and can find more help for you." Each time she said this she
patted Gertrude's hand, pity and guilt on her face. The older
woman muttered and mumbled as the niece turned to me and
said, "She hates to leave her apartment." The husband followed
with a brisk, "Well, it can't be helped."

Later, I asked Karen Burgher whether there were many
residents like Miss Loman. "No, thank God!" she replied vehe-
mently. "I think it is ridiculous to live that way, cooped up in

your apartment all the time with strangers, who are often uncaring, looking after you. And causing so much trouble for that nice couple. You'd think the nursing unit was some hellish place. But you've been there, so you know better."

Karen, as head of the nursing unit volunteers, spent a great deal of time there. In fact, she had conducted me on my first tour. The infirmary—a large, square, windowless room at one end of the corridor, with two beds for emergencies, a couple of desks, and walls lined with sinks, counters, and cabinets— was the only area that had the look of a hospital. Doors to the doctor's consultation room, an examining room, and a wide-open doorway to the adjacent nurse's station were ranged along one wall. A long counter open to the corridor formed one side of the nurse's station, which was bright with posters, paintings, and plants.

Next came the day room—large, rectangular, with one wall of windows overlooking the gardens and the lake. It, too, was decorated with wall hangings and plants and served as an activity and dining room for the patients. Two long tables against one wall held craft supplies and some partly finished colored tissue-paper flowers, painted boxes, and clay figures wrapped in clear plastic. Four large round tables, dining chairs, a few club chairs, a television set, and a piano completed the furnishings. Large glass-paneled doors separated the day room from the smaller solarium, which had three glass sides constructed like greenhouse windows.

Stretching along the opposite side of the corridor were the patients' rooms, 15 in all. Each room was divided by an opaque accordion screen that could be closed from wall to wall, folded back completely, or left partially open. There were two beds, two windows, and two doors—one on each side of the screen—in every room. The beds, placed parallel to the screens, could not be seen from the doors opening on the corridor; you had to step into the room to see the occupants, who faced windows on the opposite wall, enabling them to see the outdoors instead of gazing through the doorways at patches of hallway.

Except for the bed and a nightstand, each half-room was furnished with the patient's things: rugs, chairs, a table, a

dresser, perhaps a small bookcase or cabinet, lamps, photographs, paintings, trophies, whatever the person cared to bring
that would fit without creating a safety hazard.

There was more activity on this floor than I had anticipated. At about ten o'clock in the morning, people in wheelchairs were moving along the corridor, going to and from other
rooms and the day room. Greetings were exchanged, and con-
versational voices came from some of the rooms, but most of the
patients were silent and self-absorbed. In the day room two
women worked on paper flowers at the long table, a man and
two other women in wheelchairs watched a game show on the
large television screen, while another woman, seated in a club
chair, crocheted small colorful squares for an afghan. One
other patient, a man, dozed in his wheelchair facing the sun-
light coming through the doors from the solarium. Except for
the women at the craft table, who spoke loudly to each other
now and then, everyone else seemed oblivious of the others.

Karen greeted every patient she saw by name. Some re-
sponded brightly and asked her how she was or told her a bit of
news about themselves, others just smiled and nodded, and a
few looked blank and unseeing. One of the unresponsive patients was a tiny, shriveled woman slumped in a wheelchair
being pushed along by a nurse. The nurse touched her shoulder
and bent down to tell her that Karen was there. The small
figure raised her head, her eyes lighting up, smiled and said
softly, "How nice. I hope you're well, dear. We must have one of
our good talks again soon."

After they had passed, Karen told me the woman's name. I
recognized it at once as that of a noted psychologist, a pioneer in
the field who had written several books that are still used as
college texts. "A brilliant woman," Karen said. "She's at least
102 now, blind and almost deaf. But her mind's far from gone.
We have had the most marvelous conversations, and except for
the fact that she tires so easily I could talk with her for hours."

This woman, Karen explained, had been one of the first
residents at Lakeview. Then aged 94, frail but alert, she had
occupied an apartment for four years until her sight failed
completely. "She still listens to talking books through a set of

special earphones. But I'm afraid her body can't keep up with
her spirit. She seems to be fading away." And, indeed, she died
quietly in her bed not long afterward, two days short of her
103rd birthday.

The centenarian was the oldest resident of Lakeview. She
had outlived all the known members of her family—a brother,
his wife, and their son—and had only one outside visitor, an
elderly academician who had been her student and then a
colleague. But four or five house friends from the years of
apartment living visited with her regularly while she lived in
the nursing unit. Among staff members and volunteers, she
was a favorite; they admired her for her intelligence and her
calm, uncomplaining nature.

Resident volunteers (NUVs) usually arrived on the nursing floor at ten, a different team of two or three each day. They
were needed to clear away breakfast trays and help patients
dress by the time visiting hours began at eleven. On days when
the nursing unit's part-time activity director was there, she
took charge of the day room. Otherwise, one volunteer played
the part, organizing craft materials, encouraging patients to
participate, reading aloud, showing slides or films. The other
one or two women and Karen Burgher, who was there most
days, spent time reading or talking to patients confined to their
beds. "Sometimes when the person's very ill," Karen told me,
"we just hold their hand for a little while, to show them someone cares."

NUVs also helped feed the patients in bed and in the day
room, where most of them had lunch and dinner. On the days
the ten or so more able patients had lunch in the dining room,
volunteers accompanied them, pushing wheelchairs and sup-
porting those on walkers. In nice weather a patient might be
wheeled downstairs and out onto the garden terrace by a nurse,
a visitor, or a volunteer. Unaccompanied patients were not
permitted to leave the floor, with one exception—a short, thin,
nattily dressed man who had no visible physical impairment
and walked about quite spryly.

His name was Calvin Tucker. I saw him first standing in
the doorway of his room. After Karen introduced us and

explained who I was, he was eager to talk to me and invited me into his room. He said, "Would you believe I'm 85?" I answered no, that he looked at least ten years younger. And he did.

Tucker told me he was a geologist and had done a great deal of traveling in his work. "We had a home in the East, not far from here. But we spent a lot of time in our trailer, Cassie and me. Good times. Cassie, that's my wife. . . ." His voice broke as he brought me the framed photo from his dresser. In a few moments he picked up the thread. "She loved the life—the outdoors, seeing new places, meeting new people. Always said she had gypsy blood. No life for children though. Then we got tired of it. Settled down in our house. But she worried about what I'd do if anything happened to her. So we came here. . . ." He droned on. I had the feeling that he had repeated this litany of truncated sentences many times before. When I interrupted to say I had to leave, he shook his head hard a couple of times and said, "Oh, I drifted off again. I'm sorry."

After that, whenever Calvin Tucker saw me, he would stop and ask how my work was coming along. In the dining room, where he had dinner most evenings, he would wave or, if I were within earshot, give me a cheerful "Hello there." He was free to go anywhere he wanted to and, by all reports, was a prodigious walker, covering miles each day. He also worked with several men residents who formed a landscaping crew, weeding and trimming trees and shrubs on Lakeview's grounds.

"A most unlikely nursing patient!" I exclaimed to Nurse Parsons. "It seems so from outward appearances," she said. "Nevertheless, he's emotionally incapable of living alone. After his wife died, he stopped sleeping, eating, shaving, taking care of his clothes. He'd walk around town all night, even in stormy weather. When he came down with pneumonia, we kept him here six weeks and he improved. But no sooner did he get back to his apartment than he began slipping into the same crazy pattern. And back he came to the nursing unit. After the third try, Ben and I decided it might be best if he remained here. We talked it over with him, and he agreed to give up his apartment."

It was interesting that none of the women who were widowed at Lakeview suffered such a serious setback.

After Frank Smithson died suddenly of a massive coronary, his wife Doris, shocked and grief-stricken, was taken to California by her son and his family, "for as long as she wanted to stay," they assured her. She returned to Lakeview three weeks later.

The Smithsons and I had become good friends during the two years we had known each other. But I was not at the house when Frank died, and I was unable to attend the funeral, so I did not see Doris until several weeks after her return. She was quieter and thinner, and some of the old sparkle was gone. Her skin was chalky, the network of wrinkles more intricate, and her eyes sadder—and my expressions of sorrow brought tears welling into them. "You're very kind," she said softly. Then, bracing herself, she went on: "Everyone misses Frank. He was a wonderful man. It's still difficult to believe he's gone. I wake every morning expecting to hear his step, the shower going, the clatter of breakfast dishes. . . . But people here are so good to me, so attentive and so loyal, they don't leave me much time for brooding."

Apparently her family had tried to persuade her to give up her apartment at Lakeview and stay in California permanently. "I wouldn't hear of it," she exclaimed. "My son and his wife are beautiful people. And I know I could be comfortable in their home. But I told them, very emphatically, that I have a home here. And after a few weeks I was very anxious to get back."

During the following year, I saw Doris frequently. She played bridge regularly, resumed her gardening in the spring, and worked as she always had with the staff substitutes, the Whatnot Shop sales volunteers, and the trip planning group, rarely missing any of the excursions.

For her 80th birthday in June, her son and his wife planned a surprise party with the cooperation of Lakeview's management. Children, grandchildren, and great-grandchildren, old friends from the prep school at which Frank had been headmaster, and all of Lakeview's residents joined in the celebration. The dining room barely held them all. Excited and happy and exhibiting some of her old verve, Doris kept saying, "I don't know what all the fuss is about. Just because I've lived so long!" Once or twice a wistful note crept into her voice as she said, "Oh, how Frank would have enjoyed this. He always loved a good party."

The major physical effects of Doris's grief were increased fragility and vulnerability to illness. Flu and bronchial infections sent her to the nursing unit several times that winter, and her hearing, which had been gradually failing, became noticeably impaired. She regained much of her strength over the spring and summer, however, and a new double hearing aid partially restored her hearing. She seemed content.

What would have happened if she and Frank were living in their old house when he died? I asked Doris months later.

"I don't think I'd have made it. Sixty years of living together . . . our whole lives really . . . it was a terrible shock. Just imagine the added pain and sorrow of having to sort and pack all our belongings, and getting rid of the house." She shuddered. "At least Frank and I had done all that together before we moved here. I'd never have had the strength to do it alone. And I don't think I'd have survived without the friendship and encouragement of so many people here. It's important to me, too, that they all knew Frank well. It's comforting, a link with the past."

The Winifords, close friends of the Smithsons, told me they had despaired of Doris's recovery for a while. "She's so frail, and all the life seemed to drain out of her," Lydia said. "But I knew she was on her way to recovery when she gave Frank's favorite walking stick to Calvin Tucker after he sprained his ankle last winter. Calvin was so pleased that he presented her with a brooch he said Doris had once admired when his wife wore it. That was a big step for Calvin."

"Here you have two good examples of how beneficial it is to have the nursing unit in the same building," Craig Winiford said. "Just think how much more difficult it would have been for Doris if she'd had to go off to the hospital every time she was ill last winter. It would have been lonely and depressing. Here, in the familiar surroundings of the nursing unit, friends visited

her every day—chatting, bringing news, trying to cheer her up
and keep her from giving in to her grief. And because the place
is small and the staff isn't overloaded, she got the kind of
attention that's not often available in a larger medical facility.
The Lord only knows whether she'd have pulled through
otherwise.

"As for Calvin, he might have ended up in a mental institution long ago. That's why I can't understand the people
here who pretend the nursing unit doesn't exist. And that's
very easy to do; it's very unobtrusive. All you have to do is avoid
the second floor. But the patients aren't invisible. And they are
sometimes in the community areas, as they have every right to
be. Just watching some people's reactions to them can be an
education in human frailty."

Indeed, much could be learned about individual residents
by watching their reactions to patients in community areas,
reactions ranging from overt friendliness to pronounced aversion. A few, for example, would not enter an elevator with a
wheelchair in it, and I had seen some at the door to the terrace
lounge wheel about and head in the opposite direction when
they noticed a patient or two there. The people who practiced
these evasive tactics were a handful, perhaps 5 or 6 percent of
the 200 residents. But it was this small group that created the
big furor over allowing patients to lunch in the dining room.
And that administration-generated policy became an attitudi-
nal testing ground at Lakeview.

A majority of the residents accepted the practice with
indifference or gave it grudging support. A typical reaction was
that of Sally Pratkind: "I suppose it's all right. After all, it could
be me someday. One never knows. And every time I see some of
the patients, I think, there but for the grace of God . . ."

Sally, a pleasant and stylishly dressed woman in her early
seventies, had been secretary to the senior partner of a large
city law firm before her retirement seven years before. She was
a new resident and had been at Lakeview only a few weeks
when the policy took effect. Soon after she settled into her
apartment, she invited four good friends from the city to lunch.
"The funny part was that I had raved so about the place and the
people and how lively they are. But the first thing we saw when

we walked into the dining room were the wheelchairs and the walkers and some pretty crotchety specimens sitting around the tables near the door. My friends looked at me as though I were crazy, and one of them said, 'I thought you said this wasn't like an old age home!' "

A tour of the building and gardens after lunch cleared up her friends' poor first impression, Sally said. But after they left she asked Ben Gordon why the patients were seated so close to the doorway instead of somewhere in the back where they would be less noticeable. The administrator explained that it was done so they could be moved quickly in case of fire or some other emergency. In fact, he told her, dining room hostesses were instructed to seat all residents with walking difficulties near the entrance to the room whenever possible.

Once she had recovered from her initial embarrassment and explained the situation to her friends, Sally was amused by the incident. And it was in this spirit that she related it to me. In a more serious vein, she talked of the uncharacteristic dissension that had developed among the residents. "People at both extremes tried to pressure their friends to take a stand on the issue. If you refused, you lost friends. I think a few went along with the complainers for that reason. And I think a lot of people, who didn't care one way or the other, ended up with the supporters. I know I did. But because I was new here, I have the feeling I've been cut off from some friendships I might otherwise have made."

Not long after this conversation, I ran into Sally in the nursing unit. Karen Burgher had enlisted her as a volunteer. "I can't say I like it very much," Sally confessed. "I still have trouble eating my own dinner on Thursday, my duty day, after feeding my patients. But I know it's important, and I feel useful. And the other NUVs tell me I'll get used to it."

Craig Winiford was, of course, one of the staunchest supporters of the dining room policy. "We all ought to realize that the nursing patients are former residents. And returning to the large dining room is good for their morale. It helps them feel they are still part of the community."

Many of the residents who felt as he did were also regular visitors of friends who had moved to the nursing unit. Several residents actually visited patients who had been strangers to them, at the request of the minister of their church or of one of the NUVs, because these patients had no other visitors. And members of the house choir entertained patients with an hour of song each week, inviting them to sing along.

Residents who had spent periods of illness and convalescence in the unit often had the most positive attitudes. Kate Nolan and Betty Reardon, who had each spent three or four convalescent periods of up to a week, thought the service there was excellent. "The staff is concerned and caring. At the same time, they don't treat the patients like babies. Even those who are completely non compos mentis are treated like adults," Kate averred.

Betty agreed and added, "It's really not bad once you get used to the deficiencies of the patients and stop seeing them as a mirror of your own future. The first few times I set foot in the nursing unit I got awfully upset. I'd look at the worst cases and think, 'God, I hope I die before that happens to me!' "

"I guess we all feel that way. But some people can't bear it. They close their eyes and pretend this floor doesn't exist. They like to think of Lakeview as the Grand Hotel. And they work real hard to clear their minds of the truth, that we're a bunch of decaying ancients hovering on the brink of extinction. And that our friends in the nursing unit are just a little closer to the edge than the rest of us," Kate said with a wicked gleam in her nearly blind eyes.

"Oh, Kate, you exaggerate," Betty countered good-naturedly. "Look at Arlene Clark and Cal Tucker. They're in nursing because they couldn't manage in their own apartments anymore, but they're still going strong, and they may outlive you and me."

"Betty always comes round to seeing the cup as half full—an incorrigible optimist," Kate said fondly. "And, in truth, anyone who has to bed down in nursing would do well to follow her example and look at the best of the lot. In any case," she concluded, "though it's much better to be in your own apartment, it's good to know there's a friendly place to stay when you're ill."

Appreciation for the existence of the nursing unit was

virtually universal among residents and their families. Even those who shunned it and ignored the patients were grateful for its presence. Ilana Gross, who would never enter an elevator with a patient and who, with Nellie Blackmore, led the very small but vociferous group opposed to the dining room policy, once admitted, "Just because I don't want to be around disease and decay doesn't mean that I think it can't happen to me. I know it can. And I'm glad the skilled care is here in case I ever need it. But I don't want to be reminded of that possibility constantly. I've seen enough illness and death in my life. Now I want to enjoy each day as it comes."

According to her friend Ella Compton, Ilana had always been an "escapist." The two had met as young nurses working at the same hospital. "Why Ilana chose nursing as a career has always been a mystery to me. I suppose it was because her family was very poor and there weren't many job choices for women then. But she always hated it. As soon as she married she left the hospital, and she never turned back. Once in a while when I visited her, she'd wrinkle up her nose and say, 'You smell like the hospital.' Still, she's lots of fun to be with and we always got along real well."

Nellie Blackmore, the resident who so carefully avoided her dauther-in-law's mother and her fellow resident, the confused Deirdre Danivan, was in complete agreement with Ilana. "I know the nursing unit is here. That's enough. I don't want to see it or hear about it. And if I ever have to be put away there, it should be just that—*away!* No need to spoil everyone else's pudding."

So strong was Nellie's antipathy that after she broke her leg and pelvic bone in a bad fall and had returned from the hospital, she insisted on staying in her own apartment with round-the-clock aides. "Which she could hardly afford," Ella told me, adding, "I believe her son paid for them." During Nellie's recovery, her bridge group held all of its games in her apartment. But the women would not have lunch or cocktail parties there until she was up and about again. And Nellie understood; the sickroom atmosphere was not to their liking.

Neither Nellie nor Ilana nor their other socialite friends were critical of the nursing unit volunteers. "I can't see it. But if that's what they want to do, why not?" Nellie said with a shrug. Ilana was more positive: "I admire them, just as I've always admired Ella for all the years she's put in at hospitals. It's just not for me. I can't stand being around sick people."

The work done by the NUVs was praised throughout the house by residents and staff alike. "They perform a very necessary service for difficult people, and they're of invaluable help to us," head nurse Margaret Parsons said. "Not all of our patients are as sensible and appreciative as our precious professor [the centenarian] and Mrs. Clark. Many are cranky and some are paranoiac, accusing others of stealing belongings they've squirreled away. Occasionally we even have an hysterical patient. It can be very unpleasant for the volunteers."

I had been in the unit during one such episode. Frightening nightmarish shrieks filled the corridor. A young nurse coming from the hysterical patient's room caught sight of Karen, who had just stepped off the elevator with me. She ran up to her saying. "Oh, Miss Burgher, I'm so glad you're here. Miss Fugate is at it again."

A few minutes after Karen entered the room, the piercing cries subsided. Karen came out, shaking her head sadly. "Poor, unhappy woman. She can barely move anymore, and her stroke has made her speech unintelligible. It's terribly frustrating for her. And to think she once ran a newspaper. She took over the *Watertown Weekly Courier* from her dad when he died—the third generation to do so—and she put the paper out almost single-handedly for more than 35 years."

"Karen is a saint," Nurse Parsons told me. "She manages the volunteers with a velvet glove. She inspires and encourages them, but she never lets them get out of line. As you know, we try very hard to treat the patients with dignity. It's the last shred of pride for some of them. And it isn't always easy. Now, as far as I'm concerned, it would be disastrous to have people working with the patients who used baby talk or played children's games with them. I won't tolerate it from the staff, and Karen keeps tabs on the NUVs. She seems to revere old people and to understand them instinctively, no matter how bad their condition. And they respond in kind."

How had Karen Burgher come by this talent? "I'm not sure

myself. Maybe it's because I loved my grandparents so," she answered as we talked in her apartment one evening. The one-bedroom apartment was neat and orderly, furnished simply and sparely. Except for one wall covered with family photographs, the only ornamentation in the living room was a large painting of a full-rigged schooner at sea and some faded hand-hooked rugs atop the beige carpeting.

Karen herself was as neat and as simply dressed as the room, her long steel-gray hair arranged at the back in a bun. She was of medium height, slender, and quite erect for her 76 years. She had been born exactly at the turn of the century, January 1, 1900. If I had to characterize her in one phrase, I would call her a "no-nonsense person." Her hazel eyes could turn dark with anger but took on a warm glow when she was with people, as they did while she spoke of her past.

"We lived in a sort of family compound. And I spent the happiest times of my life in the big, rambling house my grandfather had built. My grandma's maiden sister and bachelor brother lived there, too. So it was a house full of old people who gave me all the love and attention anyone could want."

Karen's grandfather had come to Maine by way of Canada from his native Germany as a very young man. He started a lumber and pulp mill and married a native of the town he had settled in. Three of his sons worked with him in the mill, but Karen's father, the youngest, preferred the life of a peripatetic scholar, moving from medicine to law to theology and back to law. "I believe he really wanted to be an actor, but that wasn't considered a serious occupation. Perhaps it was his love of the theater that attracted him to my mother. He met her in New York, where he spent some of his student years. She had come over from Paris with a French theatrical troupe and spoke scarcely two words of English. Imagine bringing a young woman like that to a rural town in Maine!"

Karen described her parents as a tempestuous pair. Her father set up his law practice in the house his father built for the young couple, as he had built houses for his three other sons when they married. Except for the legal business of the mill, she could not recall that her father actually practiced much in the way of law. "He was always borrowing money and getting

involved in get-rich-quick schemes that never paid off. Poor
mother. She had six children in quick succession and all those
strange relatives to contend with. She was very harried and
very voluble about her discontents. So I was always running off
to grandma's. We'd talk about all sorts of things while I helped
her cook, bake, and fix preserves. Or I would sit with my
great-aunt and listen to the poems she composed about knights
and ladies, which seemed always to be in quatrains. Or I might
spend some time in the big shed behind the house where
grandma's brother had his workshop. He made furniture with
exquisite care and, to me, excruciating slowness, hobbling
around on his peg-leg and telling me stories of his seafaring
days. That desk under the ship painting is his work," she
added, pointing to the polished, finely crafted piece against the
wall.

Of the six children Karen's mother bore, only she remained. One had died in infancy, two had died of childhood
diseases, and an older brother had been killed in France during
the first world war; the youngest, wounded in World War II,
had died in 1970, two years before Karen moved to Lakeview.

"It was because of him that I left home and settled in
Boston in the forties," Karen explained. "I'd been teaching
grade school in our town, living at home, and looking after my
mother and grandmother. But there were all the cousins and
uncles and their wives to do that, so I came down to Boston to
take care of Jimmy when he was released from the veterans'
hospital. He'd lost both his legs. I couldn't bring him home even
if he'd wanted that, and he was dead set against it, because he
needed treatment and therapy at the hospital. So we took a
small apartment near there. For a long time he'd do nothing
but lie in bed or sit in his chair and stare at the walls or out the
window—absolutely nothing. But I began to leave him alone
for longer and longer periods of time until, at his therapist's
urging, I went to work full-time, teaching French at a girl's
school. Jimmy soon began cooking our meals. Later, he did the
cleaning as well. And still later, some of the shopping. Eventually, we got him a specially equipped car, and he went to work
in an electronics plant, doing assembly work."

I thought it strange that Karen had not returned to the

family home after her brother's death. "An awful lot of changes take place in 30 years," she answered thoughtfully. "The mill had been sold and all of the family houses. The family had scattered. Only one old cousin and her daughter's family still live in the town. There was really nothing for me to go back to."

How had she discovered Lakeview? "The Gilberts are old friends. Dr. Gilbert counseled many of the veterans. He was especially helpful to my brother. As we all grew older, we often discussed life after 70," Karen laughed. "Well, Mayhew—Dr. Gilbert, that is—became very enthusiastic about congregate living for the elderly. He and Alice, his wife, took me with them to visit several places on the eastern seaboard. Of all that we saw, we liked Lakeview best."

Dr. Gilbert was a large, imposing man in his late eighties, with a fringe of ear-length white hair surrounding a shiny pink bald spot. Though he counseled prisoners at the state penitentiary for a few hours each week, much of the rest of his time was spent in his study, an efficiency apartment he used for that purpose alone. He and his wife also occupied a one-bedroom apartment on the floor above. Either because he towered over most people in the house or because he had his mind on his books, he appeared aloof and abstracted. This impression quickly vanished when he was engaged in conversation.

Mayhew Gilbert was a warm advocate of congregate housing in general and of Lakeview House in particular. "Where else could a woman like Karen Burgher live so well? She devoted most of her life to her brother. And there was no way she could go home again. Home wasn't there anymore! Here she is comfortable and secure, surrounded by friends, and she can still make use of her considerable abilities."

He approved highly of having the nursing unit in the same building for several reasons. "However much any of us may dislike the thought, a few of us are headed that way if we live long enough. And it's salutary to be reminded of it. Furthermore, if we do have to go and we are still mentally competent, we have the advantages of familiarity with the staff and other patients. And our friends in the house can visit us conveniently. It spares us the trauma of having to be moved to completely strange and perhaps more institutional surroundings if we should need nursing care."

Dr. Gilbert maintained that he and his wife had frequently discussed what should be done if one of them died or had to enter a nursing facility. "If we hadn't recognized and talked about these things, we never would have looked at retirement housing. It was the realization of how difficult it would be for the remaining partner that drove us to leave our old way of life, much as we loved it."

Alice Gilbert was as sensible as her husband but less loquacious. A tall, plump woman with a pleasant face and soft blue eyes behind thick-lensed glasses, she bustled about the apartment serving tea and her home-baked cookies while her husband talked. They both wore hearing aids, and it was said that she sometimes turned hers down when he went on for too long.

When we had finished our tea and Dr. Gilbert left for his study, Alice and I sat at the table and talked.

The Gilberts were both middle-aged when they married. He was an army chaplain and she a missionary in North Africa when they met in 1935, but they waited to marry until they returned to the United States soon after the outbreak of the war in Europe. Alice went to work in the mission headquarters in Boston. Hew, as she called him, divided his time between the pastorate of a small church and pursuit of a doctorate in psychology. They lived in the church parsonage. After obtaining the degree, he continued as minister while also serving as a counselor at the veterans' hospital.

"Hew is a little sanctimonious sometimes," Alice said with the trace of a smile. "Actually, our coming to Lakeview wasn't as carefully planned as he made it sound. I was very ill for several months during which he found life very difficult. Beside all the household things, he had relied on me to do all the driving, especially at night. So his activities were seriously curtailed. Even visiting me at the hospital was a problem, though friends like Karen helped out. It was this near catastrophe that frightened us and, more than anything else, gave us the determination to make the move."

Alice thought that the other couples at Lakeview had been impelled by similar crises. "Haven't you noticed how much older the married people are than most of the singles? I don't believe there's one under 80. That's why the nursing unit is so important to us. It's a terrible strain on an old person to have to look after a partner who's ill. Merely getting to a doctor or visiting a hospital or convalescent home can become a trial, especially when you have no family to turn to."

Having been in the nursing unit for several short stays, Alice was well qualified to comment on it. "I have no serious criticism of the care or the surroundings. They're fine. But two things do worry me and a lot of other people here. One is, will there be enough room for me if I ever have to stay permanently? And my other question is, does it make sense to put people who are ill and feeling low in among nursing patients who will never recover? Wouldn't it be better to have another kind of facility for convalescents and for people who are not completely helpless?"

Other residents had expressed these same concerns—fear that the nursing unit was running out of space while, with the house population growing older, the need might be increasing; and the desirability of having an intermediate care facility. And I had discussed these concerns with the administrator, Ben Gordon. His contention was that the nursing unit was large enough to accommodate the residents. "Even though our new residents are older, because of the long waiting time between application and the availability of apartments, they seem to be healthier. Perhaps it's because of advances in medical and health care over the past ten years. As for an intermediate care unit, I think it's an excellent idea. But we'd have to sacrifice apartments to make space for it, and apartments are desperately needed now. We'd also have to increase staff, which would raise our expenses. Believe me, though, the trustees are considering it. But the thinking is that, for now at least, we've got to make do with what we have."

What the residents of Lakeview did have was a very supportive system, in sickness and health. It was not perfect, but what is? Serious illness or a worsening handicap could have a very depressive effect. Increasing memory failure, hearing or vision loss, arthritis, broken bones slow to mend, pneumonia, even a bad case of the flu might cause periods of depression. But with the help and encouragement of the people around them, most of whom had similar or worse problems, invalids usually bounced back and managed to compensate for any permanent losses. The avid gardener, who could no longer bend or kneel, tended her garden plot seated on a small, low stool. A cane with a crook end was used to remove items from the below-counter refrigerator and a stovetop baker to avoid bending down for access to the oven. The near-blind pianist had music written in large black script for her by another resident musician and was able to continue playing. Talking books, hearing aids, canes, bathtub seats for sitdown showers, raised toilet seats and grab-bar frames, any device that could compensate for a handicap and maintain independence was tried and used.

It was clear, too, that a relatively small number of residents ever had to enter the nursing unit on a permanent basis and that the active lifestyle, strong social structure, good nutrition, and prompt medical attention lessened the probability of residents becoming nursing patients. As for those few who did, they received fine care in a small, minimally institutional type of facility. And some of them were able to prove, despite their handicaps, that life can still have its pleasures.

One such exemplary patient was Arlene Clark, a widow and a former neighbor of Addie Padgett in a suburban town near Watertown. Her husband had died when she was 56, and she continued to live alone in the house they had occupied for 30 years. A son and daughter, both married, lived in distant parts of the country. Arlene went to work in the admissions office of the Watertown Hospital and stayed until she reached mandatory retirement age ten years later, switching then to volunteer work at the hospital.

During those years, on visits to her children and to friends who had moved away, Arlene looked at retirement communities in various areas. "Mostly out of curiosity," she said, "because, for some odd reason, I didn't expect to live long enough to need it. But after I turned 80, I knew I'd better think about it seriously. My health was still good, and it began to dawn on me that I might live to be 100. At the same time, I'd seen so many old people suddenly take ill and enter the hospital, only to be taken from there to nursing homes because there was no one at their own homes to look after them."

Despite this realization, Arlene told me, she continued to

delay, finding fault with every retirement community she investigated. Her children tried to coax her out to places near their homes. But somehow none of the possibilities pleased her. "When I heard about Lakeview, even before it was built, it seemed like the answer to my prayers. I understood then why I'd rejected everything else. I really didn't want to leave the Watertown area. I'd spent my whole life here. I still did some work at the hospital, and a few of my friends still lived here. I knew the shops, the banks, the hairdressers. It was home."

Arlene claimed that everything about the prospect of living at Lakeview pleased her—the location, the concept, the church sponsorship—except the high-rise building. She had never lived in an apartment and had pictured herself spending her last years in a little cottage in a small community in a sylvan setting. "It took a little self-persuasion to overcome that," she said, laughing. "Fortunately for me, I did. I was 85 when I moved in with the first batch of residents. I certainly wouldn't recommend that most people wait until they're that old! It was sheer luck that I was still healthy enough to get in and to enjoy the wonderful community life for a few years."

In her three years as a resident, Arlene continued her volunteer work at the hospital and helped start several committees in the house. Her energy began to wane after a year or so, however, and she suffered attacks of vertigo and palsy. After extensive examination and testing, her condition was diagnosed as Parkinson's disease. She was able to keep her apartment for a few more years, alternating with periods in the nursing unit that gradually grew in length and frequency until she had exceeded the 60-day limit and had to give up her apartment.

When I first met Arlene, the tremors and weakness were severe enough that she was confined to a wheelchair. But she propelled the chair by herself; she managed to dress and feed herself, very slowly and carefully; she read a great deal, using a folding bookstand she could clip to the side of her bed or chair; and she kept up a fairly extensive correspondence using an antique typewriter. "My children telephone often, but I like to keep in touch with the grandchildren and with old friends far away, and I can't use a pen any longer." She received a great deal of mail, too, and amused patients, staff members, and resident friends, who visited often, with anecdotes gleaned from her letters, some so outlandish she was accused of fabricating them.

Arlene also managed her own finances and her responsibilities as a trustee of a foundation established by her husband. Her attorney, a man in his seventies, visited once a month to deliver statements and reports and to collect her typewritten comments and instructions on foundation and financial business. To the delight of the nurses, she always teased him by announcing that he looked terrible and it was time he thought about retiring, and "since Lakeview's the best there is," urged him to pick up an application on his way out. "Don't wait until it's too late," she would admonish him as he left.

The nurses also informed me that Arlene used to read to patients, but that her voice had gotten so soft and tremulous that very few of them could hear her any longer.

On my farewell visit to the nursing unit, I stopped in to say goodbye. Arlene was then approaching her 96th birthday. Her white hair, cut very short by a local beautician who came in to do it every couple of months, shone under the lamp over her bed. A large-type book was propped on the stand next to her. She gave me a warm smile when I entered. Her words came very slowly and were barely audible. "I've enjoyed your visits, my dear, and I'll miss you. At my age, though, one is used to departures. How many there have been! All in all, I consider that God has been very good to me. I've had a fine family life. I've done interesting work. And I've had good health and been able to hear and see quite well for more years than most people get. And I found a pleasant haven in my old age." Patting my hand with her thin, trembling fingers, she wished me success.

I kissed her cheek and said, "If I can learn to be as gracious and courageous as you, I'll consider myself very successful."

7. A MODEL OF SUCCESSFUL OLD AGE: A Sociological Appraisal

It may seem paradoxical to advocate communal living as the best way to achieve independence. But the Lakeview community convinced us that the two go very well together, that the support and interaction with an empathetic community of our peers can make us stronger even when we are more frail.

—The Authors

What is your vision of a good old age? Is it a time merely to be free of work and family cares? Or a time to do the things you never had time to do before—writing poetry, painting pictures, going to school, traveling? Are you determined to go ahead with your lifelong work? Or do you see yourself switching tracks and embarking on a new career? Perhaps you picture yourself in a rocking chair on the front porch, shelling peas or whittling, surrounded by adoring grandchildren listening to your tales of yesteryear.

Anything is possible. But, for most of us, the likelihood of the last image coming to pass is slim. We may be out there on our rocking chairs, but the children and grandchildren will probably be scattered around the world. Family life is too unstructured and uprooted today to save a special niche for anyone, let alone an old parent. Our children and grandchildren are brought up to be independent, to find and follow their own paths, of which there are many more now than there were 20 or 30 years ago. The affirmation of individual independence is the keynote of twentieth-century America, the aim of social and civil rights legislation, labor laws, universal education, women's liberation, and a host of other modern movements.

The Idea of Disengagement

With the graying of America, more old people are demanding their independence, too. And as we grow older, each of us strives to maintain it. At the same time, if we have lost our role as wage-earners, parents, spouses, or whatever identity we most cherished, we must try to create new niches for ourselves in society. Or, we can simply withdraw.

In social gerontology, these alternatives are expressed as the theories of disengagement and activity. *Disengagement* is explained as the advance preparation, by society and the individual, for the "ultimate 'disengagement' of incurable, incapacitating disease and death by an inevitable, gradual, and mutually satisfying process of disengagement from society."[1] In other words, it is natural for older people to want to withdraw more and more from social situations and for society to approve of this withdrawal.

On the other hand, some professionals think this process of disengagement is not voluntary on the part of old people but is imposed by society. Nor is it beneficial to either. On the contrary, activists claim to have found that higher levels of social interaction mean greater life satisfaction in old age. This is the theory most widely accepted today, although it is believed to supply only a partial explanation of the social pattern of aging.

What researchers have found is that older people do not willingly drop out, but neither is activity the sole determinant of morale. An important component is positive identification with a group of people of the same age—a group with common interests, common problems, and common role losses, a group often created in response to rejection by the general culture.

The Makings of a Subculture

Culture is usually defined as the shared norms, beliefs, and values of a group of people. A subculture is a group that develops in response to isolation and negative evaluation by the larger general culture. The subculture is strengthened when group solidarity and heightened interaction among its members are sufficient to sustain their common values and beliefs.

Various factors may foster an aging subculture. One gerontologist, Arnold Rose, says, "Retired people—who can no longer earn a living, whose physical abilities to get 'around' and engage in sports are limited, and whose prospects for new achievements and successful competition are slim—experience a sharply diminished status. This is abetted by the absence of special marks of prestige attached to aging which are found in other societies, such as the attribution of special wisdom, the automatic succession to higher political positions. . . . Thus . . . the elderly tend to interact with each other increasingly as they grow older and with younger people decreasingly and hence develop an aging subculture."[2]

Conditions existing now and expected to continue in the future will increase the probability of this subculture formation. Those conditions include the larger number and increasing proportion of older people, the improved health of the 65-plus population which should lead to more people living into advanced old age, larger concentrations of old people remaining in urban centers with greater accessibility to each other, increases in social programs to bring them together; and the growing number of elderly, particularly single and widowed women, living alone.

Certainly, income level affects the degree and strength of this subculture. Higher-income elderly tend to stay in contact with the larger society more than do lower socioeconomic groups and may not, therefore, develop a distinctive aging subculture. Other factors that might interfere with subculture development are greater contact with family, continued employment, and, perhaps most important, denial of one's own aging and resistance to identification with other old people.

Without aging awareness and acceptance leading to aging group consciousness, a subculture of the aged is not possible. Denial of the reality means that the individual must face alone (and presumably ignore) the social stigma attached to being old, the loss of status and the ambiguity of this last stage of life—ambiguous because there are no publicly recognized roles for old people. "This means that who he is, what others think of him, and how he is to act remain vague. Such a person is faced with a life situation devoid of relatively structural expectations on behavior," says Jaber F. Gubrium, who agrees with Arnold Rose that aging group consciousness is very important.[3] But Gubrium also emphasizes that the key to a successful aging subculture is its ability to create socially meaningful roles.

Aging group consciousness occurs when older persons begin to think of themselves as members of an aging group and can discuss their problems in constructive ways. It is indicated by recognition and acceptance in a positive way of one's own aging and by the ability to make peer friendships and accept peer role models.

The lack of understanding by older people of this stage of life has been thoroughly explored by Irving Rosow, who contends that most elderly people not only do not identify with the old but are most reluctant to do so because of the way our society favors youth and youthful values. Based on assumptions that society will continue to devalue and exclude the elderly and that adjustment to old age is desirable, Rosow believes that the "insulation of the elderly from other age groups and their increased association with age peers" would provide a critical condition for developing a viable alternative, and "the concentration of socially similar older persons within a local setting, preferably residential" would raise self-esteem, facilitate group supports, provide new and substitute roles, and foster friendships and informal associations.[4]

Another dimension of adjustment to old age, according to Rosow, is that these age-homogeneous settings must also facilitate "the formulation of a distinctive new role, new expectations and norms appropriate to it, and a set of eligible role models."[5] This is more likely to occur when residents are also homogeneous with respect to ethnicity, socioeconomic class, and marital status. A concentration of similar people maximizes opportunities for informal and formal social interactions and relationships, which are essential to their well-being. Such a residential environment would encourage acceptance of old age by providing group support, new group memberships, new role sets, a positive reference group, qualified role models, and new self-images. Rosow argues that unless society's current institutions and values change dramatically this is the only viable alternative for the aged.

Study Finds Vibrant Community Life

Impressive support for Rosow's hypothesis comes from Arlie Hochschild's study of a small public housing project for the elderly in San Francisco. Hochschild began her research with the idea of testing the disengagement theory, but she found the project's residents very much engaged and participating actively in a vibrant community life. They had developed a strong consensus around central values that became the basis for role expectations. Not only were role standards articulated and supported through social rewards and controls but other features of cohesive groups had also developed: rituals, taboos, private humor, mutual aid, and so on. Their values, group embeddedness, and new roles enabled the residents to cope with many problems of aging much more successfully than old people who lived outside this housing community.

Hochschild's findings also support Rosow's argument that a residential setting with a concentration of socially homogeneous members—homogeneous not only in age but also in sex, marital status, social class, and regional background—fosters an aging subculture that enhances its members' lives.

Hochschild made another discovery. Not only was there a healthy aging subculture, but it was based on a particular kind of relationship, the "sibling bond." That is, in addition to being social siblings and equals among themselves, the residents were remarkably similar in what they wanted and what they could give one another. This sisterhood of the housing project was no substitute for relationships with their children, but it offered a full and meaningful life independent of children. Hochschild contrasted this sibling bond with the parent-child bond found in institutions where old people are "patients," not "residents," and dependent on staff members who reinforce this parent-child relationship, a childlike dependence as opposed to the adult autonomy found among the public housing project residents.[6]

Does Congregate Housing Meet Needs?

So far we have discussed the theoretical elements of an aging subculture. Since this is a book about congregate housing, let us be more specific. Is a congregate housing environment conducive to the formation of an aging subculture? What about the quality of life? Do its residents live longer? How does it help them deal with loneliness, role loss, relationships with children, and other common problems of the elderly?

Research focused on congregate housing, which is a relatively new type of living arrangement, is still somewhat sparse. But the findings of several major housing studies do indicate that congregate housing forestalls institutionalization and significantly prolongs life. Kurt G. Herz, in an analysis of Kissena Apartments in Queens, New York, reported an unusually low death rate, about 4 percent in five and a half years, with only one tenant leaving to enter a home for the aged. This is particularly significant since the average age of the 200 tenants was 74 to 75 years.[7] Another example is Riverview in New York City, a project with 188 tenants whose average age was 79.2 years, studied by Leon Kalson. During a five-year period, 36 residents left to enter old age homes and 30 tenants died. According to the Standard Ordinary Mortality Table, "this mortality rate is actuarially remarkable."[8]

You will remember, too, that actuarial predictions of a complete turnover in Lakeview's population after the first five years were confounded by the residents, more than half of whom were still there at the end of ten years. And the median age at Lakeview was 83.

Then there were the results of an extensive longitudinal study conducted by Frances M. Carp. She matched the original residents of Victoria Plaza in San Antonio, Texas, with their counterparts living in the community over a period of eight years. When compared with the housing tenants, community elderly had a larger number of deaths, significantly greater moves to nursing homes and other institutions, and had spent more time in institutions prior to death. Carp felt that the congregate facility had not only increased the life span of its residents but had also improved the quality of life of those extra years. She found, for example, that after eight years residents had enlarged their circle of friends, improved relationships with their families, and improved their own self-images.[9]

A positive relationship between congregate housing and life satisfaction is frequently cited by researchers. Elaine Brody's study of Community Housing for Elders in Philadelphia (see chapter 8 for more on this project) and other studies support this conclusion.

As a corollary to improved life satisfaction, congregate housing also seems to supply one answer to the devastating problem of loneliness in old age. Here again, Carp and others have confirmed that increases in social interaction resulted in less isolation and loneliness.

In a study of four types of housing for the elderly in California, Daniel M. Wilner and Rosabella Price Walkley observed that "special group housing serves to concentrate rather than diffuse the field of potential friends and support, thereby maximizing the condition of social interaction."[10] Arlie Hochschild, too, stated that the communal life at her study project gave the residents some measure of dignity and helped insulate them against society's treatment of them as marginal people. On an equal footing with fellow residents and with their mutual support, they were able to solve problems that would have been much more difficult if faced alone. And, reporting on his study of a New York City congregate residence, Kurt Herz cited loneliness in former housing as the residents' most important reason for moving. After five years in the new housing, residents had established many new social contacts and associations and reported a marked decrease in alienation, loneliness, and depression. David S. Greer, in his study of Fall River, Massachusetts, special housing for the elderly and handicapped, came up with similar findings.[11]

New Roles in Life Found

Congregate living also seems to aid in maintaining roles and in providing new ones. M. Powell Lawton analyzed community spaces in a sample of 12 housing projects and compared those projects offering services with those offering none. "The provision of resources within the housing environment can heighten the probability of effective role maintenance," he concluded.[12] Irving Rosow's studies also led him to the conclusion that group living facilitates the older person's transition to a new aged role and that age peers provide role models on which a person may pattern himself or herself. In addition, the group generated new activities that crystallized new role dimensions. Expanding on this concept was Hochschild's finding that older residents, who had lost their roles as wives, mothers, workers, and so on, were able in this new setting to take on new roles in organizational, political, recreational, and service activities.

A most interesting study on social organization in a French retirement residence in a working class suburb of Paris was done by Jennie Keith Ross. Her findings revealed that previous occupational level had no effect on status in the residence community. Instead, those who took on work roles within the project attained high status. Greater participation in either of the two types of organizations, formal or informal, led to higher status in the residence. In the formal organization, residents with job or work roles were accorded high status. In the informal organization, those with many friends in the residence and those with a few friends with whom they visited frequently also had high status. "The residents who feel most happy are those whose social lives and emotional energies are focused on the community. . . . The key to happiness is not the amount or type of social activity, but a general acceptance of the community as the focus of day-to-day social life."[13]

On the question of how residence in communal housing

affects family relationships, there are only a few comparative studies. Almost all indicate that relationships between adult child and old parent continue unchanged in age-segregated housing, with some suggesting that this type of housing actually improves them. Susan Sherman, who interviewed 100 residents two years apart at six age-segregated sites, found that when distance was held constant no significant differences were found in tenants' contacts with children as compared to outside groups.[14] In Frances Carp's study, there was greater satisfaction with family among the public housing tenants than in the outside community group. Carp felt the improved kinship relations probably reflected the generally higher morale of the residents.

Several researchers have suggested that "services for elderly which take some of the burden away from their children may enhance better relationships between the generations and facilitate more involvement between elderly parents and adult children if and when more serious problems develop."[15] In addition, one great advantage of age-segregated environments—the ready source of friends available—relieves elderly residents of complete dependence on their children for companionship and entertainment. Obviously, it relieves the children as well.

Decided Contrast in Lifestyles

Before we leave this general discussion of research in communal housing, it might be wise to take a brief look at how this lifestyle compares with life in institutional settings. First and foremost, communal housing respects and permits gratification of reasonable individual tastes, preferences, and needs. In the area of health perception, in institutions health is usually defined in terms of absence or decrease in illness, while in congregate facilities health is looked upon as the capacity for living, with emphasis on building on and cultivating this strength even in the face of adverse circumstances.

Erving Goffman, who has done extensive research on institutions, defines a total institution as "a place of residence and work where a large number of like-situated individuals, cut off from the wider society for an appreciable period of time, together lead an enclosed, formally administered round of life."[16] He amplifies this by pointing out that institutions suppress self-esteem and autonomy, and the staff regards inmates as inferior. The institution completely controls the inmates, stripping them of their self-images, lowering their ability to exercise their own discretion, lessening their ability to cope, and causing them to suffer some loss of identify. In addition to these indignities, exposure and contact with others are not voluntary but are forced on inmates because of the close group living arrangement.

In contrast to the lives of inmates in an institution, residents in a congregate facility have full control over their own lives, live in family units, are free to make their own friendships, determine their own activities, and mingle with the outside community. A small group in congregate living does lose some control over their lives; they are the more seriously impaired elderly who are homebound and have very limited social and physical mobility, which makes them more dependent on staff and services.

Lakeview Put to the Test

Now to return to Lakeview. Does it measure up to the sociologists' criteria for a beneficial environment for old people? Does it result in longer life, better health, and improved life satisfaction and self-esteem?

Since no other group was used for comparison, we cannot verify terms like "longer" or "better" in regard to Lakeview residents. With respect to longer life, however, we do know that, with a median resident age of 83 and an actuarial prediction in 1968 that the facility would have a complete turnover in five years, approximately 50 percent of the original move-ins were still very much alive ten years later.

Good health or at least very good functional ability among Lakeview's elderly was evident from the high level of activity observed there: daily shopping, walking, gardening, extensive participation in house-sponsored programs and excursions, volunteer work both in and outside the apartment building, and travel by a small number of residents to nearby cities and on more extended tours. The fact that more than half of the residents were able to be actively involved in leadership or service aspects of the Residents Council speaks volumes about the state of their health, both physical and mental.

Praise for life at Lakeview was expressed so often and so naturally, it could not have been done merely to impress the researcher. Besides, this satisfaction was communicated to others and, as a result, many of the residents' friends moved into the house. And the large number of friendships made there, continuing good relationships with families, and the extent of volunteer service to the house and to the outside community demonstrated the residents' positive self-esteem.

For these benefits to have emerged, a flourishing subculture had to have developed. It is true that many aspects of the Lakeview community are shared by older people in the same socioeconomic group in society, but this is true for subcultures in general. It is the extent of these behavioral patterns and shared values that is different for the study residents: the large number of new friendships, the high degree of mutual aid and support, the unusual amount of volunteerism, the frequency of social interactions, the large number of new and substitute roles, and the investment of large proportions of time in an age-graded organization, the Residents Council. In addition, the shared perceptions—in relation to the acceptance of one's own functional limitations, the fierce attitude in regard to the right to independence and freedom of choice, the need to live apart from and not be a burden on children and other relatives—were some of the outstanding characteristics of this group.

Most important of all, these residents became adjusted to old age by means of the community's many role models of people who had not only learned to accept their own physical limitations but felt it important to be as useful and active as their levels of functioning would permit, and who accepted with good grace having to forego some of their former activities and roles. Of equal importance, a great majority, in recognizing and planning for future support needs as they aged, chose a congregate living arrangement in order to continue leading an independent life, one that offered maximum opportunities for choosing friends, activities, hobbies, and family relationships.

The manner in which Lakeview residents accepted and planned for advanced old age differed strikingly from that of their age peers who remained in their own homes, moved to adult communities, or moved in with their children. And they were very proud of having selected this living arrangement and of their foresight in planning properly for their old age. Frequent references were made to the plight of outside friends. A typical remark was, "I think we deserve credit for choosing a place like this. I have friends who live in a retirement village and don't have the things we have here. Now that they are older, they will have to look for another kind of place to live."

Significantly, most residents were not placed at Lakeview by others, such as family, physicians, or agencies, but sought out a congregate facility as a solution to present or anticipated aging needs. This is in sharp contrast to other older middle- and upper-income elderly who choose to remain in their own homes, either because they believe this is a better solution for them or because they are not willing or able to face the increasing decrements of old age. Lakeview residents were not afraid to select a congregate lifestyle, despite society's negative stereotypes and frequent opposition from family and friends. They were able to accept an independent living arrangement with support services that would enable them to continue to pursue their own lifestyles within the physical and social limitations imposed by the aging process.

Strong Friendships and Social Life Develop

The setting at Lakeview stimulated social interactions that resulted in the highly developed Residents Council and informal social groups as well. The basis for all program activities, the Residents Council, involved about 75 percent of the residents, with 50 percent actively involved and participating in the organization and its offshoot committees. The remaining 25 percent, though not as active, attended programs and meetings. People working together in committees and other formal group activities formed friendships and gave one another support and aid. Hostess committees, myriad programs and activities, and informal bridge games and cocktail hours advanced adjustment to Lakeview. Welcoming committees made new residents feel more comfortable, introduced them to other residents, and familiarized them with programs and activities, thus facilitating their integration into the community.

One of the most outstanding aspects of this vital social network was the number and quality of new and substitute roles it created. The roles of friend, worker, leader, and volunteer were abundantly evident. And the residents displayed great admiration for one another, particularly those who assumed leadership roles over a period of time. What is particularly striking is not that there were people who were looked up to—because in any group of well-educated, middle-class, older adults some outstanding persons can be found who are role models for their peers. But at Lakeview there were far more than the researcher expected to find in a relatively small group of about 200 people. In addition, there were role models among the very old, those close to 90 years and older, so that the younger residents had a positive image of advanced old age.

Residents who were leaders and those who were service volunteers constituted the major types of role models at Lakeview. Although they had different backgrounds and personalities, those who were role models had two important traits in common: they had learned to cope with their increasing frailties and physical limitations and had continued to have a satisfying lifestyle within these limitations, and they had continued to take an affirmative view of life and to look forward to tomorrow.

Other shared perceptions among the residents were shown by their attitudes toward the congregate residence, their reasons for selecting it, and their feelings about privacy, freedom, and independence. Enthusiasm and great satisfaction with living at Lakeview were themes repeated countless times. These positive feelings were consistent over the three-year study period and were expressed by both old-timers and recent move-ins. "There's sort of a missionary atmosphere here. We are so satisfied and think it's such a great place to live that we have sold the idea to our friends. Most of the people who have come in the last few years are here because they knew someone at Lakeview who told them what a good place it is," was the way one resident put it. Others elaborated on this by telling stories of friends who were much opposed to their moving into the house but had subsequently filed applications themselves. In one case, a friend was so embarrassed about her original attitude that it took her a long time to admit that she was on the waiting list.

Why They Chose Lakeview

The primary reason given for selecting Lakeview was for the security and support services it offered. This was true even for the small minority that was somewhat critical of management. Although the usual reasons given in other studies for moving to a congregate residence, such as a health crisis or loss of a spouse, were also given at Lakeview, the unique aspect here was that many residents had made the move before they actually needed this type of living arrangement. They did this because they foresaw the possibility of needing a supportive environment as they aged and expected the housekeeping and meal services to help them conserve decreasing energies for other activities.

This attitude ties in with their strong belief in independence and freedom, expressed as the need "to keep control of our own lives" and the recognition that the atmosphere created by both management and other residents fostered these conditions. Curiously and in contrast to the generally held belief that a person is most free in his or her own home, Lakeview residents felt that remaining in one's own apartment or house led to greater immobility, isolation, and insecurity. For them, the personal and physical security, support services, and opportunities for social activity and friendship in an unregimented and lively environment afforded more freedom than confinement in their former residences.

After freedom and independence, privacy was valued most highly. The fact that Lakeview offered complete apartments, so that residents did not have to share bathrooms or kitchens, was considered essential. Most enjoyed the communal dinners and programs but liked to be able to retreat to the privacy of their apartments whenever they wished. "The nice thing is that you can close your door and be by yourself anytime you want to," was a common statement. And the accepted form of behavior for ensuring that privacy was described thus: "You just don't barge in on anyone else. You either telephone in advance or slip a note under the door when you want to arrange a visit." This need for privacy was so pervasive that the researcher had to be extremely careful to observe the unwritten rule.

Although there was a small group that was fearful of the nursing unit and tried to pretend it did not exist, on the whole residents were realistic in talking about their health and handicaps. Among the residents who were seriously ill or who had suffered bad accidents during the three-year research period, a few might be depressed for a time. But most displayed amazing inner strength and resiliency and bounced back with renewed vigor after they had recovered.

Other shared values were strong commitment to family, high regard for volunteers, low regard for constant complainers, the desirability of mutual support among neighbors and friends, and the avoidance of controversial subjects like politics and religion.

The last—the reluctance to engage in controversy—may have been the reason for one important component of an aging subculture being absent at Lakeview, for there was no discernible group political action or any observed interest in public action on age-related issues. This remoteness from political issues may have stemmed from the residents' backgrounds, since few, if any, had been politically active in their younger years. Also, most had sufficient income to take care of their needs. Another important factor may have been that the congregate environment offered enough support to shield the residents against many of society's negative attitudes toward the elderly.

Similar Backgrounds and Values Strengthen Sense
of Community

As we said earlier, two expected elements of an aging subculture are homogeneity and sibling-bond relationships. This study of Lakeview strongly supports these conclusions. Its residents basically were white, native-born, middle- and upper-middle-class, with above-average educational and vocational backgrounds, and a large majority were single and widowed women. And the large number and high quality of friendships among residents gave ample evidence of sibling-bond relationships. We were more concerned, however, with identifying other factors in the congregate environment that might contribute to a successful aging subculture. And, in addition to homogeneity and sibling bonds, we did find other resident characteristics that produced cohesiveness and a high degree of involvement at Lakeview.

Although there were a few men, particularly former ministers who were mentioned frequently in reference to leadership roles, the population was essentially female, and most of the leadership and service responsibilities were assumed by women. Therefore, the type and composition of this cohort was most significant. It was fairly obvious that in order to achieve the most free and least institutional environment an important component had to be the characteristics of the residents. Because an unusually high percentage had chosen to live in a congregate setting and had not been placed by relatives or doctors, we must assume they had high reserves of inner strength and relatively good self-images to begin with.

Examination of the demographic data for patterns that could explain this degree of life control despite advanced age revealed that close to 40 percent of the population were single women (never married) and an equivalent number were widows, and that the singles comprised almost half of the total female resident population. This is quite remarkable when compared to the elderly female population in the United States at the time, 9 percent of whom were single, 39 percent widowed, and 52 percent married. If we look at the statistics from a concurrent survey of a sampling of age-segregated, specially designed housing (without support services) in a state in the same geographical area, with a median and mean age of about 76, we find more than 80 percent females with only 11 percent never married and 70 percent widowed or divorced.

The figures on vocations of Lakeview's women residents also showed that only 21 percent were housewives (women who did not work outside their homes), so we know that half of the widows held jobs. If it is assumed that the single women had to work because of economic necessity, then a picture emerges of a very high percentage of female residents who worked during their adult lives in relatively responsible, service-connected jobs. More than 30 percent were administrators, social workers, teachers, librarians, nurses, and the like. Single women and widows who had lost spouses relatively early in their marriages—of whom there were a number at Lakeview—had had to take on the responsibility for their own lives. In addition, the single women had held jobs decades before, at a time when they belonged to a very small population of employed women, and their marital status also placed them in the minority group of unmarried women of their generation. Altogether, Lakeview's women bear a remarkable resemblance to today's women in terms of work experience, marital status, and self-dependence.

Advantages of Single Building and Urban Location

Another factor that became apparent during this study was the importance of building design and location. Since most residents did not own cars, the advantages of having services and facilities within walking distance were incalculable, and the effect of the one-building design on in-house activities and socializing was extremely advantageous.

In appreciation of the building's design, most residents avowed that the single building fostered togetherness. One resident expressed it this way: "We see each other all the time, coming and going, on the way to the dining room, in the lobby to pick up or drop off mail, or going out and coming into the building. Once you leave your apartment, you can't help but see other people and stop and talk. Because of the design of the high-rise, you have to pass places like the library, where you might stop and look at a book. In the lobby, you stop to read the bulletin board. Or you might stop in our little store. And the staff is always visible, too—Caroline at the front desk, and Ben, whose office door is always open."

The downtown location was heartily approved by all of the residents, who regarded it as essential for keeping people active and involved. Many said it was this accessibility to outside services and activities that attracted them to Lakeview, that it increased the possibilities for them to remain active, and that it stimulated even less active residents to be more engaged with the outside community. The people with more limited mobility often expressed their pleasure at being able to walk to and from the bank and the small grocery, which were only a block away. Other shops and bus stops and the railroad station were close enough to be reached conveniently, the last two making it relatively easy to get to cultural events in nearby cities and to visit friends and family. The location in Watertown also enabled residents to do volunteer work in the larger community and promoted other interactions with the townspeople, who were extremely helpful to the residents and appreciative of their economic and service contributions.

A resident, summing up the strong feeling on the desirability of a downtown location, said, "If you take nothing else back from your study, I hope you will take back the importance of this kind of location. Towns tend to oppose downtown locations and want to put elderly housing in the boondocks or at the edge of town. They shouldn't be allowed to do this."

While policy makers generally agree on the importance of designing buildings for the elderly to encourage social interaction, many feel that congregate facilities for frail and aged people can be built in more isolated, less accessible areas. This research contradicts this latter point of view and clearly indicates the importance of a downtown location for handicapped and older residents.

Management Encourages Freedom and Independence

Another characteristic of Lakeview that helped define its environment was the degree of autonomy and freedom found there. We have seen how administration policies tended to foster a free and independent atmosphere by having a minimum number of rules and regulations and by encouraging a tenants' organization separate and apart from management. Another factor, whether intentional or not, was the absence of programs when Lakeview was first occupied, as a consequence of which residents had to organize their own or do without. The residents established a library, because there was none. They developed music and lecture programs, because there were none. In residences with more staff to perform this function, the degree of resident involvement may be lower and the environment more regulated. At Lakeview, the staff maintained a low profile, allowing residents to follow their own interests and lifestyles and to take complete responsibility for themselves.

This study was not designed to compare the residents' former cultural patterns with their present modes of behavior. Nevertheless, because of their advanced age, their retirement status (80 percent had worked), and their widowhood (40 percent were widowed), we know they must have suffered losses in their social activities and relationships, losses in mobility, physical losses, and role losses. Despite these losses, however, most residents led active social lives: bridge games, cocktail hours, in-house programs, informal visiting, entertaining family and friends, lunching in restaurants, and enjoying cultural events in the local community and nearby urban centers with other residents and friends. An unusually large number of in-house friendships, a high degree of involvement in the formal structure (Residents Council), and active pursuit of hobbies (reading, music, art, needlework) resulted in taking on new and substitute roles as leader, worker, volunteer, service provider, and friend. These roles helped replace lost status and, in some cases, raised formerly lowered status.

Beliefs That Shape Behavior

A sense of group identification had developed through involvement in the Residents Council, through new peer friendships, and through the development of positive role models for aging. Although many residents continued to share society's cultural norms of, among others, the work ethic, political conservatism, politeness, consideration for others, and independence, certain perceptions were unique to Lakeview people. The most uncommon was the belief that remaining in previous places of residence was too insecure, restrictive, and confining, and would become even more so with advancing age. Communal attitudes on the value of mutual aid, friendship, volunteerism, privacy, and continued involvement with old friends, family, and the outside community were similar to but seemed more intense than those of the larger culture.

Pride in Lakeview, its management, and other residents in no way interfered with family relationships; rather, it seemed to strengthen them. Warm and frequent interactions with family members were revealed in conversations and by observations at Lakeview. Further, the data suggest that some of the older residents who were more handicapped would have been a greater burden on their families were they not living in a semiprotected congregate facility.

Many older people in the same socioeconomic group have chosen to live in adult communities where they pursue more hedonistic lifestyles. In direct contrast, while most of Lakeview's residents believed in the importance of leisure and hobby activities, they felt it was even more important to continue to be of service to the community. Moreover, looking at an adult community with the more middle-aged fun and leisure norms and social club activities, it becomes apparent that not all age-segregated settings produce successful adjustment to old age. But when conditions such as those found at Lakeview combine with meaningful social interactions to produce a positive aging subculture, then an appropriate adjustment to old age can take place. More than that, the resulting environment nurtures a rich and active community life that is most beneficial to its residents.

A Look into the Future

What is the relevance of all this to future generations of old people?

Most gerontologists and a growing number of legislators and government officials are aware that the congregate facility is a necessary option in the housing continuum for the elderly and that the need for this type of housing can only increase. There are already long waiting lists for existing residences (Lakeview has 200 residents and approximately 300 people on its waiting list), and most of these are for middle- and upper-income people, leaving an even greater void for the majority of low- and moderate-income elderly in need of this living arrangement. In addition, the older old, those 75 and older who are more likely to need a service-enriched environment, is the fastest-growing segment of the 65-plus population and is expected to constitute 45 percent of the elderly by the year 2000.

New generations of the old, however, are likely to be quite different from today's elderly. It is in this connection that Lakeview stands out as a possible model, since its residents are more akin to estimated future elderly than the low-income groups usually studied in public housing and other subsidized housing projects. Expectations are that older people will be in better health, will have higher incomes, and will be more educated as we approach the end of this century. "They will want a wide range of options and opportunities both for self-enhancement and for community participation. . . . As the young-old articulate their needs and desires, the emphasis is likely to be upon improving the quality of life and upon increasing the choices of lifestyles."[17]

Another difference will be in the proportion of foreign-born to native-born. Before 1950, almost one-third of those entering old age were foreign-born; by 1980, this had decreased to about 10 percent. Also, at the beginning of the 1900s, only 10 percent of the population had completed high school; today, more than 70 percent are high school graduates. Further, the number of older women is increasing, so that the ratio of men to women will be 65 to 100 by the year 2000. And finally, the number of women in the work force has jumped dramatically in the last decade alone, a trend expected to continue well into the future. Concomitantly, with the expansion of the service economy and the shrinkage of the industrial and agricultural segments, we can safely predict a large cohort of service career retirees.

Because the large majority of Lakeview residents were

older women, in relatively good health, native-born, middle-income, with better than high school educations, and more than half of them had been employed, many in service careers, they would seem to fit the description of a large proportion of the elderly in the year 2000.

One big question remains. Will the attitudes of both society and the elderly change toward congregate and similar types of communal housing? Can those now coming into old age be persuaded that a communal lifestyle offers a free, independent, and meaningful old age?

We began this chapter by speaking of the importance of individual independence. It may seem paradoxical to advocate communal living as the best way to achieve independence. But the Lakeview community convinced us that the two go very well together, that the support of and interaction with an empathetic community of our peers can make us stronger even when we are more frail.

If planning for old age were to include communal living as a positive alternative, it is conceivable that it would eventually be regarded as the preferred housing model for older people in the same way that owning a house is seen as desirable by adults in their child-rearing years. If it were an accepted norm, people could plan for this type of housing in their late middle years; they could explore and carefully evaluate different modes of congregate and communal living and then be able to make appropriate choices for their later years.

In the hope that this book has thus far projected that favorable image, we now move on to describe various communal housing options, some guidelines for evaluating them, and some suggestions for the future, which, to some extent at least, will be what we make of it.

8. YOU DON'T HAVE TO LIVE ALONE:
Communal Housing Choices

Although my adjustment to communal living took a little time, I soon began to realize that life here is very desirable. . . . When I want congenial companionship, persons my own age, younger or older are usually to be found. And those considerably older come to be thought of not as "old people," but as valued friends. Holidays are no longer lonely, they are celebrated by congenial groups. One of the greatest advantages is a sense of safety, of security.

—Helen Kingsbury Wallace

A popular film in 1982, *On Golden Pond,* broke new ground in the public's perception of aging. It celebrated the romance of an old couple—not, as in so many other films, by using an aged individual as a device for flashbacks to youthful years but by concentrating on the here-and-now in the life of a man and woman during the summer of his 80th birthday.

Without being grim or solemn, the film cast light on changes that may come with growing older—memory lapses, carelessness about household chores, yearning to regain work status—and the rage and frustration accompanying these failures. It also balanced the weaknesses by showing the strengths of endurance, loyalty, knowledge, and understanding. No one could see the film without feeling better about growing old or being old.

What Happened Next?

Still, it left many questions unanswered about the protagonists, superbly portrayed by Henry Fonda and Katharine Hepburn. What happened after they packed their summer gear and returned to their year-round home? Did they live in a large, old house near the college campus where the husband had been a professor? Or had they moved to a smaller house or an apartment after his retirement? The summer cottage we saw in the film was rustic but spacious and in a splendid lakeside setting. Did this mean they were fairly affluent? Or was their income limited? Did they have many friends? Only a few? Or were they solely dependent upon each other for companionship?

Aside from some personal characteristics and their deep love and need for each other, we learned little more about the couple from the film than that Fonda's character suffered from some sort of heart ailment and that the relationship with their only child was strained. One theme of the story was the reconciliation of the daughter, played by Jane Fonda, and father at the end of that summer.

What would a sequel to *On Golden Pond* be like? Given the statistics of the real world, the most likely scenario would have to include the death of the man in the next few years, probably in a repeat of the heart attack episode at the end of the film. (At age 65, the average life expectancy for white males is 79.5.) Hepburn's character, who can be assumed to have been two to five years younger, would then face (again using statistical probability as our crystal ball) about ten years of widowhood. (Life expectancy for white females at age 65 is close to 84 years.)

What would our heroine's life be like without our hero? Since she seemed a spunky, resourceful person, is it safe to predict a good recovery after a period of intense grief? Yes, if she doesn't fall ill or have a serious accident or descend into a deep depression. The death of a spouse often triggers a decline that, though it may be reversible, can lead to a crisis situation. How well our widow comes through this, with her own inner resources weakened, may then depend on external forces—family, friends, professional assistance. The daughter would

148

undoubtedly be of some help. But we know that her home is distant and that she is involved in a career and a new marriage, which would tend to make her impatient to get back to her own life.

Since we are writing this script, we will give our heroine a group of devoted and intelligent friends to comfort and encourage her and to see that she gets the proper medical and psychological care she needs. Once recovered, she will go through a period of gradual adjustment, during which she seeks and finds new outlets for her restored energy—volunteer work, cultural pursuits, travel, other recreation. And during the busy days her life takes on renewed color. Will that be enough? For some women, yes. Others, even with a full schedule of activities, are lonely when they return to their empty rooms. As they grow older and it becomes more difficult to go from place to place, some activities may have to be dropped and more time spent in those same empty rooms.

The Way One Widow Lives

Let us look in on the widow five years after her husband's death. She lives in the house that has been home for more than 45 years. The house on Golden Pond was sold years before. She has just passed her 80th birthday and is still spry despite a moderate arthritic condition that affects her arms and legs. A fall from her bicycle the previous year resulted in a broken hip, which mended slowly and left her slightly lame, so she no longer cycles the two miles to the village center. Using a cane, she now walks there once or twice a week. Cataract operations have left her with poor vision, and she drives her car only on short trips during daylight hours. Several times a month she drives to the railroad station and takes the train into the city to lunch with a friend or two or to keep a doctor's appointment.

In the spring and summer, gardening is her joy, and she harvests and preserves some of her fruit and vegetable crops in the fall. Much of this bounty is given away to friends and to the local church for distribution to poor families in the county. A few special treats are saved for her daughter and her son-in-law when they come to spend Christmas at the old house. She flies out to stay with them over Easter week. Except for the winter holiday and an occasional overnight visitor when the big bedroom is opened and aired, the four upstairs bedrooms are unused. She lives downstairs, using the large den–library as her bedroom. There's a lavatory downstairs, but she must use one of the two upstairs bathrooms for a bath or shower. Since her fall, she has become increasingly uneasy about climbing into the old-fashioned, high-sided tub while alone in the house. Of late, she takes baths only on days when the maid is there. It has occurred to her that installing a shower in the downstairs lavatory might be a good idea, but she hasn't yet done anything about it.

A woman comes in twice a week to clean and cook her meals for two days. Since the elderly housekeeper who held the job for many years died, a succession of younger housemaids have come and gone. To her, none of the new maids seems as reliable and trustworthy as the old housekeeper, and she feels intimidated whenever she makes a request or tries to give them directions. The various men sent to care for the grounds by the gardening service sometimes frighten her, too. Even the postman delivering the mail seems to change more frequently than in former days.

On dismal, wet days when she stays indoors, she catches herself catnapping quite often. At night, if she is unable to sleep, she imagines she hears prowlers at the doors or windows and wanders about the house checking the locks, then turns on the television set to drown out the creaks and groans of the old house, and falls asleep to the murmured voices and flickering images. Taking an occasional nip of brandy before bedtime seemed to relax her and make falling asleep easier, so she has made it part of her bedtime routine, carefully measuring the liquor out into the glass. Two of her friends became alcoholics after their husbands died—one had to be put in a nursing home and the other had a fatal fall at home—and she is acutely aware of the danger. On the nights she forgets to have dinner, which seem to be more frequent of late, she feels quite lightheaded after her nightcap.

A few remaining friends in the area occasionally ask whether she minds living "way out there" alone, and her daughter has tried to persuade her to give up the house and move to a less isolated setting. But everyone who knows her says she is "doing very well." And she feels the same way. She knows she is lonely much of the time but accepts it as part of the territory of independent widowhood. In many ways, she counts herself luckier than most, being able to maintain her old home and to continue living in lovely and familiar surroundings.

How Others Live

Figuratively speaking, this widow was not alone. Roughly half of the 15.2 million women over age 65 counted in the 1980 census and 70 percent of the 5.4 million over 75 were widows. More than a third of all elderly women—widowed, single (never married), and divorced—lived alone. If we had written our sequel differently and the husband had outlived the wife and remained in his home, he would have joined the ranks of 14 percent of elderly men (in a total 65-plus male population of 10.3 million) living alone. Had he remarried he would have been counted among the 7.6 million (78 percent) older men who were married, about a third of them to women younger than 65.

Living in her own home in a suburb was also more typical than our widow might have thought. In a reversal of the pattern of previous decades, the 1980 census found that "more than half of the older people [65 plus] in metropolitan areas lived in the suburbs rather than the central city, primarily because of the 'aging' of the inhabitants of the suburbs . . . in the larger (over a million) metropolitan areas."[1] This graying of the suburbs applied mainly to white middle- and upper-income elderly. Lower-income and nonwhite elderly were still concentrated in central cities.

Home ownership, that long-cherished tradition, was also common among older people; almost three-fourths of all elderly heads of households owned their own homes. More than half of their houses were built before 1950 and about 40 percent before 1940. Many were difficult to maintain and in need of costly repairs their owners could not afford. Many were in deteriorating neighborhoods in cities and older suburban towns.

This is not exactly a cheerful picture. But neither is the

one of our widow living in a large house in lonely, if comfortable, isolation. If, however, we could endow her with a different mind-set and release her from emotional bondage to her home, what would her options be? Since we are dealing with a fictitious character, we are free to change her destiny. In this new scenario, we can have our heroine gather up her native courage and rebel against her lonely lifestyle. She has the financial means to do a number of things. First, she might consider sharing her house with one or two friends or working out an arrangement for sharing a friend's house or apartment. Or she could try converting the second floor of her house into an apartment and rent it to a single person, a couple, or a small family. Other possibilities would be a house, apartment, or condominium in or near the city, in an adult/retirement community, or in a special housing complex or congregate/life care residence for the elderly.

Mulling over the Possibilities

Mulling over the advantages and disadvantages of the first option, she came up with these thoughts. Sharing her own home would enable her to stay in familiar and beloved surroundings and also have companionship, household responsibilities could be shared, and she would feel safer and more secure with someone there to rely on in emergencies. Except for having to adjust to other surroundings, sharing a friend's home would offer the same benefits. As for renting part of her house to a tenant, it would bring in some income, and an agreement might be worked out for caretaking services in lieu of part of the rental.

On the other hand, there were definite disadvantages to home-sharing. Remaining in her own house meant being far from community and cultural activities; the pressures of running a household—paying bills, taxes, insurance, supervising the help, and shopping—would still be with her, though shared; it might be difficult to adjust to living in close proximity to another person and giving up some of her privacy; and her friends were as old as she and equally vulnerable to illness and accident and, in a crisis, would become an added burden she wasn't sure she could carry at this stage of her life. As for an upstairs apartment, it would require construction work with all the fuss and mess that entailed; a zoning variance from the town might be difficult or impossible to obtain; she felt uneasy about having strangers, however good their references, living in the house; and it would involve additional financial and legal complications.

After weighing all of these considerations, she was not terribly enthusiastic about these home-sharing arrangements and decided to explore some of her other options. Despite the allure of living closer to the city, she almost immediately discarded the idea of an individual house. One of her objectives in making a change was to free herself from the responsibilities of caring for a house, and even a small house would demand more attention than she was willing to give. In addition, proximity to the city and new neighbors was no guarantee that she would feel less isolated. The idea of a city apartment was more appealing but also more frightening. She could get about more easily. But was it safe? Could she become accustomed to living in a large building surrounded by strangers? Would they be unfriendly and impersonal? Some of her friends who had moved to apartments complained about how difficult it was to get to know their neighbors, and about street crime, frequent rent increases, and the problems of getting service. The prospect of buying a condominium fell somewhere between a house and an apartment; it entailed fewer responsibilities than owning a house yet was less restrictive than apartment living. In a condominium outside the city, however, mobility could be a problem; within the city, safety could be a problem.

Adult/retirement communities were part of her review of options, too. She knew they were springing up everywhere, especially in areas with warmer year-round climates. Some of her friends had moved to such places in Florida, California, and Arizona. She had visited them years before with her husband, always with a feeling of amazement at how these spanking new towns seemed to appear magically out of nowhere. She understood the necessity for building in isolated areas where land was cheaper in order to avoid astronomical costs. And to compensate, each retirement village seemed to be entirely self-contained, boasting shopping centers, medical clinics, restaurants, cinemas, libraries, and recreational facilities of all kinds. Retirement communities offered a wide variety of housing choices, too; rental apartments, coop or condominium apartments, conventional single-family homes, even mobile homes. Some had minibuses that made it possible to get around the community without a car, and most provided good maintenance and security services.

But the basic question she had to ask herself was whether she would enjoy the lifestyle, a steady diet of organized recreation, hobby, club, and social activity. She remembered how amused she had been on entering a retirement village and seeing a sign announcing, "Caution: Grandparents at Play." Did she want to spend the rest of her life at play? What would happen if she couldn't keep up with the older "go-go jet set"? And even if she could, would she soon tire of it? A few of her older friends had grown weary of games and entertainments and had left what one of them called "the grandparents' playground." Several had moved back to new quarters in or near their old home towns, but they were having increasing difficulty maintaining their independence as they grew older. Others had moved to retirement residences where they had a combination of private living quarters and services like congregate meals, housekeeping, security, and, in some cases, the assurance of lifetime care—including medical and skilled nursing care—should they need it. At the age of 80, she reasoned, once she moved from her house, another move a few years later would be out of the question. Whatever choice she made, she wanted her new home to be permanent for the rest of her life.

What would you do if you were this widow? Stay in your own home? Convert your home to accommodate companions? Try to make a new home somewhere else, in a more stimulating environment? If the latter, what would your requirements be—companionship, privacy, security, services, recreation, volunteer or paid job opportunities?

Will Isolation Grow in an Aging Society?

Obviously, we are not all like the character in our movie sequel. We are younger or older, richer or poorer, in various states of health, with a wide range of likes and dislikes, abilities and disabilities. This is as true for the 26 million individuals over age 65 as it is for the rest of the population.

Nevertheless, several demographic patterns differentiate the elderly as a group. For one thing, population growth between 1970 and 1980 was three times greater for that group than for the under-65 group, up from one and a half times in the previous decade. Then, because of the longer life expectancy of females as compared to males, there are many more women than men. Three-fifths of all elderly persons are women, and the ratio of women to men increases with age: 131 to 100 in the 65-to-74 age group, 180 to 100 aged 75 and over, and 229 to 100 aged 85 and over. Also, as we said before, more than half of all older women are widowed. In addition, four out of ten older women live alone, compared to one out of ten older men. So what we have is a rapidly growing elderly population, composed in large part of women, coexisting in a society with fertility rates below zero population growth since the end of the postwar baby boom. "A continuation of these trends over a lengthy period of time will bring us an aging society with an increasing median age," says gerontologist Herman B. Brotman in *Every Ninth American*.[2]

In this aging society, the major problem may be isolation, as it is today, but multiplied by the larger number of old people who will be alive and alone. And isolation has little to do with income. It cuts across all lines, and it is more dependent on factors like housing location, the availability of family or other sources of support, access to transportation, and an individual's health than on affluence. Despite feelings of isolation and loneliness, however, older people tend to remain where they are and to make the best of it. But where they are, whether it's a small apartment or a large house, can become a prison.

"It is true that when an environment does not satisfy an individual's needs, the human being has shown a remarkable ability to adapt. However . . . it is our very adaptability that may do us in. Adaptability to an inappropriate environment consumes energy and personal resources better put into an enhancement of life, or goal reaching. Not all people are capable of such adaptability, and one pays a price to adapt."[3]

Because we believe that isolation exacts too high a price and is so widespread and pernicious among the elderly, we have concentrated on communal living in this book. As a society, we have become conditioned to think of independent living as synonymous with occupancy of a single dwelling unit, in solitary splendor or squalor, as the case may be. But it is a custom, not an immutable law. You do not have to live alone! And the alternative does not have to be an institution.

Exploring Communal Housing Options

Communal housing options are available, and more are being developed. Congregate housing is one of the very best. "Congregate housing can be the flexible alternative to the current extremes of custodial care versus complete self-sufficiency. Congregate housing can provide for changing needs and varied populations in ways that reduce isolation and stress while encouraging independence."[4] Other communal living arrangements involve sharing a large house or apartment or a cooperative arrangement among people in a group of houses or apartments.

The advantages of congregate living for old people who find living in their own homes lonely, insecure, or burdensome have been covered in detail in our description of Lakeview House. The residents there had the privacy of separate apartments and the convenience and conviviality of a communal dining room and community spaces for social and recreational activities of their own choosing; they had a cooperative staff to help with household chores and to depend on for health needs and emergencies; they had the companionship and support of other residents; and they had the freedom to come and go as they wished for as long as they were able and the comfort of knowing they could live in a clean, comfortable, congenial, and stimulating environment even after their mobility had diminished. Nothing about Lakeview was institutional, nor would there be anything institutional about any good congregate residence.

Bruce C. Vladeck, a former commissioner in New Jersey's Department of Health, said, "In a well established and managed congregate housing project, people take care of one another. They act as good neighbors. That is an awful lot cheaper than paying strangers to take care of program clients, and also clearly preferable from the point of view of desirability and humanity."[5]

Although it may be less expensive than institutional care, congregate housing is not cheap and that is its major limitation; the cost of the housing-plus-service package makes it available mainly to older people of middle to upper incomes.

Another way for people to look after one another is in shared housing, a broad term that covers various types of communal living arrangements. Basically, shared housing involves a group of people who pool their resources and live together, each having his or her own rooms but sharing other common spaces. Shared housing can be organized and managed by the home-sharers themselves, or by a nonprofit corporation or agency.

"Some innovative living arrangements for older people have been developing in recent years for which there are no generally accepted names. . . . Their most visible characteristics are that they are usually small, usually serving no more than 20 people under one roof, often use ordinary housing which may be renovated for that purpose, and provide one or more supportive services. They are viewed as noninstitutional and as promoting independence and continued community living," according to Elaine M. Brody and Bernard Liebowitz of the Philadelphia Geriatric Center (PGC).[6]

A shared housing project, called Community Housing for the Elderly (CHE), was developed by PGC in 1971. It is still in operation and consists of ten renovated one-family detached houses on two streets bordering the PGC campus. PGC, a nonprofit social agency, serves 1,100 elderly people in the city as residents of two high-rise buildings, a nursing home, and a hospital. The old neighborhood houses used for the CHE project belonged to the PGC, which financed the renovation with the aid of federal funds. Each house was converted to include three efficiency apartments—bed and sitting room, kitchen, and bathroom—and a living room shared by all three residents. Dinner meal delivery and cleaning and linen services are optional at modest cost from PGC, and a hotline telephone link in each house connects with the center for emergency calls.

Periodic evaluations of the CHE residents, comparing them to other elderly people in the neighborhood, some of whom had moved to other locations and some of whom had remained in their old homes, showed a greater degree of satisfaction with their mode of living and fewer illnesses, complaints, and nursing home placements among the CHE people. Maurice B. Greenbaum, a PGC administrator, says, "I truly believe that other kinds of agencies, with ingenuity, can produce a similarly useful housing program involving rehabilitation of single dwellings."[7]

The Transformation of Castoff Buildings

In areas where single- and two-family houses predominate, home-sharing can be a good solution to the needs of the elderly for housing, companionship, and support. And there are advantages for the community as well, whether it is urban, suburban, or rural. First, there is the satisfaction to be gained by filling an important human need. Second, it makes good economic sense. Shared living in renovated houses is usually more cost-effective than building new dwelling units. In 1980, a new one-bedroom, specially designed unit for the elderly cost approximately $35,000 to $40,000. Whereas a unit in a renovated old house usually cost no more than $25,000.[8]

Costs vary, of course, depending upon location and the type of building being renovated, and rehabilitation costs can sometimes exceed those for new buildings. Proposals for converting empty school, factory, and institutional buildings into "senior citizen housing" have proliferated during recent years of spiraling construction costs. A wry comment on this trend by M. Powell Lawton and Sally Hoover is that "the elderly seem very frequently to become the gratuitous beneficiaries of cast-off buildings of all kinds."[9]

Nevertheless, some communities are making very good use of castoff buildings. A notable example is New Britain, Connecticut, where an old high school building has been converted to house 153 of the community's elderly in 127 apartments. Some of the tenants are graduates and have children who are graduates of the old school.

Renovation and remodeling of the large Gothic-style building was contracted out to a company specializing in this kind of work. Much of the spaciousness and ornamentation of the original building, parts of which date to 1850, were retained: the old oak paneling, carved classroom doors, leaded Gothic window, beams framing walls and ceilings, wide corridors, and open foyers. In the old library, which together with adjacent classrooms on the second floor was converted into a residents' center, two murals done by the WPA during the Depression years of the 1930s were left on the walls. The 18-foot-high ceilings give even the smaller efficiency apartments an open, airy look, and the thick, old interior walls, many of which remain, help soundproof the apartments.

Although no supportive or medical services are supplied, a director manages the building and live-in superintendents are available in all emergencies, even during hours when the administration office is closed. Building security is good, and buzzers in the bedroom and bathroom of each apartment can be used to summon help at any time. In addition, the tenants organized a council and elected monitors who regularly check on floor neighbors. The council also plans activities, trips, and entertainment. Meetings and programs are held in the large community room, which is the main part of the second-floor residents' center. As a result of a tenants' petition, a volleyball and badminton court has been built outdoors. Some residents have part-time jobs in the nearby downtown area, and most are out at least part of each day shopping or visiting in the familiar neighborhood.

During the original tenant selection process, particular care was taken to dispel any notion that the School Apartments building was a convalescent home. Helen Gaydosh, the building director, said, "One thing we never let happen was to allow them to say they were coming here to die. If that was the idea, then we told them they were in the wrong place. These were homes for the living. And while we're here to help them in real cases of emergency, they were to look after themselves."[10]

It has worked out extremely well, so well that the small city of New Britain—on the basis of this first experience, which is also believed to be a first for the state—was considering two more schools for conversion. With the decrease in school-age population, turning excess school space into apartments for older area residents—many of whom, as is the case in New Britain, are former schoolmates—is a sensible solution to some of their housing problems, particularly since the buildings are often located close to town centers and in the home neighborhoods of prospective tenants.

This is not just an exercise in civic altruism. It turns out that what is good for its older residents is good for the community as well. For one thing, what could become a deteriorating eyesore can be transformed into a well-kept building again. For another, older residents in safe and comfortable housing stay in the neighborhood where they serve as a stabilizing influence. In areas where housing is in short supply, there is the added dividend of freeing up large houses and apartments occupied by only one or two people. Sometimes, too, the elderly occupants, no longer physically or financially able to care for their homes adequately, have allowed them to deteriorate, to the annoyance of their neighbors and the detriment of the neighborhood. State and local programs to help homeowners with repairs and maintenance, though they exist in some communities, are not always available or well publicized; and even an older person who is aware of an assistance program may be reluctant or unsure about how to apply.

It may be only a partial solution to housing shortages, but where there are numerous older singles and couples living in large apartments and houses, alternative living arrangements should be made available to them. As Bruce Vladeck said at a housing conference, "From a simple, common-sense point of view, when there are many elderly people, each somewhat disabled but desirous of maintaining their independence, each living in their own house—which is probably much too large for them to maintain comfortably [and] for their current needs—it must make more sense to find a way for them to pool their resources and move in with one another. Sell some of those houses to all the people who can't now afford to buy homes for their young families, and encourage the sharing of houses among widows and widowers."[11]

A Program Matches Homeowners with Homeseekers

Where opportunities for better housing exist, some older persons will take advantage of them. But there will always be those who are adamant about remaining in their own homes, no matter how adverse the circumstances. A program developed in Nassau County on Long Island, New York, works toward bringing the two groups together. Called SHARE, for Senior Housing at Reduced Expense, it matches older homeowners living alone with compatible peers who wish to share a house or apartment.

Nassau County—a suburban area close to New York City, with a population of about 1.4 million and a critical housing shortage—is primarily an area of single-family homes. Mounting taxes, maintenance, fuel, and utility costs have been particularly hard on its many moderate-income elderly homeowners who are "forced to neglect the upkeep of their homes; this tends to alienate their neighbors, to result in safety hazards, and to lower the sale value of the house," in the words of Robert Sunley, associate director of the Family Service Association (FSA) of Nassau County, which operates the SHARE program. Sunley also painted a grim picture of the lives of tenants in the county, some of whom pay 50 to 90 percent of their fixed incomes on rent and are trapped in poor locations far from friends, senior centers, and shopping by the lack of public transportation and less expensive housing.[12]

The object of the SHARE program is to bring together those struggling to stay in their own homes and those desperate to find new homes. The first step was to publicize the program and to establish one registry of homes available for sharing and another of applicants for tenancy. FSA personnel then check the homes and interview prospective participants. After the initial screening, a meeting of the individuals is arranged so they can decide whether to go ahead with the sharing arrangement. Even after it is established, the agency maintains regular contact and will assist in resolving any problems that may arise. No pressure is exerted by FSA staff, however, and final determination of compatibility and all financial arrangements are left up to the individuals.

"SHARE is not simply a listing of available housing, nor a housing exchange. The essential ingredient is careful matching of two people," Sunley emphasized. In the first four years, he said, "over 300 applicants have been matched, most with good and lasting results."[13]

An illustrative case is that of an 80-year-old widow, Mrs. W, who shared her home with Mrs. C, a 70-year-old who needed a place to live that would accept her and her dog. The FSA worker making a follow-up call after four months reported, "Mrs. C answered the phone, as Mrs. W had gone away for a few days. . . . Mrs. C sounded very happy. She said that she and Mrs. W eat together and have become wonderful companions. Mrs. C kept talking about what a wonderful woman Mrs. W is. Mrs. W's home is kept very clean, and a new kitchen (stove, sink, and washer) was recently installed. Mrs. W and Mrs. C have been working on a tablecloth doing cross-stitch. It's a gift for Mrs. W's daughter. Mrs. C concluded our conversation with the statement that she 'never had it so good.' "[14]

SHARE, New Britain's School Apartments, and Philadelphia's Community Housing project are just a few examples of the ferment going on in the field of housing for the elderly. Although their success rate is high, the numbers are very small. Yet each was greeted with an inordinate amount of attention. Elaine Brody and Bernard Liebowitz of the Philadelphia Geriatric Center gave the following assessment of this unexpected attention: "A striking fact about these innovative arrangements is that the amount of interest in them evinced by professionals, government, the general public, and the media is not proportionate to the number of older people involved. Since data about them is sparse, no accurate estimate of the population served is possible. It is safe to say, however, that the likelihood is that only a tiny fraction of the elderly population is involved. One can only conjecture about the source of the tremendous appeal of such arrangements. It may lie in their small scale, their resemblance to 'normal' living, the fact that they permit continuity of lifestyle, and in their contrast to large age-segregated apartment buildings and negatively regarded institutions."[15]

Lifestyle Choices Depend on Us

The lesson in this is that the need is great, and people everywhere are searching for alternatives. And while we have been told that the vast majority of people over 65 do not move from their homes, the popularity of these programs indicates that this immobility is not entirely voluntary and that more old people would move if they knew they could improve their housing situations. Long waiting lists for apartments in community housing projects and congregate facilities also testify to that. In 1977 it was estimated that 500,000 were on waiting lists for specially designed housing for the elderly in the United States. Yet, the most recent figures indicate, only 3 percent of the elderly population live in community housing projects.

Clearly, planned housing units can never keep up with the demand, especially when we consider the steadily burgeoning elderly population. But it is not just a question of building more units, though that is important. As we have seen, existing structures can be put to creative use. And policy planners and community organizations are moving toward an understanding that living accommodations and environments should be designed with consideration for the varying lifestyles and situations found among aging individuals: the differing needs of those who are 65 from those who are 85, those in poor health from those in good health, those who have family support from those who are alone. Above all, housing policy is beginning to take into account the American values that stress independent living and the right of free choice.

In a free society we do have free choice, including the freedom not to exercise it. But free choice is meaningless if we have not thought about what we want or have little to choose from. René Dubos—scientist, environmentalist, and self-styled "despairing optimist"—once said, "In human affairs, the *logical* future, determined by past and present conditions, is less important than the *willed* future, which is largely brought about by deliberate choices—made by the free will. Our societies have a good chance of remaining prosperous because they are learning to anticipate, long in advance, the shortages and dangers they might experience in the future. . . ."[16]

To will the future, we must face the future. But how many of us can face even our own personal futures? How many of us can ask ourselves, "If I live to be 100, where and how do I want to live when I may no longer be as sturdy and self-sufficient as I am now?" Until we can ask and answer this question, we cannot make informed choices; indeed, we cannot even discern whether the options we would want to choose from exist.

Those who are willing to look ahead to old age can anticipate some of the problems and work toward solving them before it is too late. There are now unprecedented numbers of old people—both proportionate and absolute—and continued growth is expected well into the twenty-first century. If present trends continue, however, coming generations of the elderly will be better educated, healthier, and in better financial shape. Continually shifting family patterns may result in people being more flexible in old age but may also presage less family support. In addition, fewer daughters will be available to care for aging parents because of the increased participation of women in the work force. At the same time, the daughters as they age could be better fortified by their work experience— more self-reliant, more knowledgeable about financial management, and more capable of independent decision making.

Plan for Your Own Future

Will more of the future elderly—who in a very real sense are *us*—consider communal living? And if we accept the hypothesis that Lakeview residents constitute an advanced guard, can we expect congregate living to be a wave of the future?

The authors of this book have arrived at this conclusion; in fact, it was the motivation for this book. We also believe every reader should come to his or her own conclusions about life beyond 65 . . . 70 . . . 75 . . . Do not, however, just sit on your ideas. Do a bit of research, investigate, talk to your friends. Find out how you can plan for the lifestyle that pleases you most. Whether it's some form of informal shared living with friends or a more structured arrangement under the aegis of an organization, you may have to help in its creation. In the latter case, get your local government, church, synagogue, or fraternal organization to form a committee that will poll the community and assess present needs. Be sure to include representatives of the group in need of the housing. (The opinions of those most deeply affected by the decisions are too often overlooked.) Explore the possibilities. Investigate other areas of your state, and find out what is being done to solve housing problems and what is being done elsewhere in the country. State units on aging, listed in appendix 1, can offer information and guidance.

In some communities, home-sharing will be the favored solution to the housing needs of the elderly, and you can work with an existing agency or set up a new framework for bringing homeowners and companionable tenants together. Trouble on the local level usually involves zoning laws. In many suburban towns, "accessory apartments" and doubling up by unrelated individuals in one-family houses are prohibited, no matter how large the houses or how lonely and financially strapped their occupants. Local fears of down-zoning frequently squash housing proposals for anything from small shared housing to congregate apartment buildings.

Fighting for changes in local zoning law can be a tough, frustrating, and expensive battle, which is probably one of the main reasons why rehabilitation of school and other abandoned town center buildings is becoming so popular. Instead of waging a bitter and protracted struggle, your committee might want to consider this alternative and look around for a suitable building or site.

Whatever course you take, it will not be easy. Every step of the way will be fraught with multiple problems: reaching consensus, financing, construction and design, and much more. It helps to remember that what you are building today, if it is not for you personally, will be there when you need it.

Community action isn't for everyone, of course. Some will be interested only in finding their own way, and every person who is able to do that is one less responsibility for a community and a family. But the same kind of foresight and diligence should go into an individual's or a couple's search for an independent old age.

If you are determined to live alone always—whether in your present home, in a new one, or in a retirement village— you ought to be sure you know where help will be available when you need it.

If you plan to share your home with a tenant or tenants, inform yourself about local laws, construction requirements, and available financing.

If you favor informal shared living, you should be making plans and preparations with those who are going to join you.

And if you prefer the idea of living in a congregate community, set about investigating them as soon as possible; there may be long waiting lists.

Above all, do these things while you still have enough energy and strength of will to do them.

The enormous variations among lifestyle choices precludes discussion of guidelines to follow in your exploration of all but the last—the congregate lifestyle—which, after all, is the theme of this book.

How to Find the Right Residence

In your search for a congregate residence, one of the first questions you will have to ask yourself is, "In what part of the country do I want to live?" Should you decide to stay in your home community, your choices may be very limited. What if you were to find nothing suitable? Well, then, you can go back to square one and work with a community organization to plan and build a residence, or you can widen your horizons.

An equally important decision is whether you want a life care arrangement in the congregate community you choose. Congregate housing with its self-contained apartments, meals, and housekeeping services, can but does not always include

medical care and various levels of nursing care. Residence in a
life care (sometimes called "continuing care") community is, of
necessity, more expensive and requires a sizable entry fee. For
those who can afford the costs, life care communities provide
the security of knowing they will obtain all needed services
should they become disabled or infirm in the future. Some life
care residents may find themselves paying more than the actual cost of the services they receive over the life of a contract,
while others may benefit more by being assured of housing and
services they might not have been able to afford over an extended period of time.

The financial investment in a life care community is
greater; therefore, the criteria for selecting among them are
more complex. But many of the following suggestions will
apply to all types of congregate communities.

Once you have decided on the area of your search, get a list
and as much information as you can about the facilities located
there. Life care and other congregate communities, listed by
state in appendix 2, can help you get started. Please note that
we have made the list as complete as possible, but inclusion in
this list does not constitute a recommendation. Check those
that meet your needs and your bank account, and arrange to
visit, at least for a day but preferably for longer.

Tour buildings and grounds, and note their appearance.
Are they generally attractive, well tended, and in good repair?
Is the layout of the building or buildings convenient and safe?
Are the community spaces—corridors, meeting rooms,
lounges, and recreation areas—adequate, clean, and attrac-
tive? Is building security good?

See as many apartments as you can to determine whether
they have the space and equipment you think you will need.
Are there emergency buzzers and safety equipment in the
bathrooms, smoke alarms or sprinkler outlets, carpeting, air
conditioning? Do kitchens and appliances seem convenient and
adequate? Are windows well placed to let in air and daylight? Is
the view pleasant?

Talk to residents and staff members. Are they lively,
cheerful, friendly? Do you feel comfortable with the residents?
Are they the kinds of people you would like to have as friends?

What kinds of activities do residents engage in? And who

plans them, residents or staff? Are they activities that interest you? Is there a residents council? Is it active? How often does it meet? Are there job and volunteer opportunities in the residence and out in the community? What about transportation?

Services will probably be listed in a brochure. But during your visit try to ascertain whether the services are actually provided and how well they are performed.

A list of the written rules should help clarify the amount of regulation imposed by management. But try to discover from residents how they feel about them and whether there are any other rules.

Take several meals in the dining room, and judge the quality of the food and the service. Is the room clean and uncrowded, the atmosphere pleasant and congenial?

Ask to see the infirmary, intermediate, and nursing care facilities. Are they clean and bright? Does the staff seem efficient and unharried? Do the patients look well cared for? Are there visitors about? If the residence lacks any or all of these facilities, are there plans to add any or all in the future? If not, what provisions are made for residents who need medical, personal, or skilled nursing care? How far away are hospitals and medical, dental, and other professional offices?

Tour the area surrounding the residence. Is it too urban or too rural for your tastes? Does the neighborhood seem stable and pleasant? Are there shops, churches, and recreational and cultural facilities nearby? Is public transportation conveniently accessible? Does the house provide any transportation services? Before you leave, buy a local newspaper for more insight into the town.

By the time you have completed this physical tour, you should have a fairly good idea of whether you would like living in the community.

Investigate Ownership and Management

If your response is positive, the next phase of your investigation might well concern ownership and management. Is the residence owned and operated by a proprietary (for profit) organization? Or is the sponsor a religious, fraternal, or other nonprofit organization? Most life care communities in the United States are owned and operated by nonprofit organizations that appoint boards of directors to handle the finances and set policy.

"The board of directors provides direction and continuity to a life care community. To learn whether the board is responsible and interested in the community, the prospective resident should ask for a list of board members with biographical information, how board members participate in the community, and frequency and location of board meetings. If the board meets on the premises and the members are at the community on occasions other than board meetings, it is more likely that the board will be accurately aware of what is happening."[17]

The board of directors generally hires a manager/administrator who is in charge of the operation of the community. Sometimes a management firm is retained, in which case the administrator is an employee of the firm that reports to the board. Your visit and conversations with community residents and a perusal of the rules and regulations will give you a sense of the reliability and understanding of the management.

Understand Fees and Finances

Basic questions about fees and finances were probably answered even before you visited the community, assuming that you selected only those you thought you could afford. But the ramifications require careful study. For example: "Communities have different procedures for waiting lists, deposits, refunds of deposits if a person decides not to enter the community, processing fees, and so on. The applicant should clearly understand what he or she must do to stay on the list. Some places permit those on the waiting list to refuse an accommodation a certain number of times before forfeiting their places or having to pay additional fees.

"Applicants should also clearly understand what happens if their situations (health or other) change before they take occupancy. Direct entry into the health center or refund if a person is no longer eligible for admission are among the possibilities.

"Admission processes vary among communities, with most requiring at least an interview, visit, and financial and health data. Full disclosure of assets and income is usually not requested; applicants must merely show they can pay the necessary fees."[18]

Before signing a contract, be sure to have your attorney examine it. You should clearly understand the charges and the method by which you will be expected to pay for the shelter and services you receive. Methods of payment vary, and some communities have more than one method of payment and allow residents to choose the method most convenient and beneficial to them.

The most common type of life care arrangement requires payment of a one-time entry fee in addition to monthly payments. Fees vary depending on the type of shelter and services provided. Entry fees should be refundable if you wish to leave after a reasonable trial period.

A contract should also clearly state what is included in the regular fees and what is available only at extra cost. This includes changes in fees that may result from a move to the nursing unit, death of a spouse, moves to a smaller apartment, and so on.

After the costs of services are clear, you will want to make a judgment about the financial soundness of the community. Ask to see current financial statements. Another way to gauge the community's long-term financial health is by its waiting list and apartment occupancy rate. It should be operating at close to 100 percent within a year after opening.

Communities under construction present a certain amount of risk. First, refund of deposits or entry fees if you decide to withdraw may not be possible. Then, the entry fee may also be at risk if the project is not successfully completed. If, however, the community pledges to spend none of the entry fees until signed contracts and entry fee payments are received for 60 to 80 percent of the planned apartments, firm contracts have been negotiated for all construction work, all approvals and permits have been received, and construction and permanent financing have been arranged, you are assured that the community will be able to open. This is also true if entry fees have been placed in escrow until the same conditions have been met or until you enter the community. Escrowing entry fees after construction begins, however, does increase the project cost, because more construction funds must be borrowed.

When, after all this careful investigation and a waiting period, you have signed a contract and have settled into a congregate residence that meets most of your requirements, we think you will enjoy the community life, the companionship and support of your fellow residents, and the freedom from much of the stress our society imposes on its elderly people. Here is the testimony of one resident of a congregate community of her choice: "Although my adjustment to communal living took a little time . . . I soon began to realize that life here is very desirable. . . . When I want congenial companionship, persons of my own age, younger or older, are usually to be found. And those considerably older come to be thought of not as 'old people,' but as valued friends. Holidays are no longer lonely because instead of spending them alone, they are celebrated by congenial groups. One of the greatest advantages is a sense of safety, of security. I know that if illness strikes [there is] a well-staffed infirmary . . . and a fine hospital only blocks away. Yes, I'm glad I came and came when I did. The house now has a four-year waiting list."[19]

Before we close and just for fun, we'd like to go back to our *On Golden Pond* sequel and rewrite the entire scenario.

Let's suppose that the Hepburn and Fonda characters both decided, after their Golden Pond summer, that it was time to move out of their big suburban house and into a congregate residence. We can have them conduct a search like the one through which we led you. Upon discovering a community with which they feel comfortable, they apply for a two-bedroom apartment. For the sake of dramatic unity, we are going to say they chose Lakeview House. After a wait of several years, during which they unburden themselves of many of their household possessions, they are notified that an apartment is ready for them. Putting their house up for sale, they proceed with their packing and moving and join our old friends in the high-rise building overlooking the lake.

Before very long, the wife is gardening, working in the

Whatnot Shop, helping Lynne Battelle with trip plans, and, as she loves to do, occasionally baking cookies, cakes, and pies in her little kitchen. She is more cheerful than ever. The husband tutors students at Watertown High School three times a week, reads, writes, and has revived a practice of long bygone days— playing the clarinet, but only when his wife is out of the apartment. He has lost some of his old irascibility and has become almost affable. His heart still acts up once in a while, but so far immediate attention from the second-floor staff has kept him going.

The couple visits their daughter, her dentist husband, and his son during Easter week, and the daughter and her family visit them at Lakeview during the Christmas holidays. Summers are, as always, spent at the house on Golden Pond.

It is tempting to say that they lived happily ever after. The truth is, they lived quite happily for all the rest of their long lives.

APPENDIX 1:
State Units on Aging

ALABAMA

Rebecca B. Beasley, Acting
  Executive Director
Commission on Aging
State Capitol
Montgomery, Alabama 36130
(205) 832-6640

ALASKA

Elizabeth Muktarian, Director
Division of Adult and Aging
  Services, Dept. of Health and
  Social Services
POUCH "HOIC"
Juneau, Alaska 99811
(907) 465-3250

ARIZONA

Michael Slattery, Director
Aging and Adult
  Administration, Dept. of
  Economic Security
1400 W. Washington St.
Phoenix, Arizona 85007
(602) 765-4446 (FTS)
(602) 255-4446 (commercial)

ARKANSAS

Bryan Tilley, Acting Executive
  Director
Office on Aging and Adult
  Services, Dept. of Social and
  Rehabilitation Services
Donaghey Building, 1031S
Little Rock, Arkansas 77201
(501) 371-2441

CALIFORNIA

Janet J. Levy, Director
Department on Aging
1020 19th St.
Sacramento, California 95814
(916) 322-5290

COLORADO

William J. Hanna, Director
Division of Services for the
  Aging, Colorado Dept. of
  Social Services
1575 Sherman St., Room 503
Denver, Colorado 80220
(303) 839-2586

CONNECTICUT

Marin J. Shealy, Commissioner
Department on Aging
80 Washington Street, 312
Hartford, Connecticut 06115
(203) 566-3238

DELAWARE

Eleanor Cain, Director
Division of Aging, Dept. of
  Health and Social Services
Newcastle, Delaware 19720
(302) 421-6791

DISTRICT OF COLUMBIA

D. Richard Artis, Executive
  Director
Office on Aging, Office of the
  Mayor
1012 14th St., N.W., 1106
Washington, D.C. 20005
(202) 724-5622

FLORIDA

John Stokesberry, Director
Program Office of Aging and
  Adult Services, Dept. of
  Health and Rehabilitation
  Services
1323 Winewood Blvd.
Tallahassee, Florida 32301
(904) 488-2650

GEORGIA

Troy Bledsoe, Director of Aging
  Section
Dept. of Human Resources
618 Ponce de Leon Ave., N.E.
Atlanta, Georgia 30308
(404) 894-5333

GUAM

Franklin Cruz, Ed.D., Director
Public Health and Social
  Services, Government of
  Guam
Agana, Guam 96910
011 (671) 734-2947

HAWAII

Renji Goto, Director
Executive Office on Aging, Office
  of the Governor
1149 Bethel St., 307
Honolulu, Hawaii 96813
(808) 548-2593

IDAHO

Rose Bowman, Director
Idaho Office on Aging
Statehouse
Boise, Idaho 83720
(208) 334-3833

ILLINOIS

Peg Blaser, Director
Department on Aging
421 E. Capital Ave.
Springfield, Illinois 62706
(217) 785-3356

INDIANA

Jean Merritt, Executive Director
Commission on the Aging and
  Aged
Graphic Arts Building, 201
215 N. Senate Ave.
Indianapolis, Indiana 46202
(317) 232-1190

IOWA

Glenn Bowles, Executive
  Director
Commission on Aging
415 W. Tenth St.
Des Moines, Iowa 50319
(515) 281-5187

KANSAS

Sylvia Houghland, Secretary
Department on Aging
610 W. 10th
Topeka, Kansas 66612
(913) 296-4986

KENTUCKY

Fannie Dorsey, Director
Division for Aging Services,
  Dept. of Human Resources
275 E. Main St.
Frankfort, Kentucky 40601
(502) 564-6930

LOUISIANA

Larry Kinlaw, Director
Office of Elderly Affairs
P.O. Box 44282, Capitol Station
Baton Rouge, Louisiana 70804
(504) 342-2747

MAINE

Patricia Riley, Director
Bureau of Maine's Elderly,
  Community Services Unit,
  Dept. of Human Services
State House
Augusta, Maine 04333
(207) 289-2561

MARYLAND

Matthew Tayback, Director
Office on Aging
301 W. Preston St.
Baltimore, Maryland 21201
(301) 383-5064

MASSACHUSETTS

Thomas H. D. Mahoney, Ph.D.,
  Secretary
Dept. of Elder Affairs
38 Chauncy St.
Boston, Massachusetts 02111
(617) 727-7751

MICHIGAN

Kenneth Oettle, Director
Office of Services to the Aging
300 E. Michigan Ave.
P.O. Box 30026
Lansing, Michigan 48909
(517) 373-8230

MINNESOTA

Gerald A. Bloedow, Executive
  Director
Minnesota Board on Aging
Metro Square Building, 204
Seventh and Robert Streets
St. Paul, Minnesota 55101
(612) 296-2544

MISSISSIPPI

Jay Moon, Executive Director
Mississippi Council on Aging
802 N. State St., 301
Jackson, Mississippi 39201
(601) 354-6590

MISSOURI

Floyd Richards, Director
Division on Aging, Dept. of Social
  Services
P.O. Box 570
Jefferson City, Missouri 65101
(314) 751-3082

MONTANA

Norma Vestre, Administrator
Community Services Division
P.O. Box 4210
Helena, Montana 59604
(406) 449-3865

NEBRASKA

Nell Culver, Acting Executive
  Director
Commission on Aging
301 Centennial Mall South
P.O. Box 95044
Lincoln, Nebraska 68509
(402) 471-2306

NEVADA

John B. McSweeney,
  Administrator
Division of Aging, Dept. of
  Human Resources
505 E. King St., 101
Carson City, Nevada 89710
(702) 885-4210
(702) 470-5911 (FTS)

NEW HAMPSHIRE

James McKay, Chairman
Council on Aging
14 Depot St.
Concord, New Hampshire 03301
(603) 271-2751

NEW JERSEY

Jacques O. Lebel, Director
Division on Aging, Dept. of
  Community Affairs
363 W. State St.
P.O. Box 2768
Trenton, New Jersey 08625
(609) 292-4833

NEW MEXICO

Ernesto Ramos, Director
State Agency on Aging
440 St. Michael's Dr.
Santa Fe, New Mexico 87503
(505) 827-2802

NEW YORK

Lou Glasse, Director
Office for the Aging, New York
  State Executive Dept.
Empire State Plaza, Agency
  Building 2
Albany, New York 12223
(518) 474-5731

NORTH CAROLINA

Nathan H. Yelton, Assistant
  Secretary
North Carolina Dept. of Human
  Resources, Division of Aging
708 Hillsborough St., 200
Raleigh, North Carolina 27603
(919) 733-3983

NORTH DAKOTA

Loretta Knight, Acting
  Supervisor
Aging Services, Social Services
  Board of North Dakota
State Capitol Building
Bismarck, North Dakota 58505
(701) 224-2577

NORTHERN MARIANA ISLANDS

Edward Cabrera, Administrator
Office of Aging, Dept. of
  Community and Cultural
  Affairs
Commonwealth of Northern
  Mariana Islands
Civic Center, Susupe
Siapan, Northern Mariana
  Islands 96950
Tel 9411 or 9732

OHIO

Martin A. Janis, Executive
  Director
Commission on Aging
50 W. Broad St.
Columbus, Ohio 43215
(614) 466-5500

OKLAHOMA

Roy R. Keen, Supervisor
Special Unit on Aging, Dept. of
  Human Services
P.O. Box 25352
Oklahoma City,
  Oklahoma 73125
(405) 521-2281

OREGON

Robert Zeigen, Director
Office of Elderly Affairs, Human
  Resources Dept.
772 Commercial St., S.E.
Salem, Oregon 97310
(503) 378-4728

PENNSYLVANIA

Gorham L. Black, Jr., Secretary
  of Aging
Dept. of Aging
Finance Building, 404
Harrisburg, Pennsylvania 17120
(717) 783-1550

PUERTO RICO

Alicia Ramirez Suárez,
  Executive Director
Gericulture Commission, Dept.
  of Social Services
P.O. Box 11368
Santurce, Puerto Rico 00908
(809) 722-2429

RHODE ISLAND

Anna M. Tucker, Director
Dept. of Elderly Affairs
79 Washington St.
Providence, Rhode Island 02903
(401) 277-2858

AMERICAN SAMOA

Tali T. Maae, Director
Territorial Administration on
  Aging
Office of the Governor
Pago Pago, American Samoa
  96799
011-(684) 633-1252 Com. Direct
  Dial

SOUTH CAROLINA

Harry Bryan, Executive Director
Commission on Aging
915 Main St.
Columbia, South Carolina
(803) 758-2576

SOUTH DAKOTA

Carole J. Boos, Administrator
Office on Aging, Office of Adult
  Services and Aging
State Office Building
Illinois St.
Pierre, South Dakota 57501
(605) 773-3656

TENNESSEE

Emily M. Wiseman, Executive
Director
Commission on Aging
535 Church St.
Nashville, Tennessee 37219
(615) 741-2056

TEXAS

Chris Kyker, Director
Governor's Committee on Aging
210 Martin Springs Rd.
P.O. Box 12786, Capitol Station
Austin, Texas 78704
(512) 475-2717

TRUST TERRITORY OF THE PACIFIC

Augustine Moses, Acting Chief
Office of Elderly Programs,
Community Development
Division
Saipan, Mariana Islands 96950
Tel. 9335 or 9336

UTAH

Louise Lintz, Acting Director
Division of Aging, Dept. of Social
Services
150 W. North Temple
Box 2500
Salt Lake City, Utah 84102
(801) 533-6422

VERMONT

Mary Ellen Spencer, Director
Office on Aging, Agency of
Human Services
State Office Building
Montpelier, Vermont 05602
(802) 241-2400

VIRGINIA

Wilda Ferguson, Director
Office on Aging
830 E. Main St., 950
Richmond, Virginia 23219
(804) 786-7894

VIRGIN ISLANDS

Gloria M. King, Executive
Secretary
Commission on Aging
P.O. Box 539
Charlotte Amalie, St. Thomas,
Virgin Islands 00801
(809) 774-5884

WASHINGTON

Charles Reed, Chief
Office of Aging, Dept. of Social
and Health Services
OB-43G
Olympia, Washington 98504
(206) 753-2502

WEST VIRGINIA

Raymond Leinback, Director
Commission on Aging
State Capitol
Charleston, West Virginia 25305
(304) 348-3317

WISCONSIN

Douglas Nelson, Assistant
Administrator
Division of Community Services,
Bureau on Aging
One W. Wilson St., 535
P.O. Box 7851
Madison, Wisconsin 53702
(608) 266-2536

WYOMING

Scott Sessions, Director
Commission on Aging
720 W. 18th St.
Cheyenne, Wyoming 82002
(307) 777-7986

APPENDIX 2: Life Care Congregate Communities in the United States

This list was compiled from the *Membership Directory* of the American Association of Homes for the Aging (1983), and the *Directory of Life Care Communities* published by Kendal-Crosslands (1980). It is meant to be as comprehensive as possible, but inclusion in this list should not be regarded in any way as a recommendation by the authors or publishers of this book.

* Indicates a congregate residence that does not offer life care to its residents.

ALABAMA

Mount Royal Towers
2099 Medical Center Dr.
Birmingham, Alabama 35209
(205) 870-5573

Wesley Manor
210 Honeysuckle Rd.
Dothan, Alabama 36301
(205) 792-0921

Westminster Village
P. O. Box 670
Spanish Fort, Alabama 36527
(205) 626-5588

ARIZONA

Desert Crest Retirement Home
Crestview Lodge Nursing Care
2101 E. Mayland Ave.
Phoenix, Arizona 85016
(602) 264-6427

Glencroft Retirement
  Community*
8611 N. 67th Ave.
Glendale, Arizona 85302
(602) 939-9475

Mesa Christian Home*
255 W. Brown Rd.
Mesa, Arizona 85201
(602) 833-3988

Orangewood
755 N. 16th St.
Phoenix, Arizona 85020
(602) 944-4455

CALIFORNIA

Adlai E. Stevenson House*
455 E. Charleston Rd.
Palo Alto, California 94306
(415) 494-1944

Aldersly
326 Mission Ave.
San Rafael, California 94901
(415) 453-7425

Alexander House*
2120 Santa Barbara St.
Santa Barbara, California 93105
(805) 682-7313

The Alhambra
2400 S. Fremont Ave.
Alhambra, California 91803
(213) 289-6211

Ararat Home of Los Angeles*
3730 W. 27th St.
Los Angeles, California 90018
(213) 733-5502

Atherton Baptist Homes
214 S. Atlantic Blvd.
Alhambra, California 91801
(213) 289-4178

Bay Area Catholic Homes
50 Oak St.
San Francisco, California 94102
(415) 864-7400

Bethany Center Senior Housing*
580 Capp St.
San Francisco, California 94110
(415) 821-4515

Brethren Hill Crest Homes
2705 Mountain View Dr.
La Verne, California 91750
(714) 593-4917

British Home in California
647 Manzanita Ave.
Sierra Madre, California 91024
(213) 355-7240

California Christian Home
8417 E. Mission Dr.
Rosemead, California 91770
(213) 287-0438

California Home for the Aged
P. O. Box 7877
Fresno, California 93747
(209) 251-8414

California P.E.O. Home
5203 Alum Rock Ave.
San Jose, California 95127
(408) 251-9030

California P.E.O. Home
700 N. Stoneman Ave.
Alhambra, California 91801
(213) 289-5284

Cambrian Center*
2360 Samaritan Dr.
San Jose, California 95124
(408) 559-0330

Canterbury Woods
651 Sinex Ave.
Pacific Grove, California 93950
(408) 373-3111

Carlsbad-by-the-Sea
2855 Carlsbad Blvd.
Carlsbad, California 92008
(714) 729-2377

Carmel Valley Manor
8545 Carmel Valley Rd.
Carmel, California 93923
(408) 624-1281

Casa de Verdugo*
155 N. Girard St.
Hemet, California 92343
(714) 658-2274

Casa Dorinda
300 Hot Springs Rd.
Montecito, California 93108
(805) 969-8011

Channing House
850 Webster St.
Palo Alto, California 94301
(415) 327-0950

Covenant Village
2125 N. Olive Ave.
Turlock, California 95380
(209) 632-9976

Episcopal Residence
2770 Lombard St.
San Francisco, California 94123
(415) 346-6300

Eskaton-Sunrise Community*
7501 Sunrise Blvd.
Citrus Heights, California 95610
(916) 726-3315

Faith Gardens Village
740 Mesa Ave.
Vista, California 92083
(714) 941-1480

Forester Haven
12249 N. Lopez Canyon Rd.
San Fernando, California 91342
(213) 899-7422

Forest Hill Manor
551 Gibson
Pacific Grove, California 93950
(408) 375-5125

Fredericka Manor*
183 Third Ave.
Chula Vista, California 92010
(714) 422-9271

Good Shepherd Manor*
4411 11th Ave.
Los Angeles, California 90043
(213) 299-5735

Grand Lake Gardens
401 Santa Clara Ave.
Oakland, California 94610
(415) 893-8897

The Heritage
3400 Laguna St.
San Francisco, California 94123
(415) 567-6900

Hollenbeck Home
573 S. Boyle Ave.
Los Angeles, California 90033
(213) 263-6195

Inland Christian Home
1950 S. Mountain Ave.
Ontario, California 91761
(714) 983-0084

Lake Park Retirement
  Residence*
1850 Alice St.
Oakland, California 94612
(415) 835-5511

Lincoln Glen Manor for Senior
  Citizens*
2671 Plummer Ave.
San Jose, California 95125
(408) 265-3222

Long Beach Brethren Manor*
3333 Pacific Pl.
Long Beach, California 90806
(213) 426-6547

Los Gatos Meadows
110 Wood Rd.
Los Gatos, California 95030
(408) 354-0211

Lytton Gardens
656 Lytton Ave.
Palo Alto, California 94301
(415) 328-3300

Monte Vista Grove
2889 San Pasqual St.
Pasadena, California 91107
(213) 796-6135

Motion Picture and Television
  Country House and Lodge
23450 Calabasas Rd.
Woodland Hills, California
  91364
(213) 347-1591

Mount Miguel Covenant Village
325 Kempton St.
Spring Valley, California 92077
(714) 479-4790

Mt. San Antonio
  Gardens/Congregational
  Homes
900 E. Harrison Ave.
Pomona, California 91767
(714) 624-5061

Neighborhood Manor*
1200 Woodrow Ave.
Modesto, California 95350
(209) 526-0308

Our Lady's Home*
3431 Foothill Blvd.
Oakland, California 94601
(415) 523-7034

Paradise Valley Manor*
2575 E. 8th St.
National City, California 92050
(714) 474-8301

Piedmont Gardens
110 41st St.
Oakland, California 94611
(415) 654-7172

Pilgrim Haven
373 Pine La.
Los Altos, California 94022
(415) 948-8291

Pilgrim Tower for the Deaf
1207 S. Vermont Ave.
Los Angeles, California 90006
(213) 387-6541

Pioneer House*
415 P St.
Sacramento, California 95814
(916) 442-4906

Plymouth Square*
1319 N. Madison St.
Stockton, California 95202
(209) 466-4341

Plymouth Village of Redlands
900 Salem Dr.
Redlands, California 92373
(714) 793-1233

President James Monroe Manor*
3225 Freeport Blvd.
Sacramento, California 95818
(916) 441-1015

Quaker Gardens
12151 Dale St.
Stanton, California 90680
(714) 530-9100

The Redwoods*
40 Camino Alto
Mill Valley, California 94941
(415) 383-2741

Redwood Terrace Lutheran
Home and Health Center
710 W. 13th Ave.
Escondido, California 92025
(714) 747-4306

Regents Point
19191 Harvard Ave.
Irvine, California 92715
(714) 851-1655

Rosewood Retirement
Community
1301 New Stine Rd.
Bakersfield, California 93309
(805) 834-0620

Royal Oaks Manor
1763 Royal Oaks Dr.
Duarte, California 91010
(213) 359-9371

St. Paul's Manor and Health
Care Center
2635 2nd Ave.
San Diego, California 92103
(714) 239-2097

Saint Paul's Towers
100 Bay Pl.
Oakland, California 94610
(415) 835-4700

Salem Lutheran Home*
2361 E. 29th St.
Oakland, California 94606
(415) 534-3637

Samarkand of Santa Barbara
2663 Tallant Rd.
Santa Barbara, California 93105
(805) 687-0701

San Joaquin Gardens
5555 N. Fresno St.
Fresno, California 93710
(209) 439-4770

Scripps Home
2212 N. El Molino Ave.
Altadena, California 91001
(213) 798-0934

Sequoias-Portola Valley
501 Portola Rd., Box 8500
Portola Valley, California 94025
(415) 851-1501

Sequoias-San Francisco
1400 Geary Blvd.
San Francisco, California 94109
(415) 922-9700

Solheim Lutheran Home
2236 Merton Ave.
Los Angeles, California 90041
(213) 257-7518

Southland Lutheran Home and
Geriatric Center
11701 Studebaker Rd.
Norwalk, California 90650
(213) 868-9761

Sun City Gardens*
28500 Bradley Rd.
Sun City, California 92381
(714) 679-2391

Sunny View Lutheran Home
22445 Cupertino Rd.
Cupertino, California 95014
(408) 253-4300

Sunset Haven*
275 Garnet Way
Upland, California 91786
(714) 985-0924

Tamalpais
501 Via Casitas
Greenbrae, California 94904
(415) 461-2300

Town and Country Manor
555 E. Memory La.
Santa Ana, California 92706
(714) 547-7581

Town Meadows*
115 W. Murray Ave.
Visalia, California 93291
(209) 627-2220

Trinity House*
2701 Capitol Ave.
Sacramento, California 95816
(916) 446-4806

Twelve Oaks Lodge*
2820 Sycamore Ave.
La Crescenta, California 91214
(213) 249-3361

Valdez Plaza*
280 28th St.
Oakland, California 94611
(415) 836-1800

Valle Verde Retirement Center
900 Calle de Los Amigos
Santa Barbara, California 93105
(805) 687-1571

Valley Village*
390 N. Winchester Blvd.
Santa Clara, California 95050
(408) 241-7750

Villa Gardens*
842 E. Villa St.
Pasadena, California 91101
(213) 796-8162

Villa Scalabrini Retirement
  Center*
10631 Vinedale St.
Sun Valley, California 91352
(213) 768-6500

Vista Del Monte*
3775 Modoc Rd.
Santa Barbara, California 93105
(805) 687-0793

Walnut Manor
891 S. Walnut St.
Anaheim, California 92802
(714) 776-7150

Western Park Apartments*
1280 Laguna St.
San Francisco, California 94115
(415) 922-5436

Westminster Gardens*
1420 Santo Domingo Ave.
Duarte, California 91010
(213) 358-2569

Windsor Manor
1230 E. Windsor Rd.
Glendale, California 91205
(213) 244-7219

White Sands of La Jolla
7450 Olivetas Ave.
La Jolla, California 92037
(714) 454-4201

COLORADO

Boulder Good Samaritan
  Center*
2525 Taft Dr.
Boulder, Colorado 80302
(303) 449-6150

Colorado Lutheran Health Care
  Center
8001 W. 71st Ave.
Arvada, Colorado 80004
(303) 422-5088

Eben Ezer Lutheran Care Center
Box 344
Brush, Colorado 80723
(303) 842-2861

Frasier Meadows
350 Ponca Dr.
Boulder, Colorado 80303
(303) 499-4888

Golden West Manor*
1055 Adams Circle
Boulder, Colorado 80303
(303) 444-3967

Medalion Retirement Residence
1719 E. Bijou St.
Colorado Springs, Colorado
  80909
(303) 471-4800

Park Manor*
1801 E. 19th Ave.
Denver, Colorado 80218
(303) 839-7000

Rocky Mountain Methodist
  Homes
Box 2178
Longmont, Colorado 80501
(303) 772-8101

CONNECTICUT

Covenant Village and Pilgrim
  Manor
52 Missionary Rd.
Cromwell, Connecticut 06416
(203) 635-5511

King's Daughters and Sons
  Home*
168 Westport Ave.
Norwalk, Connecticut 06851
(203) 847-7494

Regina Pacis Villa*
Route 44, Box 23
Pomfret Center, Connecticut
  06259
(203) 928-5074

Thirty Thirty Park
3030 Park Ave.
Bridgeport, Connecticut 06604
(203) 374-5611

Whitney Center
200 Leeder Hill Dr.
Hamden, Connecticut 07517
(203) 281-6745

DELAWARE

Cokesbury Village
4830 Kennett Pike
Wilmington, Delaware 19807
(302) 239-2371

DISTRICT OF COLUMBIA

Methodist Home of D.C.
4901 Connecticut Ave., N.W.
Washington, D.C. 20008
(202) 966-7623

Presbyterian Home of D.C.
3050 Military Rd., N.W.
Washington, D.C. 20015
(202) 363-6116

Thomas House
1330 Massachusetts Ave., N.W.
Washington, D.C. 20005
(202) 628-2092

FLORIDA

Abbey Delray
2000 Lowson Blvd., Box 550
Delray Beach, Florida 33444
(305) 278-3249

Alliance Home of Deland
600 S. Florida Ave.
Deland, Florida 32720
(904) 734-3486

Asbury Towers
1533 4th Ave. West
Bradenton, Florida 33505
(813) 747-1881

Azalea Trace
10100 Hill View Rd.
Pensacola, Florida 32504
(904) 478-5200

Bay Village of Sarasota
8400 Vamo Rd.
Sarasota, Florida 33581
(813) 966-5611

Bishop Gray Inn
P. O. Box 668
Davenport, Florida 33837
(813) 422-4961

Bradenton Manor Retirement
  Center
1700 21st Ave. West
Bradenton, Florida 33505
(813) 748-4161

Calusa Retirement Center
2371 W. First St.
Fort Myers, Florida 33901
(813) 332-3333

Canterbury Tower
3501 Bayshore Blvd.
Tampa, Florida 33609
(813) 837-1083

Covenant Palms of Miami
8400 N.W. 25th Ave.
Miami, Florida 33147
(305) 836-4382

Covenant Village of Florida
9201 W. Broward
Plantation, Florida 33324
(305) 472-2860

East Ridge Retirement Village
19301 S.W. 87th Ave.
Miami, Florida 33157
(305) 238-2623

Florida Lutheran Retirement
  Center
431 N. Kansas Ave.
Deland, Florida 32720
(904) 734-0603

Florida United Presbyterian
  Homes
16 Lake Hunter Dr.
Lakeland, Florida 33803
(813) 688-5521

Jacksonville Regency House
33 W. Adams St.
Jacksonville, Florida 32202
(904) 358-1832

Leisure Manor
316-336 Fourth Ave. North
St. Petersburg, Florida 33701
(813) 896-4171

Miami Jewish Home and
  Hospital for the Aged at
  Douglas Gardens
151 N.E. 52nd St.
Miami, Florida 33137
(305) 751-8626

Oak Bluffs
420 Bay Ave.
Clearwater, Florida 33516
(813) 461-4466

Oak Cove Retirement and
    Health Center
210 S. Osceola Ave.
Clearwater, Florida 33516
(813) 441-3763

Orlando Lutheran Towers
300 E. Church St.
Orlando, Florida 32801
(305) 425-1033

The Palms (Florida Brethren
    Homes)
Box 2026
Sebring, Florida 33870
(813) 385-0161

Palm Shores
830 N. Shore Dr.
St. Petersburg, Florida 33701
(813) 894-2102

Plymouth Harbor
700 John Ringling Blvd.
Sarasota, Florida 33577
(813) 365-2600

Saint Mark Village
2655 Nebraska Ave.
Palm Harbor, Florida 33563
(813) 785-2576

Shell Point Village
Route 12, Shell Point Blvd.
Fort Myers, Florida 33908
(813) 481-2141

The Shores
1700 Third Ave. West
Brandenton, Florida 33505
(813) 748-1700

Southwest Florida Retirement
    Center*
950 Tamiami Trail South
Venice, Florida 33595
(813) 488-3456

Trinity Lakes
101 Trinity Lakes Dr.
Sun City Center, Florida 33570
(813) 634-3347

Westminster Towers
70 W. Lucerne Circle
Orlando, Florida 32801
(305) 841-1310

Winter Park Towers
1111 S. Lakemont Ave.
Winter Park, Florida 32792
(305) 647-4083

GEORGIA

Branan Lodge*
Box 140
Blairsville, Georgia 30512
(404) 745-5565

Branan Towers*
1200 Glenwood Ave., S.E.
Atlanta, Georgia 30316
(404) 622-5471

Canterbury Court
3750 Peachtree Rd., N.E.
Atlanta, Georgia 30319
(404) 261-6611

Christian City Retirement Home
7340 Lester Rd.
Atlanta, Georgia 30349
(404) 964-3301

Epworth Towers*
3033 Continental Colony
    Pkwy., S.W.
Atlanta, Georgia 30331
(404) 344-9400

Lanier Gardens*
801 Riverhill Dr.
Athens, Georgia 30606
(404) 546-1480

Louis Kahn Group Home
1538 Markan Dr., N.E.
Altanta, Georgia 30306
(404) 873-2112

Magnolia Manor Retirement
  Center*
South Lee St.
Americus, Georgia 31709
(912) 924-9352

Saint John Towers*
724 Greene St.
Augusta, Georgia 30901
(404) 722-2096

Wesley Woods Towers*
1825 Clifton Rd., N.E.
Atlanta, Georgia 30029
(404) 325-2988

IDAHO

Three Fountain Village
P. O. Box 1856
Boise, Idaho 83701
(208) 343-6500

ILLINOIS

Addolorata Villa
555 McHenry Rd.
Wheeling, Illinois 60090
(312) 537-2900

Apartment Community of
  Our Lady
9500 W. Illinois, Route 15
Belleville, Illinois 62223
(618) 397-6700

Baptist Retirement Home
316 Randolph St.
Maywood, Illinois 60153
(312) 344-1541

Barton W. Stone Christian Home
873 Grove St.
Jacksonville, Illinois 62650
(217) 243-3376

Bethany Home and Hospital of
  the Methodist Church
5025 N. Paulina St.
Chicago, Illinois 60640
(312) 271-9040

Central Baptist Home for the
  Aged
7901 W. Lawrence Ave.
Norridge, Illinois 60656
(312) 452-8265

Covenant Home
2725 W. Foster Ave.
Chicago, Illinois 60625
(312) 878-8200

Covenant Village
2625 Techny Rd.
Northbrook, Illinois 60062
(312) 480-6380

Danish Old Peoples Home
5656 N. Newcastle Ave.
Chicago, Illinois 60631
(312) 775-7383

Dekalb Area Retirement Center
2944 Greenwood Area Dr.
Dekalb, Illinois 60115
(815) 756-8461

Friendship Manor
1209 21st Ave.
Rock Island, Illinois 61201
(309) 786-9667

Friendship Village
350 W. Schaumberg Rd.
Schaumberg, Illinois 60194
(312) 884-5000

Georgian
422 Davis St.
Evanston, Illinois 60201
(312) 475-4100

Holmstad
Fabyan Pkwy. and Batavia Ave.
Batavia, Illinois 60510
(312) 879-4000

Lutheran Home and Service for
the Aged
800 W. Oakton St.
Arlington Heights, Illinois 60004
(312) 253-3710

Lutheran Home of Greater
Peoria*
7019 N. Galena Rd.
Peoria, Illinois 61614
(309) 692-4494

Presbyterian Home
3200 Grant St.
Evanston, Illinois 60201
(312) 492-2900

Scottish Home
2800 S. Desplaines Ave.
N. Riverside, Illinois 60546
(312) 447-5092

Wesley Willows
4141 N. Rockton Ave.
Rockford, Illinois 61103
(815) 654-2530

Westminister Place
One Calvin Circle
Evanston, Illinois 60201
(312) 492-2903

INDIANA

Altenheim Community United
Church Homes
3525 E. Hanna Ave.
Indianapolis, Indiana 46227
(317) 788-4261

Concord Village
6723 S. Anthony Blvd.
Fort Wayne, Indiana 46816
(219) 447-1591

Franklin United Methodist
Home
1070 W. Jefferson St.
Franklin, Indiana 46131
(317) 736-7185

Hamilton Grove
Chicago Trail
New Carlisle, Indiana 46552
(219) 654-3123

Indiana Masonic Homes
690 State St.
Franklin, Indiana 46131
(317) 736-6141

Kennedy Memorial Christian
Home*
210 W. Pike St.
Martinsville, Indiana 46151
(317) 342-6636

Lutheran Homes
6701 S. Anthony Blvd.
Fort Wayne, Indiana 46816
(219) 447-1591

Marquette Manor
8140 Township Line Rd.
Indianapolis, Indiana 46260
(317) 875-9700

Peabody Retirement Community
400 W. 7th St.
N. Manchester, Indiana 46962
(219) 982-8616

Summerlea Commons*
2011 Beacon St.
Fort Wayne, Indiana 46805
(219) 482-4489

Swiss Village
Berne, Indiana 46711
(219) 589-3173

Timbercrest—Church of the
  Brethren Home
P. O. Box 368
N. Manchester, Indiana 46962
(219) 982-2118

United Methodist Memorial
  Home
P. O. Box 326
Warren, Indiana 46792
(219) 375-2201

IOWA

Bishop Drumm Retirement
  Center
5837 Winwood Dr.
Des Moines, Iowa 50324
(515) 270-1100

Calvin Manor
4210 Hickman Rd.
Des Moines, Iowa 50310
(515) 277-6141

Friendship Haven
S. Kenyon Rd.
Fort Dodge, Iowa 50501
(515) 573-2121

Friendship Village
600 Park Lane
Waterloo, Iowa 50702
(319) 291-8100

Halcyon House
1015 S. Iowa Ave.
Washington, Iowa 52353
(319) 653-3523

Heather Manor
600 E. 5th St.
Des Moines, Iowa 50316
(515) 243-6195

Heritage House
1200 Brookridge Circle
Atlantic, Iowa 50022
(712) 243-1850

The Mayflower Home
616 Broad St.
Grinnell, Iowa 50112
(515) 236-6151

Meth-Wick Manor
1224 13th St., N.W.
Cedar Rapids, Iowa 52405
(319) 365-9171

Northcrest Community
1801 20th St.
Ames, Iowa 50010
(515) 232-6760

Oaknoll Retirement Residence
701 Oaknoll Dr.
Iowa City, Iowa 52240
(319) 351-1720

Ridgecrest Retirement Village
4130 N.W. Boulevard
Davenport, Iowa 52806
(319) 391-3430

United Presbyterian Home
1203 E. Washington St.
Washington, Iowa 52353
(319) 653-5473

Valley View Village
2571 Guthrie Ave.
Des Moines, Iowa 50317
(515) 265-2571

Wesley Acres
3520 Grand Ave.
Des Moines, Iowa 50312
(515) 274-3417

KANSAS

Arkansas City Presbyterian
  Manor
1711 N. 4th St.
Arkansas City, Kansas 67005
(316) 442-8700

Brewster Place
1205 W. 29th St.
Topeka, Kansas 66611
(913) 267-1666

Kansas City Presbyterian Manor
7850 Freeman St.
Kansas City, Kansas 66112
(913) 334-3666

Lakeview Village
9100 Park
Lenexa, Kansas 66215
(913) 888-1900

Lawrence Presbyterian Manor
1421 Kasold Dr.
Lawrence, Kansas 66044
(913) 841-4262

Parsons Presbyterian Manor*
3501 Dirr
Parsons, Kansas 67357
(316) 421-1450

Presbyterian Manor
1200 E. Seventh St.
Newton, Kansas 67114
(316) 283-5400

Salina Presbyterian Manor
2601 E. Crawford
Salina, Kansas 67401
(913) 825-1366

Topeka Presbyterian Manor
4712 W. 6th St.
Topeka, Kansas 66606
(913) 272-6510

United Methodist Homes
1135 College
Topeka, Kansas 66604
(913) 234-0421

Wesley Towers
700 Monterey Pl.
Hutchinson, Kansas 67501
(316) 663-9175

Wichita Presbyterian Manor
4700 W. 13th St.
Wichita, Kansas 67212
(316) 942-7456

KENTUCKY

Christian Church Home
942 S. 4th St.
Louisville, Kentucky 40203
(502) 583-6533

Christian Health Care Center*
200 Sterling Dr.
Hopkinsville, Kentucky 42240
(502) 885-1166

Eastern Star Home in Kentucky
923 Cherokee Rd.
Louisville, Kentucky 40204
(502) 451-3535

Friendship House
960 S. 4th St.
Louisville, Kentucky 40203
(502) 589-5747

Lewis Memorial Methodist
  Home
US 31W North
Franklin, Kentucky 42134
(502) 586-3461

Louisville Protestant Altenheim
936 Barrett Ave.
Louisville, Kentucky 40204
(502) 584-7417

Wesley Manor
5012 E. Manslick
P. O. Box 19258
Louisville, Kentucky 40219
(502) 969-3277

Westminster Terrace
2116 Buechel Bank Rd.
Louisville, Kentucky 40218
(502) 499-9383

MARYLAND

Asbury Methodist Village
301 Russell Ave.
Gaithersburg, Maryland 20877
(301) 926-4900

Augsburg Lutheran Home of
  Maryland
6811 Campfield Rd.
Baltimore, Maryland 21207
(301) 486-4573

Broadmead
13801 York Rd.
Cockeysville, Maryland 21030
(301) 628-6900

Carroll Lutheran Village
200 St. Luke Circle
Westminster, Maryland 21157
(301) 848-5330

Fairhaven
7200 Third Ave.
Sykesville, Maryland 21784
(301) 795-8800

Friends House*
17340 Quaker Lane
Sandy Spring, Maryland 20860
(301) 924-5100

General German Aged People's
  Home of Baltimore
22 S. Athol Ave.
Baltimore, Maryland 21229
(301) 566-3600

Pickersgill
615 Chestnut Ave.
Towson, Maryland 21204
(301) 825-7423

Revitz House*
6111 Montrose Rd.
Rockville, Maryland 20852
(301) 881-7400

MASSACHUSETTS

Cambridge Homes for the Aged
360 Mt. Auburn St.
Cambridge, Massachusetts
  02138
(617) 876-0369

Elizabeth Carleton House
2055 Columbus Ave.
Boston, Massachusetts 02119
(617) 522-2100

Frances Merry Barnard Home
50 Beacon St.
Hyde Park, Massachusetts 02136
(617) 361-0156

Hebrew Rehabilitation Center
  for Aged*
1200 Centre St.
Roslindale, Massachusetts 02131
(617) 325-8000

Malden Home for Aged Persons*
578 Main St.
Malden, Massachusetts 02148
(617) 321-3740

MICHIGAN

Burtha Fisher Home, Little
Sisters of the Poor*
17550 Southfield Rd.
Detroit, Michigan 48235
(313) 531-1565

Friendship Village of Kalamazoo
1400 N. Drake Rd.
Kalamazoo, Michigan 49007
(616) 381-0560

Gilbert Old Peoples Home of
Ypsilanti*
203 S. Huron St.
Ypsilanti, Michigan 48197
(313) 482-9498

Glacier Hills
1200 Earhart Rd.
Ann Arbor, Michigan 48105
(313) 769-6910

Independence Village
255 Mayer Rd.
Frankenmuth, Michigan 48734
(517) 652-4100

Presbyterian Village of Detroit*
17383 Garfield Ave.
Detroit, Michigan 48240
(313) 531-6874

St. Luke's Episcopal Church
Home
224 Highland Ave.
Highland Park, Michigan 48203
(313) 868-1445

Villa Francesca Home for the
Aging*
565 W. Long Lake Rd.
Bloomfield Hills, Michigan
48013
(313) 644-5390

Vista Grande Villa
2251 Springport Rd.
Jackson, Michigan 49202
(517) 787-0222

MINNESOTA

Augustana Lutheran Homes*
218 N. Holcombe Ave.
Litchfield, Minnesota 55355
(612) 693-2430

Bethany Home—Bethel Manor*
1020 Lark St.
Alexandria, Minnesota 56308
(612) 763-3105

Covenant Manor
5800 St. Croix Ave.
Minneapolis, Minnesota 55422
(612) 546-6125

Ebenezer Covenant Home*
310 Lake Blvd.
Buffalo, Minnesota 55313
(612) 682-1434

Jones–Harrison Home
3700 Cedar Lake Ave.
Minneapolis, Minnesota 55416
(612) 920-2030

Madonna Towers
4001 19th Ave., N.W.
Rochester, Minnesota 55901
(507) 288-3911

Margaret S. Parmly Residence
28210 Old Towne Rd.
Cisago City, Minnesota 55013
(612) 257-5620

Presbyterian Homes of
Minnesota*
3220 Lake Johnanna Blvd.
Saint Paul, Minnesota 55112
(612) 631-1024

Saint Otto's Home*
920 S.E. 4th St.
Little Falls, Minnesota 56345
(612) 632-9281

Samaritan Bethany Home*
24 8th St., N.W.
Rochester, Minnesota 55901
(507) 289-4031

Thorne Crest Retirement Center
1201 Garfield Ave.
Albert Lea, Minnesota 56007
(507) 373-2311

Villa St. Vincent
516 Walsh
Crookston, Minnesota 56716
(218) 281-3424

MISSISSIPPI

Flowers Manor*
1251 Lee Dr.
Clarksdale, Mississippi 38614
(601) 627-2222

Traceway Manor*
2800 W. Main St.
Tupelo, Mississippi 38801
(604) 844-1441

MISSOURI

Armour Homes*
8100 Wornall Rd.
Kansas City, Missouri 64114
(817) 363-1510

Charles Home
4431 S. Broadway Ave.
St. Louis, Missouri 63111
(314) 481-4840

Chateau Girardeau*
3120 Independence St.
Cape Girardeau, Missouri 63701
(314) 335-1281

Friendship Village of South
  County
12503 Village Circle Dr.
St. Louis, Missouri 63127
(314) 842-6840

Friendship Village of West
  County
15201 Olive St.
Chesterfield, Missouri 63017
(314) 532-1515

Gatesworth Manor*
245 Union Blvd.
St. Louis, Missouri 63108
(314) 367-9280

Good Samaritan Home for the
  Aged
5200 S. Broadway
St. Louis, Missouri 63111
(314) 352-2400

Lenoir Memorial Home
Highway 63 South
Columbia, Missouri 65201
(314) 443-4561

Little Sisters of the Poor*
3225 N. Florissant Ave.
St. Louis, Missouri 63107
(314) 421-6022

Lutheran Altenheim Society of
  Missouri*
1265 McLaran Ave.
St. Louis, Missouri 63147
(314) 388-2867

Ozarks Methodist Manor
205 S. College St.
Marionville, Missouri 65705
(417) 463-2573

Presbyterian Manor at
  Farmington
500 Cayce Ave.
Farmington, Missouri 63640
(314) 756-6768

Presbyterian Manor at Fulton
802 Court St.
Fulton, Missouri 65251
(314) 642-6646

Presbyterian Manor at Rolla
1200 Homelife Plaza
Rolla, Missouri 65401
(314) 364-7234

St. Joseph's Hill Infirmary
St. Joseph Rd.
Eureka, Missouri 63025
(314) 587-3661

St. Louis Altenheim
5408 S. Broadway
St. Louis, Missouri 63111
(314) 353-7225

Tower Grove Manor*
2710 S. Grand Blvd.
St. Louis, Missouri 63118
(314) 773-2800

Village North
11160 Village North Dr.
St. Louis, Missouri 63136
(314) 355-8010

Vista Del Rio
700 East Eighth St.
Kansas City, Missouri 64106
(816) 221-1125

MONTANA

Eagles Manor*
9th St. at 15th Ave. South
Great Falls, Montana 59405
(406) 453-6521

Faith Lutheran Retirement
    Home*
1000 6th Ave. North
Wolf Point, Montana 59201
(406) 653-1400

Missoula Manor Homes*
909 W. Central
Missoula, Montana 59801
(406) 728-3210

Penkay Eagles Manor*
715 Fee St.
Helena, Montana 59601
(406) 442-0610

St. John's Lutheran Home*
3940 Rimrock Rd.
Billings, Montana 59102
(406) 656-2710

NEBRASKA

Gateway Manor
225 N. 56th St.
Lincoln, Nebraska 68504
(402) 434-6371

Methodist Memorial Homes
    Retirement Center*
1320 11th Ave.
Holdrege, Nebraska 68949
(308) 995-8631

Skyline Manor/Skyline Villa
7300 Graceland Dr.
Omaha, Nebraska 68134
(402) 572-5750

NEW HAMPSHIRE

Havenwood Retirement
    Community*
33 Christian Ave.
Concord, New Hampshire 03301
(603) 224-5363

Home for Aged Women
127 Parrott Ave.
Portsmouth, New Hampshire
    03801
(603) 436-2435

NEW JERSEY

Cadbury
2150 Route 38
Cherry Hill, New Jersey 08002
(609) 667-4550

Collingswood Manor
460 Haddon Ave.
Collingswood, New Jersey 08108
(609) 854-4331

Francis Asbury Manor–Epworth
  Manor
70 Stockton Ave.
Ocean Grove, New Jersey 07756
(201) 774-1316

Heath Village*
Schooleys Mountain Rd.
Hackettstown, New Jersey
  07840
(201) 852-4801

Jewish Federation Plaza*
750 Northfield Ave.
West Orange, New Jersey 07052
(201) 731-2020

Masonic Home of New Jersey
Jacksonville Rd.
Burlington, New Jersey 08016
(609) 386-0300

Meadow Lakes
Etra Rd.
P. O. Box 70
Highstown, New Jersey 08520
(609) 448-4100

Medford Leas Retirement
  Community
366 Medford Leas
Medford, New Jersey 08055
(609) 654-3000

Methodist Manor*
Phillips Rd.
Box 142
Branchville, New Jersey 07826
(201) 948-3545

Mt. St. Andrew Villa*
W55 Midland Ave.
Paramus, New Jersey 07652
(201) 261-5950

Muhlenberg Gardens*
1065 Summit Ave.
Jersey City, New Jersey 07307
(201) 792-4475

Navesink House
40 Riverside Ave.
Red Bank, New Jersey 07701
(201) 842-3400

Pitman Manor*
535 N. Oak Ave.
Pitman, New Jersey 08071
(609) 589-7800

St. Joseph's Home for the
  Elderly*
140 Shepherd La.
Totowa, New Jersey 07512
(201) 942-0300

Ward Homestead
125 Boyden Ave.
Maplewood, New Jersey 07040
(201) 762-5050

Workmen's Circle Home for the
  Aged
225 W. Jersey St.
Elizabeth, New Jersey 07202
(201) 353-1220

NEW MEXICO

Landsun Homes
2002 Westridge Rd.
Carlsbad, New Mexico 88220
(505) 887-2894

NEW YORK

Elizabeth Church Manor
863 Front St.
Binghamton, New York 13905
(607) 722-3463

Findlay Home
  (Weinstein–Ratner)
1175 Findlay Ave.
Bronx, New York 10456
(212) 293-1500

Gerry Nursing Home (Heritage
  Village Health Center)*
Route 60
Gerry, New York 14740
(716) 985-4612

Hilltop Retirement Center
285 Deyo Hill Rd.
Johnson City, New York 13790
(607) 798-7818

Isabella Geriatric Center*
515 Audubon Ave.
New York, New York 10040
(212) 781-9800

Jewish Home and Hospital for
  Aged*
120 W. 106th St.
New York, New York 10025
(212) 870-5000

Loretto Geriatric Center*
700 E. Brighton Ave.
Syracuse, New York 13205
(315) 469-5561

United Presbyterian Home at
  Syosset*
378 Syosset-Woodbury Rd.
Woodbury, New York 11797
(516) 921-3900

Wartburg Home*
Bradley Ave.
Mt. Vernon, New York 10552
(914) 699-0800

NORTH CAROLINA

Brooks-Howell Home
29 Spears Ave.
Asheville, North Carolina 28801
(704) 253-6712

Carolina Village
600 Lakewood Rd.
P. O. Box 602
Hendersonville, North Carolina
  28739
(704) 692-6275

Carol Woods
Weaver Dairy Rd.
Chapel Hill, North Carolina
  27514
(919) 968-4511

Episcopal Home for the Aging
P. O. Box 2001
Southern Pines, North Carolina
  28387
(919) 692-7151

Heritage Place
P. O. Box 1573
Fayetteville, North Carolina
  28302
(919) 323-4925

Masonic and Eastern Star Home
700 S. Holden Rd.
Greensboro, North Carolina
  27420
(919) 299-0031

Methodist Home
3420 Shamrock Dr.
Charlotte, North Carolina 28215
(704) 537-9731

Methodist Retirement Home
2616 Erwin Rd.
Durham, North Carolina 27705
(919) 383-2567

Moravian Home
5401 Indiana Ave.
Winston–Salem, North Carolina
27106
(919) 767-8130

Presbyterian Home at Charlotte
5100 Sharon Rd.
Charlotte, North Carolina 29210
(704) 553-1670

Presbyterian Home
P. O. Box 2007
High Point, North Carolina
27261
(919) 883-9111

Triad United Methodist Home*
1240 Arbor Rd.
Winston–Salem, North Carolina
27104
(919) 724-7921

United Church Retirement
Centers
J. W. Abernathy Nursing Center
102 Leonard Ave.
Newton, North Carolina 28658
(704) 464-8260

Wesley Pines
100 Wesley Pines Rd.
Lumberton, North Carolina
29358
(919) 738-9691

NORTH DAKOTA

Bethany Homes*
201 S. University Dr.
Fargo, North Dakota 58103
(701) 237-0720

Missouri Slope Lutheran Home
2425 Hillview Ave.
Bismarck, North Dakota 58501
(701) 223-9407

Sunset Home*
802 N.W. Dover
Bowman, North Dakota 58623
(701) 523-3214

Trinity Medical Center Nursing
Homes*
305 8th Ave., N.E.
Minot, North Dakota 58701
(701) 857-5000

Valley Memorial Home*
2900 14th Ave., South
Grand Forks, North Dakota
58201
(701) 780-5500

OHIO

Abbot Home for Men
1258 Greenwood Ave.
Zanesville, Ohio 43701
(614) 453-2781

Baptist Home and Center
2373 Harrison Ave.
Cincinnati, Ohio 45211
(513) 662-5880

Bethany Lutheran Village
6451 Far Hills Ave.
Dayton, Ohio 45459
(513) 433-2110

Bethesda Scarlet Oaks
440 Lafayette Ave.
Cincinnati, Ohio 45220
(513) 861-0400

Breckenridge Village
36855 Ridge Rd.
Willoughby, Ohio 44094
(216) 942-4342

Brethren's Home*
750 Chestnut St.
Greenville, Ohio 45331
(513) 548-4117

Canton Christian Home*
2550 Cleveland Ave., N.W.
Canton, Ohio 44709
(216) 456-0004

Chapel Hill Home
12200 Strausser St., N.W.
Canal Fulton, Ohio 44614
(216) 854-4177

Copeland Oaks and Crandall
  Medical Center
800 S. 15th St.
Sebring, Ohio 44672
(216) 938-6126

Dorothy Love Retirement
  Community
3003 W. Cisco Rd.
Sidney, Ohio 45365
(513) 498-2391

Elyria United Methodist Home
807 West Ave.
Elyria, Ohio 44035
(216) 323-3395

First Community Village
1800 Riverside Dr.
Columbus, Ohio 43212
(614) 486-9511

Friendship Village
5790 Denlinger Rd.
Dayton, Ohio 45426
(513) 837-5581

Friendship Village of Columbus
5800 Forest Hills Blvd.
Columbus, Ohio 43229
(614) 890-8282

Good Shepherd Home*
622 Center St.
Ashland, Ohio 44805
(419) 289-3523

Grace Brethren Village
1010 Taywood Rd.
Englewood, Ohio 45322
(513) 836-4011

Healthhaven Nursing Home
615 Lathan La.
Akron, Ohio 44319
(216) 644-3914

Helen Purcell Home
1854 Norwood Blvd.
Zanesville, Ohio 43701
(614) 453-1745

Home for Aged Women*
1171 E. State St.
Salem, Ohio 44460
(216) 337-3697

Judson Park
1801 Chestnut Hills Dr.
Cleveland Heights, Ohio 44106
(216) 721-1234

Maple Knoll Village
11100 Springfield Pike
Springdale, Ohio 45246
(513) 782-2400

Maria Joseph Center
4830 Salem Ave.
Dayton, Ohio 45416
(513) 278-2692

Marjorie P. Lee Home
3550 Shaw Ave.
Cincinnati, Ohio 45208
(513) 871-2090

The Meadows*
11100 Springfield Pike
Springdale, Ohio 45246
(513) 782-2400

Llanfair Terrace Retirement
   Community
1701 Llanfair Ave.
Cincinnati, Ohio 45224
(513) 681-4230

Mennonite Memorial Home*
410 W. Elm St.
Bluffton, Ohio 45817
(419) 358-1015

Menorah Park*
27100 Cedar Rd.
Beachwood, Ohio 44122
(216) 831-6500

Methodist Home on College Hill
5343 Hamilton Ave.
Cincinnati, Ohio 45224
(513) 681-2440

Mt. Healthy Christian Home
8097 Hamilton Ave.
Cincinnati, Ohio 45231
(513) 931-5000

Mt. Pleasant Retirement Village
225 Britton Rd.
Monroe, Ohio 45050
(513) 539-7391

Otis Avery Browning Masonic
   Memorial Home
8900 Neowash Rd.
Waterville, Ohio 43566
(419) 878-4055

Otterbein Home*
585 N. State Route 741
Lebanon, Ohio 45036
(513) 932-2020

Park Vista Presbyterian Home
1216 5th Ave.
Youngstown, Ohio 44504
(216) 746-2944

Riverview Home
5999 Bender Rd.
Cincinnati, Ohio 45233
(513) 922-1440

Rockynol
1150 W. Market St.
Akron, Ohio 44313
(216) 867-2150

Schroder Manor
1302 Millville Ave.
Hamilton, Ohio 45013
(513) 867-1300

Sem Villa II*
5371 S. Milford Rd.
Milford, Ohio 45150
(513) 831-3262

Sumner Home for the Aged
209 Merriman Rd.
Akron, Ohio 44303
(216) 762-9341

Thurber Towers
645 Neil Ave.
Columbus, Ohio 43215
(614) 221-6172

Trinity Home
3218 Indian Ripple Rd.
Dayton, Ohio 45440
(513) 426-8481

Wesley Glen
5155 N. High St.
Columbus, Ohio 43214
(614) 888-7492

Westminster Thurber
   Community
717 Neil Ave.
Columbus, Ohio 43215
(614) 228-3819

Westover
855 Stahlheber Rd.
Hamilton, Ohio 45013
(513) 895-9539

Winebrenner Village
424–425 Frazer St.
Findlay, Ohio 45840
(419) 422-2957

OKLAHOMA

Oklahoma Christian Home
906 North Blvd.
Edmond, Oklahoma 73034
(405) 341-0810

OREGON

Calaroga Terrace
1400 N.E. 2nd Ave.
Portland, Oregon 97232
(503) 234-8271

Capital Manor*
P. O. Box 5000
Salem, Oregon 97304
(503) 362-4101

Fairlawn Towne*
1280 N.E. Kane Rd.
Gresham, Oregon 97030
(503) 667-1965

Friendsview Manor
1301 E. Fulton St.
Newberg, Oregon 97132
(503) 538-3144

Holladay Park Plaza
1300 N.E. 16th Ave.
Portland, Oregon 97232
(503) 288-6671

Rogue Valley Manor
1200 Mira Mar Ave.
Medford, Oregon 97501
(503) 773-7411

Rose Villa
13505 S.E. River Rd.
Portland, Oregon 97222
(503) 654-3171

Willamette View Manor
12705 S.E. River Rd.
Portland, Oregon 97222
(503) 654-6581

PENNSYLVANIA

Baptist Homes of Western
　Pennsylvania
489 Castle Shannon Blvd.
Pittsburgh, Pennsylvania 15234
(412) 563-6550

Brethren Home
P. O. Box 128
New Oxford, Pennsylvania
　17350
(717) 624-2161

Brethren Village*
3001 Lititz Pike
P. O. Box 5093
Lancaster, Pennsylvania 17601
(717) 569-2657

Carlisle Presbyterian Home
602 N. Hanover St.
Carlisle, Pennsylvania 17013
(717) 243-5714

Cathedral Village
600 E. Cathedral Rd.
Philadelphia, Pennsylvania
　19128
(215) 487-1300

Church of the Brethren Home
1005 Hoffman Ave.
Windber, Pennsylvania 15963
(814) 467-5505

Cornwall Manor*
Cornwall, Pennsylvania 17016
(717) 273-2647

Crosslands
P. O. Box 100
Kennett Square, Pennsylvania
19348
(215) 388-1441

Dunwoody Village
3500 W. Chester Pike
Newtown Square, Pennsylvania
19073
(215) 359-4400

Easton Home for Aged Women
1022 Northampton St.
Easton, Pennsylvania 18042
(215) 258-7773

ECC Retirement Village*
S. Railroad St.
Myerstown, Pennsylvania 17067
(717) 866-6541

Elm Terrace Gardens
660 N. Broad St.
Landsdale, Pennsylvania 19446
(215) 368-6087

Epworth Manor
951 Washington Ave.
Tyrone, Pennsylvania 16686
(814) 684-0320

Evangelical Manor
8401 Roosevelt Blvd.
Philadelphia, Pennsylvania
19152
(215) 624-5800

Foulkeways at Gwynedd
Meeting House Rd.
Gwynedd, Pennsylvania 19436
(215) 643-2200

Frey Village*
1020 N. Union St.
Middletown, Pennsylvania
17057
(717) 944-0451

Green Ridge Village
Big Spring Rd.
Newville, Pennsylvania 17241
(717) 776-3192

Kendal at Longwood
P. O. Box 699
Kennett Square, Pennsylvania
19348
(215) 388-7001

Landis Homes Retirement
Community
Route 3
Lititz, Pennsylvania 17543
(717) 569-3271

Lebanon Valley Brethren Home
1200 Grubb St.
Palmyra, Pennsylvania 17078
(717) 838-5406

Lebanon Valley Home*
550 E. Main St.
Annville, Pennsylvania 17003
(717) 867-4467

Lewisburg United Methodist
Home
Lewisburg, Pennsylvania 17837
(717) 524-2271

Lutheran Home
Topton, Pennsylvania 19562
(215) 682-2145

Lutheran Home at Telford
235 N. Washington St.
Telford, Pennsylvania 18969
(215) 723-9810

Martins Run
11 Martins Run
Marple Township, Pennsylvania
  19063
(215) 353-7660

Menno-Haven
2075 Scotland Ave.
Chambersburg, Pennsylvania
  17201
(717) 263-8545

Messiah Village
100 Mt. Allen Dr.
Mechanicsburg, Pennsylvania
  17055
(717) 697-4666

Oxford Manor Steward Home*
Seven Locust St.
Oxford, Pennsylvania 19363
(215) 932-2900

Passavant Health Center
401 S. Main St.
Zelienople, Pennsylvania 16063
(412) 452-5400

Paul's Run Retirement
  Community
9896 Bustleton Ave.
Philadelphia, Pennsylvania
  19115
(215) 934-3000

Pennswood Village
Route 413
Newtown, Pennsylvania 18940
(215) 968-9110

Philadelphia Geriatric Center
5301 Old York Rd.
Philadelphia, Pennsylvania
  19141
(215) 455-6100

Philadelphia Protestant Home
700 E. Gilham St.
Philadelphia, Pennsylvania
  19111
(215) 745-1986

Phoebe-Devitt Home
1925 Turner St.
Allentown, Pennsylvania 18104
(215) 435-9037

Pickering Manor Home*
226 N. Lincoln Ave.
Newtown, Pennsylvania 18940
(215) 968-3878

Quincy United Methodist Home*
P. O. Box 217
Quincy, Pennsylvania 17247
(717) 749-3151

Reformed Presbyterian Homes
  for the Aged
2344 Perryville Ave.
Pittsburgh, Pennsylvania 15214
(412) 321-4139

Riverside Presbyterian Tower*
23rd and Race Streets
Philadelphia, Pennsylvania
  19103
(215) 563-6200

Rosemont Presbyterian Village
404 Cheswick Pl.
Rosemont, Pennsylvania 19010
(215) 527-6500

Rydal Park
On the Fairway
Rydal, Pennsylvania 19046
(215) 885-6800

St. Barnabas
Meridian Rd.
Gibsonia, Pennsylvania 15044
(412) 443-0700

St. Joseph Home for the Aged
1182 Holland Rd.
Holland, Pennsylvania 18966
(215) 357-5511

St. Mary's Manor*
701 Lansdale Ave.
Lansdale, Pennsylvania 19446
(215) 368-0900

St. Paul Homes
339 E. Jamestown Rd.
Greenville, Pennsylvania 16125
(412) 588-4070

Schock Presbyterian Home
17 E. Main St.
Mount Joy, Pennsylvania 17552
(717) 653-2058

Sherwood Oaks
100 Norman Dr.
Mars, Pennsylvania 16046
(412) 776-8100

Simpson House*
Belmont and Monument
  Avenues
Philadelphia, Pennsylvania
  19131
(215) 878-3600

Springfield Retirement
  Residence
551 E. Evergreen Ave.
Wyndmoor, Pennsylvania 19118
(215) 242-9515

Tel Hai Retirement Community
P. O. Box 190
Honey Brook, Pennsylvania
  19344
(215) 273-3149

Thornwald Home*
442 Walnut Bottom Rd.
Carlisle, Pennsylvania 17013
(717) 249-4118

United Methodist Home
700 Bower Hill Rd.
Pittsburgh, Pennsylvania 15243
(412) 341-1030

United Methodist Home and
  Nursing Hospital
31 N. Park Ave.
Meadville, Pennsylvania 16335
(814) 724-8000

Wood River Village Association
3200 Ben Salem Blvd.
Ben Salem, Pennsylvania 19020
(215) 752-2370

Wyncote Church Home
Maple and Fernbrook Avenues
Wyncote, Pennsylvania 19095
(215) 885-2620

RHODE ISLAND

Ballou Home for the Aged
60 Mendon Rd.
Woonsocket, Rhode Island 02895
(401) 769-0437

Jewish Home for the Aged of
  Rhode Island*
99 Hillside Ave.
Providence, Rhode Island 02860
(401) 351-4750

Scandinavian Home for the Aged
1811 Broad St.
Cranston, Rhode Island 02905
(401) 461-1433

SOUTH CAROLINA

Frampton Hall
N. Broad St.
Clinton, South Carolina 29325
(803) 833-0386

Presbyterian Home of South
  Carolina
Highway 56 North
Clinton, South Carolina 29325
(803) 833-5190

Presbyterian Home of South
  Carolina
2350 Lucas St.
Florence, South Carolina 29501
(803) 665-2222

Presbyterian Home of South
  Carolina
C.M.R. Box 140
Summerville, South Carolina
  29483
(803) 873-2550

South Carolina Episcopal Home
  at Still Hopes
W. Columbia, South Carolina
  29169
(803) 796-6490

TENNESSEE

McKendree Manor
4347 Lebanon Rd.
Hermitage, Tennessee 37076
(615) 889-6990

St. Peter Manor*
108 North Auburndale
Memphis, Tennessee 38104
(901) 725-8210

Shannondale
801 Vanosdale Rd.
Knoxville, Tennessee 37919
(615) 588-1361

Trezevant Manor and Allen
  Morgan Nursing Center
177 N. Highland St.
Memphis, Tennessee 38111
(901) 324-CARE

Uplands*
P. O. Box 168
Pleasant Hill, Tennessee 38578
(615) 277-3511

TEXAS

Bayou Manor
4141 S. Braeswood Blvd.
Houston, Texas 77025
(713) 666-2651

Buckner Retirement Inn*
4800 Samuell Blvd.
Dallas, Texas 75228
(314) 381-2171

Crestview Retirement
  Community*
P. O. Box 4008
Bryan, Texas 77805
(713) 775-4778

Eden Home for the Aged
631 Lakeview Blvd.
New Braunfels, Texas 78130
(512) 625-6291

Good Samaritan Village*
2500 Hinkle Dr.
Denton, Texas 76201
(817) 383-2651

Hallmark
4718 Hallmark La.
Houston, Texas 77056
(713) 622-6633

Home for the Aged
  Women–Men*
920 S. Oregon St.
El Paso, Texas 79901
(915) 533-5152

Kings Manor Methodist Home*
430 Ranger Dr.
P. O. Box 1999
Hereford, Texas 79045
(806) 364-0661

John Knox Village of the Rio
  Grande Valley
1300 S. Border Ave.
Weslaco, Texas 78596
(512) 968-4575

Moody House*
2228 Seawall Blvd.
Galveston, Texas 77550
(713) 763-6437

Morningside Manor*
602 Babcock Rd.
San Antonio, Texas 78284
(512) 734-7271

Presbyterian Manor
4600 Taft Blvd.
Wichita Falls, Texas 76308
(817) 691-1710

Presbyterian Village
550 Ann Arbor
Dallas, Texas 75216
(214) 376-1701

Presbyterian Village North
8600 Skyline Dr.
Dallas, Texas 75243
(214) 349-3960

Sherick Memorial Home*
2502 Utica Ave.
Lubbock, Texas 79407
(806) 799-8600

Trinity Towers*
2800 W. Illinois
Midland, Texas 79701
(915) 694-1691

Village
4917 Ravenswood Dr.
San Antonio, Texas 78227
(512) 673-2761

Wesleyan Retirement Home*
P. O. Box 486
Georgetown, Texas 78626
(512) 863-2528

Westminster Manor
4100 Jackson Ave.
Austin, Texas 78731
(512) 454-4711

VERMONT

Vernon Hall Retirement
  Residence*
Route 142
Vernon, Vermont 05354
(802) 254-8091

VIRGINIA

Beth Sholom Home of Central
  Virginia
5700 Fitzhugh Ave.
Richmond, Virginia 23226
(804) 282-5471

Bridgewater Home*
302 2nd St.
Bridgewater, Virginia 22812
(703) 828-2531

Culpepper Garden*
4435 N. Pershing Dr.
Arlington, Virginia 22203
(703) 528-0162

Emily Green Home*
500 Westmoreland Ave.
Portsmouth, Virginia 23707
(804) 399-3442

Goodwin House
4800 Fillmore Ave.
Alexandria, Virginia 22311
(703) 578-1000

Hermitage on the Eastern Shore
P. O. Box 300
Onancock, Virginia 23417
(804) 787-4343

Hermitage Methodist Home
1600 Westwood Ave.
Richmond, Virginia 23227
(804) 355-5721

Hermitage in Northern Virginia
5000 Fairbanks Ave.
Alexandria, Virginia 22311
(703) 820-2434

Lakewood Manor
1900 Lauderdale Dr.
Richmond, Virginia 23233
(804) 740-2900

Lydia H. Roper Home
127 E. 40th St.
Norfolk, Virginia 23504
(804) 622-6979

Mary F. Balentine Home for the
    Aged
7211 Granby St.
Norfolk, Virginia 23505
(804) 489-1441

Snyder Memorial Home*
310 W. 31st St.
Richmond, Virginia 23225
(804) 232-5190

Sunnyside Presbyterian Home*
P. O. Box 928
Harrisonburg, Virginia 22801
(703) 434-4801

Virginia Baptist Home
P. O. Box 191
Culpeper, Virginia 22701
(703) 825-2411

Virginia Baptist Home
P. O. Box 6010
Newport News, Virginia 23606
(804) 599-4376

Virginia Mennonite Home
1301 Edom Rd.
Harrisonburg, Virginia 22801
(703) 434-1716

Washington House
5100 Fillmore Ave.
Alexandria, Virginia 22311
(703) 379-9000

Westminster Canterbury House
600 Westbrook Ave.
Richmond, Virginia 23227
(804) 264-6000

Westminster Canterbury of
    Lynchburg
501 Va. Episcopal School Rd.
Lynchburg, Virginia 24503
(804) 386-3500

Westminster–Canterbury in
    Virginia Beach
3100 Shore Dr.
Virginia Beach, Virginia 23451
(804) 496-1100

Williams Home
1201 Langhorne Rd.
Lynchburg, Virginia 24503
(804) 384-8282

WASHINGTON

Bayview Manor
11 W. Aloha St.
Seattle, Washington 98119
(206) 284-7330

Covenant Shores
9150 N. Mercer Way
Mercer Island, Washington
  98040
(206) 236-0600

Exeter House
720 Seneca St.
Seattle, Washington 98101
(206) 622-1300

Hearthstone
6720 E. Green Lake Way North
Seattle, Washington 98103
(206) 525-9666

Hilltop House*
1005 Terrace St.
Seattle, Washington 98104
(206) 624-5704

Horizon House
900 University St.
Seattle, Washington 98101
(206) 624-3700

Judson Park Retirement
  Residence
23600 Marine View Dr. South
Seattle, Washington 98188
(206) 824-4000

Rockwood Manor
E. 2903 25th Ave.
Spokane, Washington 99203
(509) 535-3651

Samuel and Jessie Kenney
  Presbyterian Home
7125 Fauntleroy Way, S.W.
Seattle, Washington 98136
(206) 937-2800

Warm Beach Health Care Center
  and Manor*
20420 Marine Dr.
Stanwood, Washington 98292
(206) 652-7585

Washington Odd Fellows Home*
534 Boyer Ave.
Walla Walla, Washington 99362
(509) 525-6463

Wesley Gardens
815 S. 216th St.
Des Moines, Washington 98188
(206) 824-5000

WISCONSIN

Cedar Ridge Foundation*
3011 N. Cedar Ridge Rd.
Oconomowoc, Wisconsin 53066
(414) 646-2731

Colonial View Apartments*
601 Thomas Dr.
Sun Prairie, Wisconsin 53590
(608) 837-5166

Congregational Home
13900 W. Burleigh Rd.
Brookfield, Wisconsin 53005
(414) 781-0550

Friendship Village of Milwaukee
7500 W. Dean Rd.
Milwaukee, Wisconsin 53223
(414) 354-3700

Grace Lutheran Foundation*
822 Porter Ave.
Eau Claire, Wisconsin 54701
(715) 832-3003

Luther Manor
4545 N. 92nd St.
Wauwatosa, Wisconsin 53225
(414) 464-3880

Methodist Manor and Methodist
  Manor Health Center
3023 S. 84th St.
West Allis, Wisconsin 53227
(414) 541-2600

Milwaukee Catholic Home
2462 N. Prospect Ave.
Milwaukee, Wisconsin 53211
(414) 224-9700

Milwaukee Protestant Home
Bradford Terrace
2449 N. Downer Ave.
Milwaukee, Wisconsin 53211
(414) 332-8610

Sheboygan Retirement Home*
930 N. 6th St.
Sheboygan, Wisconsin 53081
(414) 458-2137

Tudor Oaks Retirement
  Community
577 W. 12929 McShane Rd.
Hales Corners, Wisconsin 53130
(414) 529-0100

Villa Clement
9047 W. Greenfield Ave.
West Allis, Wisconsin 53214
(414) 453-9290

Wisconsin Masonic Home
Dousman, Wisconsin 53118
(414) 965-2111

Notes

Introduction

1. Florida Scott-Maxwell, *The Measure of My Days* (New York: Alfred A. Knopf, Inc., 1968), p.5.
2. Ellen Goodman, "On Learning to Grow Old," *Washington Post,* January 15, 1980 (© 1980, The Boston Globe Newspaper Company/Washington Post Writers Group, reprinted with permission.)

Chapter 2. Lingering Images

1. Joan Saunders Wixen, "How We're Coping with Anxiety," *Modern Maturity,* June-July 1981, p.31.
2. Wixen, "How We're Coping," *Modern Maturity,* p.32.
3. Wilma T. Donahue, Penelope Hommel Pepe, and Priscilla Murray, *Assisted Independent Living in Residential Congregate Housing: A Report on the Situation in the United States* (Washington, D.C.: International Center for Social Gerontology, 1978).
4. Betsy Brown, "Crisis Teams Aiding the Elderly," *The New York Times,* Westchester section, February 14, 1982, p.10 (© 1982 by The New York Times Company. Reprinted by permission.)
5. Robin Marantz Henig, *The Myth of Senility* (New York: Anchor Press/Doubleday. © 1981 by Robin Marantz Henig. Reprinted by permission of Doubleday and Company, Inc.)
6. *JASA/Brookdale News,* New York, July-August 1980, pp. 1 and 3.
7. *The Poor in Great Cities* (New York: Charles Scribner's Sons, 1895), p.68.
8. Ibid., pp.214–15.

Chapter 6. A Look at the Nursing Unit

1. Garson Kanin, *It Takes a Long Time to Become Young* (New York: Berkley Publishing Corporation, 1979), p.92. (Copyright ©

1978 by T.F.T. Corporation. Reprinted by permission of Doubleday and Company, Inc.)

Chapter 7. A Model of Successful Old Age

1. Elaine Cumming and William Henry, *Growing Old* (New York: Basic Books, 1961).
2. Arnold Rose and Warren Peterson, eds., *Older People and Their Social World* (Philadelphia: F.A. Davis Company, 1965), p.4.
3. Jaber F. Gubrium, *The Myth of the Golden Years: A Sociological Environmental Theory of Aging* (Springfield, Ill.: Charles C. Thomas, 1973), p.5.
4. Irving Rosow, *Socialization to Old Age* (Berkeley, Cal.: University of California Press, 1974), pp.156–60.
5. Ibid., p.160.
6. Arlie Hochschild, *A Community of Grandmothers* (unpublished doctoral dissertation, University of California–Berkeley, 1969), pp.191–209.
7. Kurt G. Herz, "Community Resources and Services to Help Independent Living," *The Gerontologist,* vol.11, no.1 (Spring 1971, part 1), pp.59–66.
8. Leon Kalson, "The Therapy of Independent Living for the Elderly," *Journal of the American Geriatric Society,* vol.xx, no.8 (1972), pp.394–97.
9. Frances M. Carp, "Long-Range Satisfaction with Housing," *The Gerontologist,* vol.15, no.1 (February 1975, part 1), pp.68–72.
10. Daniel M. Wilner and Rosabella Price Walkley, "Some Special Problems and Alternatives in Housing for Older Persons" in *Aging and Social Policy,* ed. John McKinney and Frank T. deVyer (New York: Appleton-Century-Crofts, 1966).
11. David S. Greer, M.D., "Housing for the Physically Impaired" in *Housing and Environment for the Elderly,* ed. T.O. Byerts (Washington, D.C.: Gerontological Society, 1973).
12. M. Powell Lawton, "Public Behavior of Older People in Congregate Housing" in *Proceedings of the Second Annual Conference of Environmental Design Research Associations* (Pittsburgh, Penn.: October 1970).
13. Jennie Keith Ross, "Life Goes On: Social Organization in a French Residence" in *Late Life Communication and Environmental Policy,* ed. J.F. Gubrium (Springfield, Ill.: Charles C. Thomas, 1974), pp.116–17.

14. Susan R. Sherman, "Mutual Assistance and Support in Retirement Housing," *Journal of Gerontology*, vol.30, no.1 (January 1975), pp.479–83.

15. Elizabeth S. Johnson and Barbara J. Bursk, "Relationships Between the Elderly and Their Adult Children," *The Gerontologist*, vol.17, no.1 (February 1977), p.96.

16. Erving Goffman, *Asylums* (New York: Doubleday/Anchor Books, 1961).

17. Bernice Neugarten and Robert J. Havinghurst, *Social Policy, Social Ethics and the Aging Society* (University of Chicago: Committee on Human Development, 1976).

Chapter 8. You Don't Have to Live Alone

1. Herman B. Brotman, *Every Ninth American* (Falls Church, Va.: March 1982 edition), p.29.

2. Ibid., p.1.

3. Louis E. Gelwicks and Maria B. Dwight, "Programming for Alternatives and Future Models" in *Congregate Housing for Older People: A Solution for the 1980s,* eds. Robert D. Chellis, James F. Seagle, Jr., and Barbara Mackey Seagle (Lexington, Mass.: Lexington Books, D.C. Heath and Company. © 1982, D.C. Heath and Company. Reprinted by permission of the publisher.)

4. Robert D. Chellis and James F. Seagle, Jr., "Preface: A Needed Alternative" in *Congregate Housing for Older People,* p.ix.

5. Bruce C. Vladeck, "Keynote Address," in *Proceedings of Conference on New Options for Independent Living: Expanding Housing Choices for the Elderly* (Princeton: New Jersey Department of Community Affairs, Division on Aging, September 29, 1980), p.12.

6. Elaine M. Brody and Bernard Liebowitz, "Some Recent Innovations in Community Living Arrangements for Older People" in *Community Housing Choices for Older Americans,* ed. M. Powell Lawton and Sally L. Hoover, p.245. (© 1981 by Springer Publishing Company, Inc., New York. Reprinted by permission.)

7. Maurice B. Greenbaum,"Urban Single Dwelling Rehabilitation" in *Proceedings on New Options for Independent Living,* p.112.

8. Carla L. Lerman, "Group Homes" in *Proceedings on New Options,* p.102.

9. Lawton and Hoover, *Community Housing Choices,* p.9.

10. Andree Brooks, "New Britain Elderly Back to School,"*The New York Times,* Connecticut section, July 27, 1980, p.15.

11. Vladeck, *Proceedings on New Options,* p.11.

12. Robert Sunley, "Home Sharing," *Proceedings on New Options,* pp.119–20.

13. Ibid., p.121.

14. Ibid., p.125.

15. Brody and Liebowitz in *Community Housing Choices,* ed. Lawton and Hoover, p.245.

16. René Dubos, *The New York Times,* Op-ed page, March 6, 1982 (© 1982 by The New York Times Company. Reprinted by permission.)

17. *Directory of Life Care Communities,* 2nd ed., compiled by Nora E. Adelmann (Kennett Square, Penn.: Kendal-Crosslands, 1980), p.7.

18. Ibid., p.7.

19. Helen Kingsbury Wallace, "I'm Glad I Came," *The American Baptist,* October 1975, p.18.

Addendum

Much of the text of this book is based on the unpublished doctoral dissertation of Dr. Vivian F. Carlin, *A Model of Successful Old Age: A Participant Observation Study of a Congregate Residence* (Rutgers University, 1981).

Index

A

Activity, vs. disengagement, 126.
Activities Director, 90.
Administration, improvements in, 89. *See also* Management.
Administrator: appointment of, 88; in congregate housing, 87–88, 169.
Admission procedures, 170. *See also* Application and entrance requirements.
Adult/Retirement communities, 37–38, 152, 153–54. *See also* Age-segregated housing; Communal housing; Congregate housing; Housing for the elderly.
Age, median of residents, vi, 5.
Age-segregated housing, vi, 65, 128–29, 133, 163. *See also* Adult/Retirement communities; Communal housing; Congregate housing; Housing; Housing for the elderly.
Aging: adjustment to, 127–29; conferences and symposia on, 24; fear of, 21–22, 24, 37, 39; Greco-Roman view of, 22–23; Judeo-Christian view of, 22–23; loneliness in, 131–32; negative attitude towards, vi; 19th century impressions of, 23–24, 36–37; refusal to accept own, 21–22, 24, 33–34, 37, 39, 69, 127–28; social problems produced by, 26; stereotypes of, 21–24, 25, 37; views of, vii, 125. *See also* Aging subculture; Death; Depression; Elderly; Illness; Loneliness; Men; Widows; Women.

Aging subculture; and congregate housing, vi, 130–32, 144; formation of, 127–29; homogeneity in, vi, 128–29, 140; influence of residential setting on, 129–30; role of single women and widows in, 140–41. *See also* Aging; Men; Widows; Women.
Aides, home health care, 103.
Apartments: availability of, 4; behavior in, 95; choice of, 95; convalescing in, 103–05; description of, vi, 9, 10–11; drinking in, 46-47, 95; kitchen in, vi, 11, 51–52; meals in, 11, 86, 104; privacy of, 96, 139, 156; smoking in, 46, 95. *See also* Meals; Privacy, right to; Residents: privacy of.
Application and entrance requirements, 93–94, 169–70.
Art exhibits, 78.

B

Birren, Dr. James E., 26.
Board of directors, 4, 88, 94–95, 169.
Booth, George, v.
Brody, Elaine M., 157, 162.
Brotman, Herman, 155.
Buildings, conversion to housing for the elderly, 152, 157–61, 165.
Butler, Dr. Robert, 21.

C

California: San Francisco public housing for the elderly, 129; study of housing in, 131.
Carp, Francis M., 131, 133.
Case history. *See* Life history.